MULTICULTURAL EDUCATION SERIES
James A. Banks, *Series Editor*

(continued)

MULTICULTURAL EDUCATION SERIES, *continued*

Culturally Responsive Teaching, Second Edition
GENEVA GAY

Why Race and Culture Matter in Schools
TYRONE C. HOWARD

Diversity and Equity in Science Education
OKHEE LEE AND CORY A. BUXTON

Forbidden Language
PATRICIA GÁNDARA AND MEGAN HOPKINS, EDS.

The Light in Their Eyes, 10th Anniversary Edition
SONIA NIETO

The Flat World and Education
LINDA DARLING-HAMMOND

Teaching What Really Happened
JAMES W. LOEWEN

Diversity and the New Teacher
CATHERINE CORNBLETH

Frogs into Princes: Writings on School Reform
LARRY CUBAN

Educating Citizens in a Multicultural Society,
Second Edition
JAMES A. BANKS

Culture, Literacy, and Learning
CAROL D. LEE

Facing Accountability in Education
CHRISTINE E. SLEETER, ED.

Talkin Black Talk
H. SAMY ALIM AND JOHN BAUGH, EDS.

Improving Access to Mathematics
NA'ILAH SUAD NASIR AND PAUL COBB, EDS.

"To Remain an Indian"
K. TSIANINA LOMAWAIMA AND TERESA L. MCCARTY

Education Research in the Public Interest
GLORIA LADSON-BILLINGS AND WILLIAM F. TATE, EDS.

Multicultural Strategies for Education and Social Change
ARNETHA F. BALL

Beyond the Big House
GLORIA LADSON-BILLINGS

Teaching and Learning in Two Languages
EUGENE E. GARCÍA

Improving Multicultural Education
CHERRY A. MCGEE BANKS

Education Programs for Improving Intergroup Relations
WALTER G. STEPHAN AND W. PAUL VOGT, EDS.

City Schools and the American Dream
PEDRO A. NOGUERA

Thriving in the Multicultural Classroom
MARY DILG

Educating Teachers for Diversity
JACQUELINE JORDAN IRVINE

Teaching Democracy
WALTER C. PARKER

The Making—and Remaking—of a Multiculturalist
CARLOS E. CORTÉS

Transforming the Multicultural Education
of Teachers
MICHAEL VAVRUS

Learning to Teach for Social Justice
LINDA DARLING-HAMMOND, JENNIFER FRENCH, AND
SILVIA PALOMA GARCIA-LOPEZ, EDS.

Culture, Difference, and Power, Revised Edition
CHRISTINE E. SLEETER

Learning and Not Learning English
GUADALUPE VALDÉS

The Children Are Watching
CARLOS E. CORTÉS

Multicultural Education, Transformative Knowledge,
and Action
JAMES A. BANKS, ED.

De**construct**ing
RA**CE**

Multicultural Education
Beyond the **Color-Bind**

JABARI **MAHIRI**

TEACHERS COLLEGE PRESS

TEACHERS COLLEGE | COLUMBIA UNIVERSITY
NEW YORK AND LONDON

Published by Teachers College Press, 1234 Amsterdam Avenue, New York, NY 10027

Library of Congress Cataloging-in-Publication Data

Names: Mahiri, Jabari, editor.
Title: Deconstructing race : multicultural education beyond the color-bind / Jabari
    Mahiri.
Description: New York, NY : Teachers College Press, 2017. | Series: Multicultural
    education series | Includes bibliographical references and index.
Identifiers: LCCN 2017014082 (print) | LCCN 2017030006 (ebook)
ISBN 9780807774861 (ebook)
ISBN 9780807757772 (hardcover : alk. paper)
ISBN 9780807757765 (pbk. : alk. paper)
Subjects: LCSH: Multicultural education—United States. | Educational
    equalization—United States. | Race—Classification—United States. | Ethnicity—
    United States. | Group identity—United States. | Cultural pluralism—United
    States.
Classification: LCC LC1099.3 (ebook) | LCC LC1099.3 .M3325 2017 (print)
DDC 370.117—dc23
LC record available at https://lccn.loc.gov/2017014082

ISBN 978-0-8077-5776-5 (paper)
ISBN 978-0-8077-5777-2 (hardcover)
ISBN 978-0-8077-7486-1 (ebook)

Printed on acid-free paper
Manufactured in the United States of America

24 23 22 21 20 19 18 17   8 7 6 5 4 3 2 1

For Generations
Ayana and Nia; Jelani, Nina, and Hélio;
Kobié, Ana Maria, Santiago, and Amado;
and Ajamu, Ahlia, Soleil, Imani, and Ade

Contents

Series Foreword

Mahiri's major project in this engaging and timely book is to deconstruct race and racial categories in order to free individuals so that they can embrace authentic identities that are fluid, complex, and consistent with what he calls their "micro-cultural identities," which make the "hidden aspects of people's identities visible." Mahiri's project to deconstruct race is a continuation—with rich insights and contributions by him—of a long and impressive tradition of social science scholars and literary writers who had similar aims, such as W. E. B. Du Bois (1994), Ralph Ellison (1947), James Baldwin (Mead & Baldwin, 1971), and Toni Morrison (1992)—who are profiled in this book. Social scientists such as Omi and Winant (1994), Gould (1996), Jacobson (1998), and Brodkin (1998) have also made rich, original, and illuminating contributions to the project to deconstruct race and detail the ways in which it is a pernicious and destructive social construction. Anthropologists Mukhopadhyay, Henze, and Moses (2014) have written a sourcebook on race, culture, and biology that complements Mahiri's project. It focuses on ways in which teachers can help students to deconstruct and acquire sophisticated and intricate understandings of race.

Race is one of the main categories used to construct differences in the United States as well as in other nations around the world. Groups holding political and economic power construct racial categories to privilege members of their groups and to marginalize outside groups (Banks, 2002). Jacobson calls races "invented categories" (p.4); Montagu (1997) describes race as "man's most dangerous myth" (p. 37); Omi and Winant (1994) state that the "determination of racial categories is an intensively political process" (p. 3).

The data and quotes from the 20 individuals that Mahiri interviewed make a compelling case about the ways in which racial categories often deny individuals the opportunity to actualize their authentic selves and reduce them to "acting White" or to "acting Black," when their micro-cultural and authentic identities are much more complex than a single racial category. Mahiri's analysis of how racial categories stigmatize and limit the possibilities of individuals is insightful and informative. However, his discussion of ways to eliminate what he calls the "color-bind" caused by racial categories and institutionalized racism reveals the intractability of the systemic barriers created by institutionalized racism, and how changing the ways in which individuals view their micro-cultures and racial identities will not necessarily change the ways in which they are categorized and treated by outside individuals and groups. However, helping individuals to identify their authentic micro-cultural identities is an essential step in a much larger project that requires institutional and structural changes.

Brodkin (1998) makes an important distinction between "ethnoracial assignment" and "ethnoracial identity" (p. 3). Ethoracial *assignment* is the way that individuals and groups are categorized by outside groups who have the power to make these categories matter economically, politically, and socially. Ethnoracial *identity* is the ways in which individuals and groups categorize themselves "within the context of ethnoracial assignment" (p. 3). Mahiri describes examples of how "people can actively and consciously reject [an] identity and, ultimately, construct ones that are more ancestrally and scientifically accurate." These examples raise the question about how sustainable authentic identities are when they are constructed and embraced by individuals within an institutionalized racist system. This question is far beyond what can be resolved in this thoughtful and comprehensive book or in this Foreword. However, deconstructing race and the color-bind requires both dismantling racial categories as well as dismantling institutionalized racism (Leonardo, 2013) and White nationalism, both of which were invigorated by the election of Donald Trump in 2016 and by the symbols of White privilege and White nationalism that he conveys to his followers (Painter, 2016).

Another complex phenomenon related to racialization and racial categories that goes beyond the boundaries and scope of this informative book and Foreword are the ways in which groups that have been victimized by racial categories and institutionalized discrimination have used that marginalization and victimization as vehicles for protest, resistance, empowerment, and to push for social justice. Racialized and marginalized groups have also been the guardians and perpetuators of freedom within U.S. society writ large. A salient example is the civil rights movement that African Americans initiated and led during the 1960s and 1970s. The civil rights movement not only mobilized and empowered African Americans, but helped to democratize U.S. society. It greatly increased social justice for diverse groups who were victims of discrimination in the United States, such as White women, Native Americans, and Asian Americans. The Immigration Reform Act of 1965—which initiated a period of massive immigration that began in 1968 and changed the ethnic texture of the United States—was a consequence of the civil rights movement. The movement also echoed throughout the world and stimulated protests from South Africa to Northern Ireland. Okihiro (1994) argues compellingly that groups in the margins of U.S. society have been the conscience of the nation and the leaders of the struggles to close the gap between democratic ideals and institutional racism and discrimination. Foner (1998) makes a similar argument:

The authors of the notion of freedom as a universal birthright, a truly human ideal, were not so much the founding fathers, who created a nation dedicated to liberty but resting in large measure on slavery, but abolitionists who sought to extend the blessings of liberty to encompass blacks, slave and free; women who seized upon the rhetoric of democratic freedom to demand the right to vote; and immigrant groups who insisted that nativity and culture ought not to form boundaries of exclusion. (pp. xx–xxi)

Because of the growing population of students from diverse racial, ethnic, linguistic, and religious groups who are attending schools in the United States, teachers and other educators need to contribute to the efforts to deconstruct race and to provide students with cultural alternatives. Although students in the United States are becoming increasingly diverse, most of the nation's teachers are White, female, and monolingual. Race and institutionalized racism are significant factors that influence and mediate the interactions of students and teachers from different ethnic, language, and social-class groups (G. R. Howard, 2016; T. C. Howard, 2010; Leonardo, 2013). The growing income gap among adults (Stiglitz, 2012)—as well as among youth, as described by Putnam (2015) in *Our Kids: The American Dream in Crisis*—is another significant reason why it is important to help teachers to understand how categories related to race, ethnicity, and class influence classroom interactions and student learning, and to comprehend the ways in which these variables influence student aspirations and academic engagement (Suárez-Orozco, Pimentel, & Martin, 2009).

American classrooms are experiencing the largest influx of immigrant students since the beginning of the 20th century. Approximately 21.5 million new immigrants—documented and undocumented—settled in the United States between 2000 and 2015. Less than 10% came from nations in Europe. Most came from Mexico and from nations in South Asia, East Asia, Latin America, the Caribbean, and Central America (Camarota, 2011, 2016). The influence of an increasingly diverse population on U.S. schools, colleges, and universities is and will continue to be enormous.

Schools in the United States are more diverse today than they have been since the early 1900s, when a multitude of immigrants entered the United States from Southern, Central, and Eastern Europe. In 2014, the National Center for Education Statistics estimated that students from ethnic minority groups made up more than 50% of public school pre-K–12 students, an increase from 40% in 2001 (National Center for Education Statistics, 2014). Language and religious diversity is also increasing in the U.S. student population. The 2012 American Community Survey estimated that 21% of Americans aged 5 and above (61.9 million) spoke a language other than English at home (U.S. Census Bureau, 2012). Harvard professor Diana L. Eck (2001) calls the United States the "most religiously diverse nation on earth" (p. 4). Islam is now the fastest-growing religion in the United States, as well as in several European nations such as France, the United Kingdom, and the Netherlands (Banks, 2009; O'Brien, 2016).

The major purpose of the Multicultural Education Series is to provide preservice educators, practicing educators, graduate students, scholars, and policymakers with an interrelated and comprehensive set of books that summarizes and analyzes important research, theory, and practice related to the education of ethnic, racial, cultural, and linguistic groups in the United States and the education of mainstream students about diversity. The dimensions of multicultural education, developed by Banks and described in the *Handbook of Research on Multicultural Education* (Banks, 2004) and in the *Encyclopedia of Diversity in Education* (Banks, 2012), provide the conceptual framework for the development of the publications in the Series. The dimensions are content integration, the knowledge construction process, prejudice reduction, equity pedagogy, and an empowering institutional culture and social structure. The books in the Multicultural Education Series provide research, theoretical, and practical knowledge about the behaviors and learning characteristics of students of color (Conchas & Vigil, 2012; Lee, 2007), language minority students (Gándara & Hopkins, 2010; Valdés, 2001; Valdés, Capitelli, & Alvarez, 2011), low-income students (Cookson, 2013; Gorski, 2013), and other minoritized population groups, such as students who speak different varieties of English (Hudley & Mallinson, 2011), and LGBTQ youth (Mayo, 2014). Three other books in the Multicultural Education Series complement this book and focus on institutionalized racism in education: *Race Frameworks: A Multidimensional Theory of Racism and Education* by Zeus Leonardo (2013); *Engaging the "Race Question": Accountability and Equity in U.S. Higher Education* by Alicia C. Dowd and Estela Mara Bensimon (2015); and *Race, Empire, and English Language Teaching: Creating Responsible and Ethical Anti-Racist Practice* by Suhanthie Motha (2014).

It is important for teachers and other educators to participate in the project to deconstruct race and to support students when they embrace identities and categories that are consistent with their ethnoracial identities and ancestry. Supporting students when they construct and embrace authentic racial categories is important in part because of the growing number of Americans who are reporting more than one race on the U.S. census. This population grew from 6.8 million in 2000 to 9 million in 2010. During that same time-frame, the number of people who self-reported as both White and Black/African American grew by more than one million, an increase of 134%; those who self-reported as both White and Asian grew by 750,000, an increase of 87% (Jones & Bullock, 2012). As teachers and other educators work to help deconstruct institutionalized racial categories, they should also help students of color to understand that, regardless of their ethnoracial identities as individuals, they must still function in a society and nation that will frequently categorize them based on what outsiders perceive as their phenotype. It is important to help students understand the difference between ethnoracial identities and the ethnoracial assignments that are given to individuals by the larger society, in order to help them to function effectively and to attain psychological health in a racist society and nation-state. James Gee's notion of "identity affinities"—which are discussed by Mahiri—enable people to use digital texts and tools to create individual identities and selective affinities with chosen groups. Identity affinities provide a means by which students can, to some extent, circumvent categories and identities imposed by others.

When educators work to deconstruct racial categories, they should respect and be sensitive to the fact that many students who are members of minoritized and racialized groups—such as African American and Latinos—have enormous pride in the ethnic cultures of their groups, find them empowering, and feel that their ethnic and racial groups enable them to "forge self-definitions of self-reliance and independence" (Collins, 2000, p. 1). Although these students have myriad micro-cultural identities, their racial identity is predominant.

I hope this visionary and timely book will stimulate rich conversations that will enable educators to participate in the deconstruction of race and the color-bind and in the reduction of institutionalized and systemic racism, as well as highlight the ways in which groups that are victimized by racism and racialized categories have used their victimization as vehicles for resistance, empowerment, and the advancement of social justice.

—James A. Banks

REFERENCES

Banks, J. A. (2002). Race, knowledge construction, and education in the USA: Lessons from history. *Race Ethnicity and Education, 5*(1), 5–27.

Banks, J. A. (2004). Multicultural education: Historical development, dimensions, and practice. In J. A. Banks & C. A. M. Banks (Eds.), *Handbook of research on multicultural education* (2nd ed., pp. 3–29). San Francisco, CA: Jossey-Bass.

Banks, J. A. (Ed.). (2009). *The Routledge international companion to multicultural education*. New York, NY and London, UK: Routledge.

Banks, J. A. (2012). Multicultural education: Dimensions of. In J. A. Banks (Ed.), *Encyclopedia of diversity in education* (vol. 3, pp. 1538–1547). Thousand Oaks, CA: Sage Publications.

Brodkin, K. (1998). *How Jews became white folks and what that says about race in America*. New Brunswick, NJ: Rutgers University Press.

Camarota, S. A. (2011, October). *A record-setting decade of immigration: 2000 to 2010*. Washington, DC: Center for Immigration Studies. Retrieved from cis.org/2000-2010-record-setting-decade-of-immigration

Camarota, S. A. (2016, June). *New data: Immigration surged in 2014 and 2015*. Washington, DC: Center for Immigration Studies. Retrieved from cis.org/New-Data Immigration-Surged-in-2014-and-2015

Collins, P. H. (2000). *Black feminist thought: Knowledge, consciousness, and the politics of empowerment* (2nd ed.). New York, NY: Routledge.

Conchas, G. Q., & Vigil, J. D. (2012). *Streetsmart schoolsmart: Urban poverty and the education of adolescent boys.* New York, NY: Teachers College Press.

Cookson, P. W. Jr. (2013). *Class rules: Exposing inequality in American high schools.* New York, NY: Teachers College Press.

Dowd, A. C., & Bensimon, E. M. (2015). *Engaging the "race question": Accountability and equity in U.S. higher education.* New York: Teachers College Press.

Du Bois, W.E.B. (1994). *The souls of black folk.* New York, NY: Dover.

Eck, D. L. (2001). *A new religious America: How a "Christian country" has become the world's most religiously diverse nation.* New York, NY: HarperSanFrancisco.

Ellison, R. (1947). *Invisible man.* New York, NY: Vintage Books.

Foner, E. (1998). *The story of American freedom.* New York, NY: Norton.

Gándara, P., & Hopkins, M. (Eds.). (2010). *Forbidden language: English language learners and restrictive language policies.* New York, NY: Teachers College Press.

Gorski, P. C. (2013). *Reaching and teaching students in poverty: Strategies for erasing the opportunity gap.* New York, NY: Teachers College Press.

Gould, S. J. (1996). *The mismeasure of man.* New York, NY: Norton.

Howard, G. R. (2016). *We can't teach what we don't know: White teachers, multiracial schools* (3rd ed.). New York, NY: Teachers College Press.

Howard, T. C. (2010). *Why race and culture matter in schools. Closing the achievement gap in America's classrooms.* New York, NY: Teachers College Press.

Hudley, A. H. C., & Mallinson, C. (2011). *Understanding language variation in U.S. schools.* New York, NY: Teachers College Press.

Jacobson, M. F. (1998). *Whiteness of a different color: European immigrants and the alchemy of race.* Cambridge, MA: Harvard University Press.

Jones, N. A., & Bullock, J. (2012, September). *Two or more races population: 2010.* 2010 Census Briefs. Washington, DC: United States Census Bureau. Retrieved from census.gov/prod/cen2010/briefs/c2010br-13.pdf

Lee, C. D. (2007). *Culture, literacy, and learning: Taking bloom in the midst of the whirlwind.* New York, NY: Teachers College Press.

Leonardo, Z. (2013). *Race frameworks: A multidimensional theory of racism and education.* New York, NY: Teachers College Press.

Mayo, C. (2014). *LGBTQ youth and education: Policies and practices.* New York, NY: Teachers College Press.

Mead, M., & Baldwin, J. (1971). *A rap on race.* New York, NY: Dell Publishing.

Montagu, A (1997). *Man's most dangerous myth: The fallacy of race.* Walnut Creek, CA: AltaMira Press

Morrison, T. (1992). *Playing in the dark: Whiteness and the literary imagination.* Cambridge, MA: Harvard University Press.

Motha, S. (2014). *Race, empire, and English language teaching: Creating responsible and ethical anti-racist practice.* New York: Teachers College Press.

Mukhopadhyay, C. C., Henze, R., & Moses, Y. T. (2014). *How real is race? A sourcebook on race, culture, and biology.* Lanham, MD: AltaMira Press.

National Center for Education Statistics. (2014). *The condition of education 2014.* Retrieved from nces.ed.gov/pubs2014/2014083.pdf

O'Brien, P. (2016). *The Muslim question in Europe: Political controversies and public philosophies.* Philadelphia, PA: Temple University Press.

Okihiro, G. Y. (1994). *Margins and mainstreams: Asians in American history*. Seattle, WA: University of Washington Press.

Omi, M., & Winant, H. (1994). *Racial formation in the United States: From the 1960s to the 1990s*. New York, NY: Routledge.

Painter, N. I. (2016, November 16). What Whiteness means in the Trump era. *The New York Times*. Retrieved from nytimes.com/2016/11/13/opinion/what-whiteness-means-in-the-trump-era.html?_r=0

Putnam, R. D (2015). *Our kids: The American dream in crisis*. New York, NY: Simon & Schuster.

Stiglitz, J. E. (2012). *The price of inequality: How today's divided society endangers our future*. New York, NY: Norton.

Suárez-Orozco, C., Pimentel, A., & Martin, M. (2009). The significance of relationships: Academic engagement and achievement among newcomer immigrant youth. *Teachers College Record*, 111(3), 712–749.

U.S. Census Bureau (2012). *Selected social characteristics in the United States: 2012 American Community Survey 1-year estimates*. Retrieved from factfinder2.census.gov/faces/tableservices/jsf/pages/productview.xhtml?pid=ACS_12_1YR_DP02&prodType=table

Valdés, G. (2001). *Learning and not learning English: Latino Students in American schools*. New York, NY: Teachers College Press.

Valdés, G., Capitelli, S., & Alvarez, L. (2011). *Latino children learning English: Steps in the journey*. New York, NY: Teachers College Press.

Acknowledgments

I thank Professor James Banks, who invited submission of this book to his thought-leading series on Multicultural Education. Jim offered insightful guidance throughout this book's development. His concepts of "microcultures" and "multiple group memberships" are two of his many ideas that have influenced my thinking. I thank Professor James Gee for his informative work on "activity-based identities" and on learning with new media. I also thank Executive Acquisitions Editor Brian Ellerbeck for shepherding this book from proposal to publication. Additionally, I thank the interviewees who graciously shared their stories. They were my teachers, and I hope this book does justice to what I learned. Because of them, my intellectual quest also became a spiritual one. I thank Professors Janaina Minelli De Oliveira, Linn Areskoug, Gesa Kirsch, Erin Murphy-Graham, and Amanda Godley, along with Dr. Isabelle Bourdon, Dr. Lanette Jimerson, and Dr. Zehlia Babaci-Wilhite, as well as Myra Oiga and Joseph Wood for thoughtful responses to the book as it developed. Also, I thank my co-instructors—Jeremiah Sims, Sepehr Vakil, Cherise McBride, Robyn Ilten-Gee, and Grace Kim—and the graduate students in my fall 2015 and fall 2016 urban education classes who shared insights into the issues addressed in this book. Particularly, I thank Shivani Savdharia, Yael Friedman, and Eva Marie Oliver for pedagogical projects connected to these two urban education classes that I discuss in the final chapter, as well as Kylie Garcia for use of her identity profile from the 2016 class and Amelia Vargas for sharing a key U.S. census document. Importantly, I thank the William and Mary Jane Brinton Family for support from their Chair endowment, which significantly enabled my research, writing, and work with the interviewees. And, of course, I thank Joelle Cheng and Nia Mahiri Crawford for meticulously transcribing the interviews and Ayana Crawford for proofreading. Nia also became a cogent collaborator in coding the interview data, working with the references, and responding to the book's themes.

CHAPTER 1

Writing Wrongs

Ethnography offers all of us the chance to step outside our narrow cultural backgrounds, to set aside our socially inherited ethnocentrism, if only for a brief period, and to apprehend the world from the viewpoint of other human beings.

—James Spradley (1979, v)

Kobié Jr. is caramel colored. He was 3 years old when this chapter was written. His family soon started calling him Santi, short for his middle name, Santiago. In the United States where he was born, he is seen as a black* boy. But his identity is more complex than that.

Santi's father was born and grew up in Chicago and identifies as African American. He majored in French and minored in math at Morehouse College. Santi's mother identifies as Latina and completed her bachelor's degree at the University of California, Santa Cruz. She was born in Popayá, a town in southwestern Colombia. At 5 she immigrated to the United States with her mother, who identifies as white and who was also born in Colombia. Santi's grandfather on his mother's side is indigenous Colombian and has lived his whole life in Colombia. Santi's mother and grandmother are fluent in Spanish and English, and he too is bilingual in these languages.

Hélio was 8 when this chapter was written. Like his first cousin Santi, he was born in the United States. His dad, like his dad's brother, grew up in Chicago; he graduated from Morehouse with a double major in physics and Spanish. Hélio's mother is a French citizen and defined in her country as Caucasian. Her mother is Polish and Italian and her father is German. She met Hélio's father while they were both completing doctorate degrees at the University of California, Berkeley. Hélio is fluent in English and French, so his uncle can communicate with him in French and English, while his father can communicate with his cousin Santi in Spanish and English. Hélio has a light complexion. When with his mother in the United States, he is seen as white; when with his father, he is seen as biracial. But his identity is more complex than that.

---

*Lowercase letters are used for color-coded designations of racial categories throughout the book (except for the Series Foreword).

Hélio and Santi are not anomalies. Like every individual in the United States (and the world), they are physically, linguistically, geographically, historically, and personal-culturally *situated* in families; in communities and communities of practice; in social, affinity, and religious groups; and in educational and other institutions within society. Their identities are constituted by rich arrays and confluences of forces and factors stemming from how each is distinctively and fluidly situated. A core motive and focus for this book is "writing the wrongs" of hierarchy and hypocrisy perpetuated by how these children are socially constructed in U.S. society.

After completing 2 years of research, the writing of this book occurred during the 2016 presidential campaign and election. Since the November 8 results, significant increases in hate crimes and harassment against Muslims, Latinos, Jews, African Americans, LGBTQ Americans, and other minority and vulnerable groups have been continually documented and reported. Trump's deliberate denigration of these groups leading up to and subsequent to the election reinvigorated and validated white supremacists' views that reject the value of multiculturalism and instead promote an imagined white, Christian European heritage. Clearly, his rhetoric and selection of people into leadership positions in his administration have emboldened white identity politics and increased discord and division in our society. One of the many painful examples is the incident at JFK Airport in New York shortly after his inauguration, in which Robin Rhodes, a 57-year-old man from Worchester, Massachusetts, physically and verbally assaulted a female Delta Airlines employee who was wearing a hijab. He kicked her and ranted profanities about Islam and also said, "Trump is here now. He will get rid of all of you" (Bever, 2017). Significantly, Trump's election was predicated on the fact that 58% of people identified as white voted for him. Deconstructing race is particularly imperative in the corrosive post-election climate facilitated by his election, and the roles of multicultural education are all the more pivotal.

Race is a socially constructed idea that humans can be divided into distinct groups based on inborn traits that differentiate them from members of other groups. This conception is core to practices of racism. There is no scientific justification for race. All humans are mixed! And, scientists have demonstrated that there is no physical existence of races. Yet, race *is* a social fact with a violent history and hierarchy that has resulted in differential and disturbing experiences of racism predicated on beliefs that races do exist. My argument for deconstructing race is grounded in insights from scholars who have guided my thinking, as well as extensive ethnographic interviews of people identified within the five most generally referenced racial categories in the United States—in essence, what I've learned from the literature joined with what I've learned from lives of others.

LEARNING FROM THE LIVES OF OTHERS

What I've learned from the literature and scholarship on race as well as prospects for deconstructing it are taken up in Chapters 2 and 3 and threaded through the subsequent chapters. This literature and scholarship provided compelling examples of writing the wrongs of race by explicating myriad false premises and contradictions in racial ideologies and narratives past and present. Initially, this book was conceived exclusively as a discussion of scholarship on these issues. However, after conversations with Relene,* who became the first of 20 interviewees, I decided to bring perspectives and stories from people's lives into dialogue with literature and scholarship. I saw the book's focus being substantively illuminated by my conscious attempt to step outside my own cultural background and, as Spradley suggested in the quote that begins this chapter, to "apprehend the world from the viewpoint of other human beings" (1979, p. v). Consequently, in-depth descriptions and stories of people's actual lives were joined with selected literature and scholarship as ways of writing the wrongs of race.

I was reminded of the critically acclaimed movie, *The Lives of Others* (Wiedermann, Berg, & von Donnersmarck, 2006), which won an Oscar for best foreign film. The story was set before the collapse of the Berlin Wall, when East Germany's population was closely monitored by the state secret police, the Stasi. Only a few citizens were permitted to lead private lives, among them a renowned pro-Socialist playwright. Eventually, he too was subject to surveillance, and a Stasi policeman was ordered to secretly monitor the conversations in his apartment to discover any incriminating activities by the group of artists who frequently met there. However, what the policeman learned in listening in on their lives ended up changing *his* life and politics.

Of course, I received permission to interview the adults who volunteered for this project, but as with the "secret sharer" in *The Lives of Others,* my personal views and understandings were shaped and changed by what I learned. Wacquant (2008) also argued for and demonstrated the significance of extending scholarship with ethnographic investigations. Spradley (1979), who provided a comprehensive framework for ethnographic interviewing, went so far as to say, "Perhaps the most important force behind the quiet ethnographic revolution is the widespread realization that cultural diversity is one of the great gifts bestowed on the human species" (p. v). Spradley (1979), Denzin and Lincoln (2003), Frank (2009), and Saldaña (2009) oriented my approach to conducting the interviews and analyzing the transcripts and field note data. Coding across data sources was converted into larger descriptive categories and later merged into the major themes discussed in Chapter 3.

---

*Pseudonyms for all interviewees have been selected to reflect real names in terms of cultural connections like ethnic, linguistic, geographic, or religious origins.

Because I feel that not only academics, but *all* readers should understand the approaches used to generate and document claims being made about people's lives, I discuss these methods as part of the Introduction to this book. Ultimately, I would like readers to respond as Joseph Wood, one of many pre-publication "ghost" readers, did. He put himself in the shoes of the interviewees and mused over inaccuracies of his own racial identity. Indeed, how do we all construct identity in contrast to how it is socially constructed for us?

The qualitative work began when I interviewed Relene at Seoul International Airport in May of 2014. I completed the remaining 19 interviews, four adults identified in each of the categories of European, African, Asian, and Hispanic American and American Indian/Alaskan Native, over the next 2 years. They agreed to be audiotaped, so in addition to their voices, I captured facial expressions, gestures, and body language as they spoke, often passionately and painfully, about these issues.

I met Relene at the 2014 Korean Association of Multicultural Education Conference (KAME), in which I co-presented a paper with Grace Kim where I introduced the concept of "micro-cultures" as a way of re-thinking identity beyond what I called "the color-bind." Kim provided illuminating examples from her research on participatory culture at a Korean website called *Dramacrazy* (Mahiri & Kim, 2016; Kim, 2016). As Relene and I discussed our research interests, I also learned that she had come to the United States with her family from the Caribbean Island of Dominica as an immigrant in late adolescence. This positioning had sharpened the focus of her "inner eyes"—an image from the "Prologue" of *Invisible Man* (Ellison, 1947) that I will discuss in Chapter 2.

As we talked about the focus of this book project, I could see the significance of pre-interview conversations. I listened for information and ideas that, if she agreed to be interviewed, would inform my questions to help her deeply probe her experiences. For example, although she has dark brown skin, she talked about how her teenage experiences in Boston made her feel like she was "passing for black." This was more than a year before Rachel Dolezal was outed by her parents on June 15, 2015 as a white woman passing for black.

I will return to the controversy surrounding Ms. Dolezal in Chapter 5, but here I provide a glimpse of how Relene came to her own sense of "passing." Of African-Caribbean heritage, she identifies as a black woman who became a naturalized U.S. citizen. She noted, "U.S. society tends to identify me as an African American woman, meaning a U.S.-born black." But her experiences in Boston not only revealed her marginalization from blacks born in the United States, they also reflected her being the victim of intense discrimination by them. Yet, she and other West Indian immigrants wanted to be accepted by the Boston black community. So she adopted cultural practices—behaviors and styles of dress, music, food, and language—that eventually allowed her to pass for black. Essentially, she performed overt cultural components of being black, in part, to avoid "blacklash." Below the surface association with being black, however, Relene's life is much more complex—as is everyone's. Her truer self, her unique and dynamic positionality, practices, choices, and perspectives were not visible through the veil of race used to define her, whether by those who saw themselves as black or white.

After interviewing Relene, I realized that gathering information and ideas in pre-interview conversations allowed me to initially have to ask only two questions of each interviewee: *How do you feel U.S. society identifies you?* And, *How do you identify yourself?* Because I was interested in how the interviewee's identities and affinities were mediated by digital media and hip-hop culture, I closed each interview with two final questions: *In what ways did you previously and do you currently participate in digital culture?* And, *In what ways, if any, did you previously and do you currently participate in hip-hop culture?* Each interview involved following up on things interviewees revealed in response to these four questions in an open-ended, dialogical way. These four questions allowed me to explore if and how the interviewees' identities and affinities that were revealed through their positioning, practices, choices, and perspectives complicated or obviated assigned racial categories.

Each formal interview lasted from 2 to 3 hours, and I also had follow-up conversations with all the interviewees to explore additional questions. I didn't record or take notes during conversations prior to or subsequent to the formal interviews, but shortly afterward, I wrote expansive descriptive and reflective fieldnotes to capture what I had learned. These notes became part of the data for analysis. Every interview was transcribed, read a number of times, and inductively coded to develop categories, as well as to identify any outlier considerations within and across racial, gender, sexual diversity, and generational designations.

Like Relene, the other 19 interviewees bravely intimated how they constructed, negotiated, rejected, erased, or deliberately distinguished key aspects of their identities. They also discussed how they saw their identities being invisibilized, homogenized, or boxed in rigid categories. They used and explained terms like "pigmentocracy," "blacxican," "Mexica," "racial indeterminacy," "gender ambiguity," "pretending to be white," "clapback," and "selective identities" that illuminated intricate aspects of their mercurial lives. Consequently, they revealed complexity, specificity, and fluidity of their personal-cultural identities and affinities that could not be contained within or explained by reductive conceptions of race.

All 20 are U.S. citizens. One criteria was that each interviewee self-identify in one of the five ascribed racial categories. One person discussed in Chapter 5 who has an African American and a German parent did not affirm an African American identity, but indicated that she is often seen that way. Within these categories, I selected two women and two men, with one of them being identified as lesbian, gay, bisexual, transgender, or queer (LGBTQ). This held for all groups except American Indian/Alaskan Natives, in which no one identified as LGBTQ. However, interviews with two of the American Indians spoke incisively to considerations of gender and sexual orientation. Another criterion was that interviewees be between the ages of 21 and 45 years old, which was true for all except one subject who was 47 when interviewed. This age specification was to get perspectives of interviewees who were born and developed into adults since the rise of the digital age and the birth of hip-hop in the early 1970s.

While honoring these selection criteria, I drew mainly on snowballing my personal, social, and professional relationships and networks to identify participants. Like the narrator in James McPherson's short story "Elbow Room" (1986), I was hunting for good stories. This may be seen as a limitation, but I feel that the significance of the study is in what is revealed about its focus through the sustained, close exploration of the practices, choices, and perspectives of the interviewees. Though beginning in self-acknowledged racial categories, the questions and dialogues allowed the interviewees to reflect on how their identities have been shaped by personal and social experiences, histories, trajectories, choices, and views that don't fit easily into assigned categories of race.

KEY CONCEPTS

We are all born into a social position and with physical features that contribute to our sense of who we are. But social positioning and physical features are not (or should not be) determinative of identity. Against the grain of social constructions, this book reveals how people's identities are ultimately determined by a wide range of personal-cultural practices, choices, and perspectives. The practices engaged in throughout our lives are tied to major and minor life choices as well as perspectives we develop about ourselves and others at the intersection of personal, social, material, and spiritual worlds. The lives of the interviewees provided evidence for how the intersections and interactions of these components reflected the actual identities of individuals, rather than the essentialized racial categories that Brodkin (1998) noted are "assigned" by white supremacy.

"Micro-cultures" (with a hyphen) is a key concept that captures the numerous components of positioning, practices, choices, and perspectives that make up the unique identities of each individual. This idea builds upon, but is distinguished from, Banks' (2013) concepts of "microcultures" (without a hyphen) and "multiple group memberships," as discussed in Chapter 9. I describe micro-cultural identities and practices as being mediated by language, and, like language, as being both acquired and learned. But they are also constituted and mediated through digital texts and tools that dramatically increase the range of how they can be engaged or enacted. At any moment, the vertical axis of these virtually limitless combinations of components—like fingerprints—reflect and define the ultimate uniqueness of individuals. On multiple horizontal axes, alignments of components also reflect similarities of individuals to specific others in shared or connected experiences within histories and geographies—within time and space. Unlike fingerprints, the combinations of micro-cultural components are dynamic and constantly changing (Mahiri, 2015; Mahiri & Kim, 2016; Mahiri & Ilten-Gee, 2017). From this perspective each life might be seen as a river fed by many distinct tributaries flowing into the sea of humanity.

The core argument of this book is that the continually emerging, rapidly changing micro-cultural identities and practices of individuals cannot be contained in the static racial categories assigned by white supremacy. Although many scholars of multicultural education have complicated these categories to illustrate more nuanced understandings of individual and group differences within them, and although individuals and groups have struggled to construct identities of themselves within these assigned categories, *the lives and literature discussed in this book challenge the very use of these categories as viable ways to identify people.* The scholarship reviewed and the people interviewed reveal the deceit of racial categories. As the multicultural paradigm continues to evolve, these categories themselves must be changed. A beginning step in this direction has already been taken in the 2010 census by backing away from identifying Hispanics as a race, as I discuss in Chapter 3. In Chapter 7, I build on the language used to identify Hispanics in the 2010 census to offer a more accurate and viable way of defining people without resorting to race as a classification. Teaching and learning that directly acknowledge and decisively build upon the micro-cultural identities and affinities of youth and adults will substantially contribute to deconstructing reductive, color-coded, racial categories and thus contribute to dismantling the hierarchies and binaries upon which white supremacy is based.

Of course, this challenge must go beyond mere recognition of microcultures. Mills (1997), along with many other scholars, recognized that "racism [as manifested through white supremacy] is itself a political system, a particular power structure of formal and informal rule, socioeconomic privilege, and norms for the differential distribution of material wealth and opportunities, benefits and burdens, rights and duties" (p. 3). Negating the effects of racism, power, and privilege wielded historically and contemporarily by groups that define themselves as white will take time and deliberate, strategic acts of deconstructing race. Some LGBTQ individuals and groups have demonstrated the viability of resisting and transforming restrictive understandings of sexual diversity, particularly over the past 50 years. It may take another 50 years of conscious work to transform understandings of human diversity before we can right the wrongs of race that white supremacy has specified and reinforced, both for its proponents and for those it oppresses and exploits. Facilitating this process in teaching and learning contexts within and beyond schools is a pivotal challenge of multicultural education.

In conjunction with micro-cultures, "identity contingencies" (Steele, 2010) is another key concept used to address how social constructions of identity can be predicated on physical characteristics and used as the basis for stereotypes and resulting stereotype responses. Steele and many other researchers building on his work have indicated how identity contingencies like skin color, facial features, hair type, and body size are linked to how people are socially constructed and treated in society, as well as how they interact with the world. Stereotypes associated with identity contingencies can forcefully and problematically shape people's identities and development. Identity contingencies and associated stereotypes underlie how individual identities are constituted and responded to in U.S. society, and they factor in as components of an individual's micro-cultural positioning that must be understood.

Digital media is also integral to micro-cultural identities. Two of Gee's (2003) 36 Principles of Learning with New Media—the "Identity Principle" and "Affinity Group Principle"—are additional concepts that clarify how individual identities move beyond racially defined categories. In defining the "Identity Principle," Gee noted that

> Learning involves taking on and playing with identities in such a way that the learner has real choices and ample opportunity to mediate on the relationship between new identities and old ones. There is a tripartite play of identities as learners relate, and reflect on, their multiple real-world identities, their virtual identities, and a projective identity. (2003, p. 208)

Individual identities are also linked to affinities with other individuals and groups in both real and virtual spaces. Regarding the "Affinity Principle," Gee (2003) noted that membership and participation in affinity groups or affinity spaces (the virtual sites of interaction) are defined primarily by shared endeavors, goals, and practices, rather than shared race, gender, nation, ethnicity, or culture (p. 212).

An additional concept from Gee (2013, 2015) that is important regarding micro-cultures is his delineation of the nature of activity-based identities. This concept focuses on the freely chosen practices of an individual that contribute to grounding a sense of self. Gee contrasted activity-based identities to relational identities. Relational identities are closely related to identities that are socially constructed and also connect to Steele's notion of identity contingencies. Gee noted that relational identities most often work to efface rather that reflect diversity, but when accepted and owned they can be like activity-based identities.

Activity-based and relational identities also were 2 of the 13 categories that surfaced in the interview data. These practices can reflect resident and emerging forms of social organization or what Gee (1991) earlier referred to as discourse communities. He described how discourse communities come with "identity kits" that include how to act, talk, and take on specific roles that others in the community recognize. Relene essentially was performing components of the identity kit needed to get recognized as black in Boston. Finally, Crenshaw's (1989) concept of intersectionality (which examines how various social, cultural, and biological categories of identity intersect) was another useful concept for seeing the complexity of numerous elements of identity that are simultaneously yet differentially impacted within oppressive systems. Again, all of these intersecting and interacting components are multiplied through the use of digital texts and tools.

CHAPTER OVERVIEWS

Chapters 2 and 3 discuss literature and scholarship that explicate crucial prospects and imperatives of deconstructing race. Chapter 2 is *not* a traditional literature review. It discusses works primarily by literary writers who I feel were inherently "Deconstructing Race." The idea was to begin discussion of the book's focus with writers who are central to American literature and, therefore, generally familiar to readers throughout the United States and the world. Although authors in this group have written many novels, Ellison's *Invisible Man* (1947) is the only novel discussed. Morrison's *Playing in the Dark* (1992) is a critique of how literature by white authors works to *make* race and difference invisible. Baldwin's *A Rap on Race* (1971, with Margaret Mead) powerfully captures racial dynamics from a half-century ago and reminds us how little things have changed. Du Bois' *Souls of Black Folk* (1994/1903) is used to frame this dialogue on race among these four American writers. The chapter begins with ideas from Derrida (1981/1972) on deconstruction and also discusses multicultural education with respect to race. It concludes with a discussion of why deconstructing race is imperative, particularly in light of the contemporary re-emergence of white identity politics.

Chapter 3 *is* a traditional review of scholarship. After discussing prospects and imperatives of "Deconstructing Race" in Chapter 2, this chapter begins with Du Bois' (1903) characterization that the problems of the 20th century is the problem of the color line. It then discusses scholarship that addresses how the problem of the 21st century is "The Color-Bind." Discussions of the color-bind in this chapter are not color-blind. Rather than not seeing or denying the reality of difference, the color-bind reflects on-going attempts to contain people in fabricated racial categories, shackling minds and imaginations in divisions of difference. Scholarship in this chapter illuminates how and why this has occurred historically and contemporarily in sections on "Prisons of Identity" and "Prisms of Identity." It reveals how these constraints on human identity are sustained for each racial group through societal forces and institutions like the U.S. census. This chapter argues that breaking out of the color-bind frees us to better appreciate and embrace our differences, but also to see vital commonalities in our human experiences beyond the blinders of race.

The next five chapters present stories and perspectives of the diverse group of interviewees whose lives, like all our lives in the United States, are forcibly fixed primarily within five general categories of race. As the final section of Chapter 2 connects the issues of this book to the current controversy of re-emerging white identity politics, the chapter-by-chapter discussions and stories of the interviewees are also connected to current controversies. All but one of the titles of these chapters came from state-ments made by individual interviewees. These titles signal a conceptual and linguistic shift toward negating the color-codes that define racial categories: "Pretending to be White," "Passing for Black," "No Body's Yellow," "The Brown Box," and "Red Rum."

Chapter 4, "Pretending to be White," has a slightly different purpose and structure from the other four chapters on the interviewees. It begins by defining and discussing the 13 key categories that surfaced in the coding of data and how they connected under three major themes that variously dis-tinguished and united the stories of all 20 interviewees. This chapter is used to demonstrate how each of the 13 categories reflected in the three major themes of "hyperdiversity," "stereotyping," and "identity constructions" are specifically evidenced in the lives of all four interviewees discussed. The same level of evidence supports the discussions of the other 16 interviewees, but with this group, the categories from the data are embedded in the telling of their stories.

Chapter 5, which presents the stories of four African Americans, is framed with a discussion of the Rachel Dolezal controversy, while Chapter 6, which presents the stories of four Asian Americans, begins with the con-troversy surrounding the response to the 2017 Oscars by Korean rapper Jonathan Park, who talked about knocking down racial walls. Chapter 7, which presents the stories of four Hispanic Americans, begins with a discus-sion of how identity is framed for Hispanics as connected to the most recent U.S. census. I suggest that this framing offers a way forward in thinking about the issue of identity for all people in the United States. Chapter 8, on Native Americans, is framed by the crisis at Standing Rock, and the stories of those four interviewees reflect ways of thinking about our humanity that also suggests a way forward.

Chapter 9 brings findings from the five chapters on interviewees to-gether within a framework of "Micro-cultures" that builds upon and is distinguished from Banks' (2013) concept of "microcultures" without a hyphen. The concept of micro-cultures with the hyphen is fully explicated as a framework for understanding the significance of the findings from the interview data of the previous chapters. The final chapter synthesizes findings and discussions from the earlier chapters and suggests "Challenges of Multicultural Education" in moving beyond the color-bind. It portrays "Multicultural Education 2.0" through discussion and examples of teaching and learning in schools that work to more fully realize the prospects of our country's diversity and humanity.

CHAPTER 2

Deconstructing Race

This deep feeling of race is at present the mainspring of Negro life . . . an attempt, fairly successful on the whole, to convert a defensive into an offensive position, a handicap into an incentive.

—Alain Locke (1925)

I use *deconstruct* in its literal meaning of exposing and dismantling the existing structure of a system. In this case it's the system of white supremacy that created the concept of race and sustains it through practices of racism. White supremacy is the formulation and institutionalization of social constructions of whiteness into systems of exploitation and oppression of all other peoples in order to generate and maintain power, wealth, privilege, and control. Virginia slave owners and colonial rulers in the 17th century began using the term *white* to distinguish European colonists from Africans and indigenous peoples and as an effort to prevent cross-racial revolts among unpaid laborers. After one such revolt, Bacon's Rebellions in 1676, in which indentured servants of European and African descent united against the colonial elite, the term *white* was established, naming a legal concept that designated those in the servant class on the basis of skin color and continental origin. Keep in mind that prior to the 18th-century increases in the African slave trade, between one-half and two-thirds of immigrants to the British colonies in the Western Hemisphere were white indentured laborers (Hoffman, 1991). Allen (2012) also connected the colonists' engagement with Indians to the invention of the notion of the white race. Although Indians were not enslaved in the ways African Americans were, they were considered not only nonwhite but also nonassimilatable, and therefore relegated to the other side of the color-line.

A major institutional force that has been critical to sustaining the idea of race and the term *white* as a racial marker is the U.S. census. From the first census, taken in 1790, through to the most recent one, in 2010, in presenting demographic data in racial categories, the census has used "white" to classify the race of some residents in this country, while the racial terms for every other group have gone through dramatic and problematic changes. As late as 1900, for example, U.S. census categories for people who were considered to be of "black" African descent included mulatto, quadroon, octoroon, and Negro or of Negro descent, as well as black. Interestingly, based on decades of U.S. census data, Palmié (2007) estimated that about 25% of Americans listed as white in 1970 probably had ancestors from Africa. Hypodescent, the one-drop-of-black-blood rule, would change the identity of many who see themselves as white. On the other hand, more than 80% of those listed as black had non-African ancestors (Palmié, 2007, p. 206). U.S. census designations for Asians, Hispanics, and American Indians and Alaskan Natives were also highly changeable over time, while the term for marking whiteness as a racial designation has remained constant from 1790 to the present.

The 2010 census recognized six racial categories: "white American," "black or African American," "American Indian and Alaska Native," "Asian American," "Native Hawaiian and Other Pacific Islander," and "people of two or more races" (U.S. Census Bureau, 2010). It classified Hispanic or Latino as an ethnicity rather than a race. As noted in Chapter 1, the definition the U.S. Office of Management and Budget (OMB) provided in 1997 for self-identifying Hispanic or Latino ethnicity is actually a more accurate and viable way for all individuals in the United States to self-identify in terms of their ancestry, inclusive of ethnic and geographical origins.

Instead, directed by the OMB, the U.S. census continues to sustain a white/black racial binary by its use of these two colors to designate racial categories. It does not use color designations for any of the other racial groups it attempts to track. Nevertheless, it sustains the notion of hypodescent in that if a person who chooses the "black or African American" category also chooses to identify with one or more additional, races including the white race, he or she is still racially identified as a member of the "black in combination" population, or the "multiple race black" population (Rastogi, Johnson, Hoeffel, & Drewery, 2011). In other words, a person could have parents who were white and black, but if both designations were chosen in the 2010 census, she or he would be identified as of the "black in combination" population. All the other categories on the census can also be in combination with other groups; however, no option is provided for a "white in combination" population.

Remarking on how race is constructed in the United States, Coates (2015) wrote, "Race is the child of racism, not the father" (p. 7). We can also see race as the child of white supremacy, the illegitimate offspring of mating power with possessiveness in the interests of capital accumulation and social control. Following Lipsitz in this regard, it is "the possessive investment in whiteness that is responsible for the racialized hierarchies in our society" (2006, p. vii). This also reflects what Feagin (2010) called "the white racial frame" that propagates and rationalizes racial inequality through a broad set of institutional structures and practices.

Leonardo (2009) defined white supremacy as a specific form of modern racism that underlies and makes other forms of racism thrive (p. 118). He separated whiteness as a force extending from a racialized collective that has fueled colonization and other forms of domination from "white ethnic cultures, some forms of which may be benign or even critical" (p. 118). However, lumping all groups together that have been variously and at different historical periods assigned as white by forces of white supremacy is problematic, rather than benign or critical. As indicated in Chapter 3, these selective assignments and their acceptances by groups not previously defined as white reflects conscious political and ideological expansions of whiteness. Consequently, the notion of "white ethnic cultures" must be dis- aggregated into specific ethnic cultures that over time have been defined as white. Building on insights from scholarship and from the 20 interviewees, I argue in this book that in contrast to identification with whiteness, people's recognition and affirmation of identities and affinities linked to but also going beyond specific ethnic identities and cultures reveal movement toward deconstructing race.

I also use *deconstruct* to connect to elements of the philosophy of de- construction (Derrida, 2005/1967) that countered the very idea of literal meanings and demonstrated that everyday language is not innocent or neu- tral. The everyday language in question is resident in the terms "white" and "black," and three other colorized referents—"yellow," "brown," and "red"*—capriciously situated between the white/black poles. These terms have been historically constructed and enforced around the core white/black binary through which white supremacy works, and they are defined and operationalized as if they have intrinsic rather than constructed meanings, qualities, and values.

Derrida's contributions to a conceptual shift, a linguistic and cultural "turn" (Bonnell & Hunt, 1999) in social and textual analysis, helped to open new modes of thinking that critiqued and challenged old paradigms and epistemological models. One premise of Derrida's concept of decon- struction is the denial of any possibility of a pure presence or intrinsic es- sence, including the denial of any essential notion of "being." Subsequently, scholars like Nakayama and Krizek (2010) and others have noted that there is no true essence to whiteness. Rather, it is a rhetorical construction—and a "state of mind" as noted by Baldwin in *A Rap on Race* (Mead & Baldwin, 1971)—that must be named and critiqued to expose how it works in in- stantiating and normalizing its values and beliefs. These frameworks were useful for illustrating how terms, like *white* and *black*, can be constituted in reciprocal determination as oppositions. Derrida contended, "In a classical philosophical opposition we are not dealing with the peaceful coexistence of a vis-à-vis, but rather a violent hierarchy. One of the two terms governs the other (axiologically, logically, etc.), or has the upper hand" (1981/1972, p. 41).

---

*In addition to quotation marks being placed around the color-coded designations in this sentence, every subsequent use of these terms to identify racial groups should be read as if they were also within quotation marks. Similarly, the terms *race* and *racial* should also be read as if they were in quotes.

For the United States to become more just and democratic—for it to truly acknowledge and affirm its multicultural identity and history—it is imperative that the terms governing its violent racial hierarchy and that give whites the upper hand be dismantled. Acknowledging that "the sheer amount of acts of violence or terror by whites toward racial minorities is overwhelming," Leonardo created a list, which I will return to in the next chapter, of 29 acts, laws, and decisions that capture a "portrait of white supremacy" (2009, p. 85). This overwhelming violence takes many forms and stems directly from ways that societal inequities are structured, perpetuated, and exacerbated through politics and law; corporations and the military; health care and employment disparities; poverty, policing, and prisons; media, sports, and entertainment; and, yes, education.

The voices and views of the scholars and interviewees brought together in this book make a compelling case that viable prospects for addressing societal inequities and their concomitant acts of violence are fundamentally connected to deconstructing race. Although not a panacea for the historically structured racial inequities in the United States, education can contribute to prospects for a more just society. Multicultural education can be a potent force that increases our understanding and expression of personal-cultural identities and perspectives outside the prisons and prisms of the color-bind. To do so, however, requires shifting the multicultural paradigm beyond essentialized categories of race.

MULTICULTURAL EDUCATION

Education and lifelong learning experiences are the most important ways we understand our world, ourselves, and our relations with others. If education is to be a vehicle for progressive personal and interpersonal transformation, issues of equity, diversity, inclusion, and building on the assets of all students must lie at its heart. But education systems in the United States have been made to privilege the cultural practices of people who define themselves as white in ways that marginalize and present obstacles to learning for students from all other cultural groups (Banks, 2003, 2013; Carter, 2012; Gay, 2010; Gregory & Weinstein, 2008; Ladson-Billings, 2006; Mahiri, 2011; Mahiri & Freedman, 2014; Nieto, 2013; Noguera, 2008; Sleeter, 2013; Sleeter & Grant, 1987; Valenzuela, 1999). Schools, in fact, are primary vehicles for separating people based on race and ability as well as gender and age. Consequently, they have historically contributed to the formulation of ideas about race, and they could play an important role in helping to break down racial boundaries in our society.

Having emerged in response to the assimilationist models, early on, *multicultural education* was defined as "a field of study designed to increase educational equity for all students and incorporated, for this purpose, content, concepts, principles, theories, and paradigms from history, the social and behavioral sciences, and particularly from ethnic studies and women's studies" (Banks & McGee Banks, 1995, p. xii). An important goal is for all students to acquire the dispositions, knowledge, and skills to effectively function in a democratic society that works for the common good. To this end, it developed and promoted approaches to learning that were culturally relevant (Ladson-Billings, 2009), culturally responsive (Gay, 2010), and eventually culturally sustaining (Paris, 2012).

Critical race theory (Bell, 1992; Ladson-Billings & Tate, 1995) pushed the multicultural paradigm beyond curricular transformation to deeper considerations of how race permeates every aspect of education as well as the larger society. Of course, some of these considerations were also addressed or implied in formulations of scholars who shaped multicultural education— like the five dimensions of multicultural education (Banks & McGee Banks, 2004), Nieto and Bode's (1992) seven dimensions of multicultural education, Sleeter and Grant's (1987) five approaches to multicultural education, and Gay and Howard's (2000) work on multicultural teaching for the 21st century. For example, Banks and McGee Banks's (2004) five dimensions, which have been widely used in creating multicultural education courses and programs, include a focus on equity pedagogy and prejudice reduction in addition to considerations for content integration, knowledge construction, and empowerment of school cultures and social structures. Similarly, Sleeter and Grant's (1987) five approaches include understanding the strength and values of different cultural groups and developing good human relationships between them. Essentially, all the dimensions and approaches to multicultural education include issues of equity along with the importance of creating greater congruence between students' cultural backgrounds and schooling experiences in order to increase academic achievement and personal and social development. But they all also take for granted the racial distinctions that have been made between different groups.

As a more radical extension of multiculturalism, critical race theory focused on whiteness as property, interest conversion of whites, critiques of liberalism, and counter-storytelling to clarify the effects of race and racism in education and society in the United States. In illuminating the pervasiveness of race, this framework also claimed that racism is permanent. Consequently, it does not work beyond the problematic categories of race that have been assigned by white supremacy. However, Crenshaw's (1989) work on intersectionality productively extends critical race theory toward a more comprehensive critique of how oppression occurs on multiple dimensions simultaneously at the intersection of an array of components of an individual's identity. And, while it widens the gaze to other categories of identity, more work is needed to directly deconstruct the ascribed categories that extend from the very idea of race. This is particularly true for the idea of a white race resulting from the critical significance of the concept of whiteness at the center of the race problem. Ignatiev and Garvey (1996), for example, argued that acceptance of the existence of races as reflected in multiculturalism and general theories of race is problematic because it normalizes race as something more than a constructed idea.

So conceptions of race continue to reflect limits in multicultural education research and scholarship. This is exemplified in the Hanley and Noblit (2009) review of 146 studies on culturally responsive pedagogy. In exploring culture and racial identity as an asset across all these studies, they framed this extensive review within the fixed racial categories of white supremacy and coined the acronym ALANA to stand for African American, Latina/o American, Asian American, and Native American. European Americans intentionally were not addressed in the numerous studies they decided to review.

Continuing the use of these categories is problematic because they are based on the notion that humans exist in distinct groups defined by inborn traits that group members share. They are problematic also because the social practices of racism operate by taking for granted that these distinctions are real despite their having no scientific basis. Consequently, though working toward progressive goals, multicultural education in the United States is constrained—if not subverted—in its important work to increase educational equity for all students. It should also be noted that another critical limitation of multicultural education practices is the negligible attention paid to differences of sexuality, gender, and social class in contrast to the amount given to race, ethnicity, and culture (Asher, 2007). A number of the people interviewed for this book talked about the centrality of these considerations in constructions of their identities.

Banks and McGee Banks (2004) insightfully noted that multicultural education must address four important questions if it is to become fully institutionalized and continue to challenge the United States to honor its democratic values and principles. Part of her concern was how one of the antecedents to multicultural education, the intergroup education movement, eventually became divided and dissolved when, over time, it did not effectively address these same questions. For the present discussion, I will focus on just one of the questions that McGee Banks outlined: "If multicultural education is to maintain its integrity, what can change and what must remain the same?" (p. 148).

Based on the scholarship reviewed and the people interviewed in this book, illuminating the specific play of micro-cultural positioning, practices, choices, and perspectives in people's lives provides the basis for an ameliorative shift in the multicultural paradigm to help it maintain its integrity and viability and increase its transformational impact as an educative force.

LEARNING FROM LITERATURE

A wealth of scholarship has convincingly argued both the fallacy of racial constructions and how they have been intentionally changed by sociopolitical dynamics and contexts, thus further indicating the absence of any ontological purity or intrinsic essence. In this present section, I highlight how specific books by four of these scholars, W. E. B. Du Bois, Ralph Ellison, Toni Morrison, and James Baldwin, have clarified and critiqued intricate issues of race in the United States and guided my thinking in this book.

During his long life of prolific scholarship and activism within and beyond the black emancipation tradition, Du Bois described and analyzed racial issues from slavery and Reconstruction; through the Jim Crow era, the Harlem Renaissance, the Great Depression, and both world wars; to the civil rights, black liberation, and Pan-African movements; and up to the doorstep of the hip-hop and digital generations. At the turn of the 20th century in *Souls of Black Folk* (1994/1903), he provided understandings of the complexity and contradictions of racial formulations that are equally incisive in the opening decades of the 21st.

Du Bois argued that the challenge was not to Africanize America, or to bleach the Negro soul in a flood of white Americanism, but to simply "make it possible for a man to be both a Negro and an American" (1994/1903, p. 3). Importantly, he also profoundly understood the ways that the color-line has always been porous and penetrable—that human passions, prerogatives, and power have never been bound by ascribed racial categories, even when policed by unimaginable cruelties of slavery, rape, torture, and lynching. He captured the dreadful complexity of these dichotomies in a provocative passage that I abridged as follows. "Amid it all, two figures ever stand to typify that day to coming ages,—the one, a gray-haired gentleman. . . . the other, a form hovering dark and mother-like . . . had aforetime quailed at that white master's command . . . aye, too, at his behest had laid herself low to his lust, and borne a tawny man-child to the world, only to see her dark boy's limbs scattered to the winds by midnight marauders" (p. 18).

Du Bois included in his formulation of the color-line "the relation of the darker to the lighter races of men in Asia and Africa, in America and the islands of the sea" (1994/1903, p. 9). But in the United States, he tried to show what emancipation meant to African Americans and, further, what life was like in "the two worlds within and without the Veil," in part, by stepping "within the Veil, raising it that you may view faintly its deeper recesses" (p. v). There were times in *The Souls of Black Folk* when Du Bois took on the role of an ethnographer, going into the backcountry/the black country of Tennessee and using his work as a teacher to gain intimate access to those communities. I humbly attempted something similar with people in each of the assigned racial categories by using ethnographic interviews to probe the deeper recesses of their personal-cultural being behind the "Veil" of the color-bind.

In the prologue to *Invisible Man*, intentionally or not, Ellison (1947) made a "signifying connection"(Gates, 1988) to the scene described above from *Souls of Black Folk*. Like Du Bois's work to lift the veil and see the deeper recesses of blackness, Ellison's invisible man took us below the superficial surface of blackness to explore its complexities, including the violence—both physical and psychological—that has been exacted. Living off the grid in New York City and siphoning electricity from Monopolated Light and Power to illuminate 1,369 lights in his underground room and play his phonograph, the invisible man might be seen as a precursor to early hip-hop DJs who plugged into lamp poles in the Bronx to mix music for their parties in the streets. Like music innovators would discover 30 years later, and with the help of a hit of reefer and sips of sloe gin, the invisible man found "a new analytical way of listening to music. . . . The unheard sounds came through, and each melodic line existed of itself, stood out clearly from all the rest, said its piece, and waited patiently for the other voices to speak" (Ellison, 1947, p. 8).

What the protagonist "mixed" was his sense of invisibility with the sounds of the blues, specifically Louis Armstrong's song "(What Did I Do to Be So) Black and Blue." This mix aided in understanding Armstrong's music and created a slightly different sense of time: "You're never quite on the beat. Sometimes you're ahead and sometimes behind. Instead of the swift and imperceptible flowing of time, you are aware of its nods, those points where time stands still or from which it leaps ahead. And you slip into breaks and look around. That's what you hear vaguely in Louis' music" (Ellison, 1947, p. 8).

In entering the music, descending into its depths, and waiting patiently for other voices to speak, the invisible man found himself hearing not only in time but in space as well. At each level there was a different scene and a different story. On the first level he saw an old woman "singing a spiritual as full of Weltschmerz as flamenco" (Ellison, 1947, p. 9). Her story echoed the same theme of power and passion between a white man and a black woman described in the passage above from *Souls of Black Folk*. On the next level he saw "a beautiful girl the color of ivory" pleading in a voice like his mother's "as she stood before a group of slaveowners who bid for her naked body" (p. 9). On a lower level still he encountered someone preaching a sermon on the "Blackness of Blackness" that arguably also is a deconstruction of blackness: "'I said black is . . . an' black ain't.' . . . Black will Make you . . . or black will unmake you. . . . Ain't it the truth, Lawd" (p. 9).

These scenes from the prologue of *Invisible Man* merge with what is seen in *Souls of Black Folk* to lift the veil of white supremacy and reveal ways it works to create and contrast itself to blackness—a blackness that often gets expressed in blues. My ethnographic interviews were also portals for slipping between the hues and descending to the depths of my informants' experiences in time and place and cyberspace.

The invisible man loved light and needed it to confirm his reality. Yet he had been "boomeranged" across his head so often that he also came to see the "darkness of lightness" (Ellison, 1947, p. 6). This oxymoron bridges to Morrison's (1992) *Playing in the Dark* and her potent critique of the authoring of invisibility of blacks in literature that is synonymous with how the invisible man understood the inability or refusal of whites to see him in the physical world. Instead, they saw only his surroundings, themselves, or figments of their imaginations because of the *inner* eyes that focused their physical eyes on which aspects of reality to discern.

As with Ellison, Morrison's quest to render a "deep story" (1992, p. v) beyond superficial views of blackness (in this case in white literary imaginations) also connected to Louis Armstrong. This connection occurred in conjunction with her critique of Marie Cardinal's (1983) autobiographical novel, *The Words to Say It*. Cardinal's intention in this work "was to document her madness, her therapy, and the complicated process of healing" (p. v) in language that would allow her understanding of this process to be accessible to readers. The precise narrative moment when the author knew she was in trouble psychologically and in danger of collapse was revealed about 40 pages into the text with a description of her first anxiety attack, her first encounter with "the Thing." It occurred during a Louis Armstrong concert while he was playing an improvisation on his trumpet. To paraphrase how Cardinal described it, the sounds of the trumpet piled up to fuse a new musical base that gave birth to one precise, unique note whose path was almost painful as it tore at the nerves of those who followed it. At this point her heart began to accelerate, shaking her rib cage and compressing her lungs so that she had to leave the concert and run out into the streets, like someone possessed.

Morrison noted how this intense scene that catalyzed Cardinal's anxiety attack was invisibilized in terms of the process of her regaining mental health because its significance was not marked or remarked on by Cardinal, her analyst, or the eminent doctor who wrote the preface and afterword to her book. This invisible presence was nonetheless embedded in and acting on the text, even if it was not the author's conscious intention. Areskoug and Asklund (2014) identified how these invisible presences act as "stowaways of fiction" or "stowaways of storytelling" (p. 35) that, like the famous stowaway in Joseph Conrad's "The Secret Sharer" (1910), definitively affect and dramatically contribute to the narrative from down below its surface meanings, whether the author's "hidings" are conscious or unconscious. In his poem "The Whipping," Robert Hayden (1966) emotively captured both the physical and psychological effects of "hidings" that must be born, even though they are not visible on the surface of skin.

Morrison's critique uncovered the stowaways hidden in Cardinal's narrative. For example, she noted how in Cardinal's *The Words to Say It*, "black or colored people and symbolic figurations of blackness are markers, metaphorical shortcuts, for the benevolent and the wicked; the spiritual . . . and the voluptuous; of 'sinful' but delicious sensuality coupled with demands for purity or restraint" (Morrison, 1992, p. ix). She built on her critique of Cardinal to demonstrate how throughout *Playing in the Dark* language and literature are able to "powerfully evoke and enforce hidden signs of racial superiority, cultural hegemony, and dismissive 'othering' of people" (p. xx). Her motive to apprehend these hidden signs and images and trace their effects on the literary imagination also guides my motive in this book to probe and illuminate how socially constructed signs and images of race affect and often constrain how we imagine ourselves and others in daily life.

Can we, as Morrison once attempted in her only short story, experiment with readings (of the world and ourselves) in which meanings are not pervasively expressed through reductive racial codes? Can we see the personal-cultural positioning, practices, and choices that constitute the identities and affinities of each individual as fluid, diverse components of what Morrison saw as possibilities for "a sharable world"? Whiteness clouds this vision through the bifocal of white supremacy that attempts to split the world into a binary of whites and others. Even when extended beyond white and black to "people of color," the constructions of these people(s) are almost always in contrast to constructions of whiteness.

Nearly 50 years ago in his first comment in *A Rap on Race*, coauthored with anthropologist Margaret Mead, James Baldwin, like many others before and after, indicated a principal driver of this racial split: "It is a question of the fears of white people. . . . That's what makes it all so hysterical, so unwieldy and so completely irretrievable. Reason cannot reach it" (Mead & Baldwin, 1971, p. 1). In the documentary film on Baldwin titled *I Am Not Your Negro*, which opened in theaters in February 2017, the hysteria and violence predicated on the fears of white people from this country's inception to the present moment are graphically and painfully displayed.

In 1970 Baldwin and Mead met for 7½ hours over a period of 2 days in late August to discuss race and society. *A Rap on Race* was published from the transcripts of those discussions. The conversation began amicably, but it ended in heated confrontation. As with the works of the other scholars addressed in this section, Baldwin's insights during this extended dialogue helped me think about key considerations for *Deconstructing race*. In some ways his conversation with Mead was a bit like an ethnographic dialogue, with both participants learning from the lives of the other. Baldwin, particularly, brought up intimate experiences of growing up in Harlem and living in the United States as well as abroad. He shared the traumatic experience of almost being beaten to death by two police officers when he was 10 years old. The core problem in the United States, he surmised, the one problem that obsessed his life, is the problem of color. Baldwin claimed, "It is not an isolated, particular, peculiar problem. It is a symptom of all the problems in this country" (Mead & Baldwin, 1971, p. 66).

Baldwin was acutely aware of speaking in "horrible generalities" of white people or black people (or any people). He spoke incisively about essential contradictions, not just among white people, but also among people who had come to identify themselves as black. He described how some had spent most of their lives trying to be white and its cost to their humanity. He discussed how difficult it was to account for this cost, except in black music or perhaps in the black church. One can hear echoes of "(What Did I Do to Be So) Black and Blue," from the prologue to *Invisible Man* as well as connections to the sermon on "the blackness of blackness" that Ellison's protagonist witnessed deep between the notes. Many of Baldwin's books might be seen as similar sermons, beginning with their explicit references to biblical themes in their titles: *The Fire Next Time, Go Tell It on the Mountain,* and *The Evidence of Things Not Seen.* He noted, "If you try to take apart a black man's sermon and really understand what he is saying, it's kind of terrifying" (Mead & Baldwin, 1971, p. 14).

Baldwin was also acutely aware of the mixing, both forced and consensual, that has always occurred among people and expressed that people who define themselves as white know all this, yet "pretend . . . that it isn't so" (p. 40). Pretense, including the pretense of being white, sustains the color-bind. At one point in his dialogue with Mead, Baldwin challenged her perception that she herself was white. "You're neither black nor white, either. Because, as Malcolm X put it, white is a state of mind. The great question, my dear, is how one begins to attack that state of mind" (p. 159). As one kind of attack, Morrison imagined a story without racial codes, and although Baldwin did not feel race could be ignored, while in France among all kinds of different people (where he said he found himself), Baldwin came to see the possibility of a different frame of reference beyond the simple binary he grew up and lived with in the United States. Importantly, he realized that once the racial bifocal was lifted, he could no longer view the social world through its dichotomous lens and instead relied on his own *inner eyes* to see realities beyond the cloud of whiteness.

Toward the end, Baldwin and Mead's dialogue became acrimonious. For one thing, Mead strongly disagreed with Baldwin's claim that history is the present. He argued, "You and I are history. We carry our history. We act in our history. . . . We *act* on it. And if one is going to change history—and we have to change history—we have to change ourselves because we *are* history" (Mead & Baldwin, 1971, p. 175). He went on to talk about the responsibility we must all have to the future, a commitment to generations unborn. In his words, "We are meant to be witnesses to a possibility which we will not live to see, but we have to bring it out. . . . It has to do with what we know human beings have been and can become" (p. 185).

Morrison and Du Bois are consonant with these views of Baldwin on activism, responsibility, and commitment to change the history of race. Along with Ellison, all have made significant conceptual contributions to understanding whiteness and white supremacy, and they have formatively influenced the development of whiteness studies that has extensively critiqued the social construction of whiteness and the invention of the white race. One reason these four scholars have been so instrumental in reconceiving race is that each has simultaneously been a part of and apart from U.S. constructions of race. Like ethnographers, they existed in interstitial spaces by being a part of cultural (and literary) practices as active participants, yet apart from them as keen observers and critics.

Du Bois described the souls of black folk in part by getting proximal and living with them as a teacher to observe and document "the two worlds within and without the Veil." Ellison used participant observations of an invisible man to focus "inner eyes" on heightening the visibility of racial contradictions. Morrison, reading like a writer, revealed the distorted constructions of blackness in white literary imaginations playing in the dark. And Baldwin grounded insights from a literary life on the boundary to deliver a rap on race that dismantled essential premises on which race in the United States is based.

While Ellison and Morrison have called attention to the continual need for whites to be reassured of superiority, Du Bois and Baldwin have called for whites to disavow their loyalty to whiteness and its conferred privileges. This latter idea is seen by some as treason or evidence of one's being a "race traitor." It might also be seen as the kind of reason that's needed to help people become "race traders"—consciously subverting loyalty to race for loyalty to a broader humanity and to a shareable, sustainable world. The idea of race traitors is that people who are identified as white and who have the strongest investment in whiteness no longer accept that identity and work to disrupt its attending structures of power and privilege. This attributes agency mainly to people defined as white. The idea of race traders is that they cannot be just whites, although they must include *just* whites. In other words, all people who are oppressed willingly or unwillingly collude in the production of whiteness and the hierarchy of white supremacy by enduring and even embracing the subordinated, racial categories to which they have been assigned. Rather than overturning hierarchies of oppression, they wretchedly reproduce them.

Additionally, since the oppressive system itself inculcates its hierarchical model of humanity, a real danger in struggling against it is that the oppressed themselves can become oppressors or "sub-oppressors" when their vision is veiled to more equitable ways of being human. According to Freire (1970), "The very structure of their thought has been conditioned by the concrete, existential situation by which they are shaped" (p. 30). This imperative, however, is superseded by prospects for deconstructing race.

PROSPECTS AND IMPERATIVES

Prospects for deconstructing race connect, in part, to a brief meeting more than 35 years ago that I was fortunate to have had with Toni Morrison. Recently out of college, I was the managing editor for a quarterly journal, *Black Books Bulletin,* that was published by an activist community organization in Chicago, the Institute of Positive Education. At the time Toni

Morrison was an editor at Random House, and our journal's editor, Don L. Lee, made a request to her to meet with me in her New York office so that I could learn more about editing and publishing. During the 45-minute meeting, one of the things she talked about was a book she was editing on the role of trains in the development of the United States. She liked the book but had indicated to the author that it had very little on how trains were integral to the history and development of blacks in this country and how blacks were integral to the history and development of trains. Initially, the author's response was to add another chapter on blacks at the end of the book. This perhaps was consistent with how for so long blacks had been segregated on trains going up North from the South and relegated to colored-only train cars. But Morrison required a complete reworking of the entire book to incorporate blacks into all the other aspects of training that were addressed, rather than just having a chapter on blacks added as a kind of caboose on the end.

This way of thinking about and narrating dynamic intersections and interactions of different people in the history and development of this country, instead of simply telling a series of separate stories, stuck with me. There was no place for this way of thinking in the formulations of white supremacy, but also there was no place for it within the formulations of the black activist organizations to which I belonged at that time. The ascription of a fictive, white racial purity created and delineated a binary opposite in blackness. But our subscription to blackness reflected the same essential problem of attempting to establish and project a racial purity that was equally fictive.

One interesting example of a formulation of black racial purity was the theorizing of "Nigrescence" by Cross (1991) to explain what he claimed to be a "Negro to black conversion experience." With the purpose of forming development theories and personality constructs that could facilitate black people's liberating themselves from oppression, Cross articulated five stages of the process of conversion from being a Negro to being a black: pre-encounter, encounter, immersion-emersion, internalization, and internalization-commitment. Interestingly, there is no real evidence that people systematically move through these neatly defined stages. More importantly, the notion that people can be divided and defined by a hierarchical, psychological, and behavioral model that maps a process of their becoming increasingly black suggests that, like white racial purity, there is a black racial purity that is possible and desirable to achieve.

I'm aware that one response to oppression and the terms through which it is expressed is to vacate some of its signifiers and infuse them with more politically positive or culturally acceptable meanings. This linguistic jujitsu leverages the accumulated weight of a negative term in order to flip it. It's argued that this has been done with the N-word. Ultimately, as constructions of white supremacy, there is nothing more redemptive in the word "black" than in the word "Negro," or its close relative the "N" word, or the plethora of other words used over time to designate "the other."

These considerations equally apply to the term "white." Human rights educator Wendy Zagray Warren noted how people she works with in the South sometimes resent exaltations of diversity by others because their generalized white identities cloud or deemphasize more specific (and potentially affirming) ethnic or national origin connections (Warren, personal communication, November 17, 2016). When whiteness is disaggregated, it is also dissipated. In another example, Olsen (2008) interviewed white high school students and discovered that they held resentment toward students of color for forming clubs based on their cultural or racial identities, such as the Black Student Club and La Raza. When the transparency of whiteness was lost, Olsen noted, these white students experienced a "crisis of identity."

In attempts to claim a more salient identity, people who have their DNA tested are almost always surprised, if not shocked, by rich, unrecognized diversity in their backgrounds. How complex and uniquely specified would an individual's identity be if it was informed by (reverse engineered by) direct connections to at least seven generations in the past? How would it be further informed by seeing its connections to at least seven generations in the future? Seven generations is a time span that could be experienced by an individual in a single lifetime. We could actually know people we are connected to seven generations in the past and appreciate the influences they have had on who we are today. And we can potentially know people whose identities we have influenced seven generations hence. Inevitably, we would see the unique pathways that brought each of us to this present moment, and the array of possible pathways into the future. Understanding human identity within a flow of generations further illuminates the false notions of racial purity that are central to the hierarchies of white supremacy.

The 2015–16 presidential contest between Hillary Clinton and Donald Trump provided numerous examples of destructive uses of race predicated on racial purity. The hope for some that was generated by Bernie Sanders was extinguished after the Republican and Democratic conventions. At the same time, the daily media feast on Trump's white identity politics incited divisions in our nation based on race, religion, gender, class, national origin, ability, and physiology. The media mania around Trump's campaign is important because media powerfully contributes to how people make sense of the world and what becomes normalized, sanctioned, or acceptable generally and with specific regard to diverse others (Jackson, 2014). The New York Times estimated that the media contributed $2 billion of free publicity or "earned media" by March 2016 (Confessore & Yourish, 2016). This media barrage also revealed how prospects for a more equitable, sustainable world were being deliberately disassembled by Trump's xenophobic narratives and actions.

Although it has always been imperative that nihilistic behaviors and views be challenged and changed, it was troubling that profit-driven motives of the media, even in strident critique, often enabled and propagated his attacks on and condemnations of so many individuals and groups. Trump constantly decried Mexicans as rapists; Muslims as terrorists; African Americans as lazy; immigrants as criminals; women as fat, ugly, and nasty; war heroes as losers; veterans with post-traumatic stress as not being mentally tough; top generals as embarrassing to the country; the disabled as targets for mockery. The list goes on and perilously includes his condoning of torture (and the torture of families of terror suspects without due process), his nuclear saber rattling, and his denial of human causes of climate change. Additionally, some of his campaign promises were clearly unconstitutional.

On August 25, 2016, Hillary Clinton released a video of some of the white supremacists who were backing Trump, and in a 30-minute speech in Reno, Nevada, on the same day, she laid out a case for why Trump was, in her words, "a profoundly dangerous racist." "The names may have changed," she said. "Racists now call themselves racialists. White supremacists now call themselves white nationalists. A paranoid fringe, a mostly online group with a mix of white nationalist beliefs, now calls itself the 'alt-right.'" These groups saw Trump as a vehicle for amplifying and legitimizing their ideas, one of which was that saying racist things was not an act of hate, but an act of freedom.

David Duke, a former leader of the Ku Klux Klan, was one of the people inspired by Trump's presidential campaign. Although Trump disavowed Duke's support, it did not stop white supremacists like Duke from attaching themselves to him. Trump said on television that he would have to do some research before denouncing the KKK. Motivated to run for the U.S. Senate seat for Louisiana to advocate for European Americans, Duke said in an interview aired on National Public Radio (August 5, 2016) that Trump's attacks on Muslims and illegal immigration had brought his own beliefs into the mainstream. As revealed in this interview, Duke's beliefs in a nutshell were that "there's massive racist, racial discrimination against European Americans . . . a vicious anti-white narrative in our national media," and political correctness inhibits people from expressing their real political views (Inskeep, NPR, August 5, 2016).

Trump—who avoided the draft and inherited considerable wealth from his father, an avowed white nationalist, to finance his businesses—laid the foundation for the white identity politics at the core of his presidential campaign by actively stoking a sense of paranoia regarding race. His derisive questioning of President Barack Obama's birthplace and citizenship beginning in 2011 propelled him into the spotlight and eventually national politics. With just weeks remaining before the election, he continued making statements such as "An extremely credible source has called my office and told me that Barack Obama's birth certificate is a fraud." Although Trump's campaign was characterized by racism, sexism, and bigotry, many people were passionately, albeit irrationally, receptive to it. It also reflected the separate standard that this country has for men identified as white. Would Obama have been elected if it had come out before his election that he had sexually assaulted a number of women? Followers proclaiming that

"Trump could shoot someone on Broadway, and I would still vote for him" (McCamon, 2016) exemplified both the passion and the irrationality of the rhetoric that was stirred up. With Trump actively propagating white identity politics and a climate of hate and distrust, acts of racial violence and aggression increased, as reported by many sources. Within a week after the election, for example, the Southern Poverty Law Center (2016) documented a significant surge in "hate incidents," with the most frequent occurring in K–12 schools, followed by businesses and universities.

A small but telling example occurred at my own university in the building that houses the Graduate School of Education, where I teach. Somebody defaced the poster of a doctoral student, T. Geronimo Johnson, that was hanging in the lobby simply because it depicted an African American man. In addition to Johnson's statement that graduate school taught him that "giving back is the greatest gift you will ever receive," the poster noted that he worked with the College Writing Programs on campus and that he was also the director of the Summer Creative Writing Program. Someone wrote in large letters: "Enough PC Bullshit, Ok. Time to promote a real writer." The racist inscription on the poster was telling because the defiling person implied by the comment that because he is black, Johnson could not be a "real writer."

While completing his doctorate, Johnson (who holds an MFA from the Iowa Writer's Workshop) had published two well-received novels, *Hold It Till It Hurts* (2012) and *Welcome to Braggsville* (2015). His first novel was selected as a finalist for the 2013 PEN/Faulkner Award for Fiction out of 350 works that had been considered. His second novel was named the winner of the 2015 Ernest J. Gaines Award for Literary Excellence and also of the 2016 William Saroyan International Prize for Writing. It was long-listed for the 2015 National Book Award, long-listed for the 2015 Andrew Carnegie Medal for Excellence in Fiction, named 1 of 10 books all Georgians should read by the Georgia Center for the Book, and included on *Time* magazine's list of the top 10 books of 2015. The tagged implication that Johnson could not possibly be a real writer reflected the kind of sentiments noted in *A Rap on Race* that "reason cannot reach" (Mead & Baldwin, 1971, p. 1) because reason is predicated on a search for truth. Particularly since the 2016 election, it's important for multicultural education to more directly incorporate considerations of moral education and the role of reasoning as central to developing youth into adults who are equipped and able to logically address and promote equity and social justice in our society (Nucci, 2016).

In conjunction with the backlash to Barack Obama's presidency, for example, it can be argued that Trump's campaign reflected what Keyes (2004) indicated by the title of his book *The Post-Truth Era*, the erasure of boundaries between honesty and dishonesty, between truth and lies. This era is enabled by media becoming entertainment that gives "exciting" (or inciting) people a platform even when it is clear that they are lying or being intentionally deceptive. Trump's media persona was built on lies, distortions and dissembling of the truth, and fake news. In his 1987 book with Schwartz entitled *The Art of the Deal,* Trump even lied about his parents being, not German, but Swedish. Trump called his proclivity for embellishing the truth "truthful hyperbole" (Trump & Schwartz, 1987), which is an oxymoron because hyperbole is, by definition, untrue. Nonetheless, the lies of "truthful hyperbole" can have considerable psychological force despite lacking logical force. His campaign's catchphrase, "Make America Great Again," harkened to a notion of the past that only existed as hyperbole. The danger to our society, to any society, is for it to be driven by powerful forces that may have psychological value for some but have no bases in truth and reason.

White supremacy is such a force. Its violent hierarchies of race confound the truth. It erects walls that divide who gets defined as "us" from who gets defined as "them." They can be physical walls, but they are more constraining as psychological ones. We may have deep feelings of race, deep attachments to it, but as Alain Locke (1925) noted in a paraphrase of the quote that began this chapter, this is merely the attempt to convert a defensive position into an offensive one, to make a handicap an incentive.

Hélio, Santi, and coming generations of children should not be handicapped *or* privileged by constructions of race. Both first cousins are ardent about solving puzzles and building things. People frequently remark that they think like engineers. Hélio has already skipped a grade in school (as his father had at about the same age), and Santi shows similar intellectual and artistic passions and promise. Unfortunately, our society responds to them differently based on their different hues. We all have skin in this game, but the game should not be fixated on skin. It's entirely illegible for readings of race.

A pressing problem in the early decades of the 21st century is to move beyond skin color as a surrogate for race and difference, to tear down the psychological walls that divide us and build more equitable, inclusive, and sustainable connections. It is the challenge to realize Baldwin's vision of "what we know human beings have been and can become" (1970, p. 185). As guest editor of a special issue of *Wired,* President Obama (2016) discussed other challenges we face: "Climate change. Economic inequality. Cybersecurity. Terrorism and gun violence. Cancer, Alzheimer's, and antibiotic-resistant superbugs" (Obama, 2016, p. 20). A plaque on his desk concisely states, "Hard Things are Hard." Yet, he also noted, "through our ingenuity, our commitment to fact and reason, and ultimately our faith in each other—[humans] can science the heck out of just about any problem" (p. 19). Intentionally, we can change our experiences of race such that the history of race is also changed to more accurately reflect what contemporary science understands about the idea of race. What I've learned from the literature and from the lives of others offers prospects for moving beyond the imperatives of the color-bind toward deconstructing race.

CHAPTER 3

The Color-Bind

I whiten my blackmen, I beckon my white, What's the hue of a hide to a man in his might!

—W. E .B. Du Bois (1899)

Du Bois characterized the key issue of the 20th century as the problem of the color-line. I argue in this book that the key issue of the 21st century is the problem of the color-bind. Scholarship in this chapter expands the conceptual framing on how whiteness in the United States was created and sustained and how it in turn creates and colors others as nonwhite. This chapter also discusses how people's identities are imprisoned within the limited spectrum of color categories that have been generated by and distinguished from whiteness as they are refracted through the prism of white supremacy. Insights from the interviewees in subsequent chapters indicate that an optic shift is needed to envision and appreciate the nuance, specificity, fluidity, and complexity in people's daily lives. Their varied human qualities are not confined within racialized color codes, and multicultural education has a crucial role in helping us break free of the color-bind. But a regrounding and sharper focusing of its lenses is needed to better see and appreciate people's personal-cultural identities and affinities beyond the prisons and prisms of race.

The work of some of the scholars presented in this chapter provides critiques of how race is constructed in the United States while also affirming or not explicitly negating the idea of a racial essence. Others critique the very idea of race as a ghastly fiction. The next section discusses scholarship from both perspectives that addresses the prison of race—how it is problematically constructed and why it must be deconstructed. The section following that discusses scholarship on the prism of race—how the limited spectrum of differences as they are refracted in relation to whiteness clouds rather than clarifies how people actually exist and engage in the world.

PRISONS OF RACIAL IDENTITY

The scholarship and activism of Du Bois beginning at the turn of the 20th century affirmed how his brilliance and work on issues of race in the

United States offered understandings of its complexity that are equally incisive in the opening decades of the 21st. As in the first chapter, I use Du
Bois to begin discussion of several important issues associated with the
color-bind. He was intimately aware of it and eventually of the need to
move beyond it. Considered the father of modern black scholarship, mil-
itancy, self-consciousness, and cultural development, Du Bois founded the
Niagara Movement in 1905 to fight racial discrimination and segregation
in the United States. In 1908 he was one of the founders of the National
Association for the Advancement of Colored People (NAACP) as well as
founder and editor of its journal, *The Crisis*. In the opening decades of the
20th century, Du Bois wrote on a wide range of topics in *The Crisis* and in
other works that included "The Talented Tenth" (1903), "The Burden of
Black Women" (1907), "Intermarriage" (1913), "Woman Suffrage" (1915),
and "The Souls of White Folk" (1920).

Importantly, as Zack (1993) has argued, "Du Bois was aware of the lack
of an empirical foundation in nature for the concept of race," and further,
"The black emancipatory tradition in the United States has recognized the
weakness of the concept of physical race for a long time" (p. 17). Yet, Zack
continued, "there is no sustained objection to ordinary racial designations
within the tradition of black emancipation" (p. 18). In other words, though
Du Bois and other major writers within this tradition resisted racism, they
often did so while accepting the concept of race. As Du Bois had written in
the last sentence of "The Forethought" of *Souls of Black Folk,* "Need I add
that I who speak here am bone of the bone and flesh of the flesh of them that
live within the Veil"? (1994/1903, p. vi).

Because the construction of race depends on its acceptance by the groups
and individuals it defines, we all face the dilemma of working against disas-
trous consequences of race in the United States without affirming and, thereby, perpetuating and remaining imprisoned by it. Du Bois clearly struggled
with this dilemma and ultimately saw beyond its constraints. During the
same period that he wrote about being bone and flesh of those who live behind the veil, for example, he also wrote "The Song of the Smoke" (1899),
from which the lines that introduce this chapter were taken. The narrator of
this poem proclaims, "I am darkening with song, I am hearkening to wrong,
I will be black as blackness can" (Du Bois, 1968, p. 359). Yet it's interesting
that the narrator also says, "What's the hue of a hide to a man in his might!"
Ultimately, this line indicates that a person's value and humanity cannot
be defined by skin color. Although the sentence is structured as a question,
it's significant that it ends with an exclamation. Building on the previous
line of "Whiten my blackmen," this section of the poem—like the sermon
on the blackness of blackness in the prologue to *Invisible Man* discussed
in Chapter 2—recognizes the limits of the color-bind and the prospect of
getting beyond it.

At the same time that "The Song of the Smoke" was published, Du Bois
was preparing a contribution of hundreds of photographs that captured

the progress of Negroes in the United States to be exhibited at the 1900 Paris Exposition. At first, the United States had not planned to incorporate African Americans in its national exhibit at all. However, important African American leaders appealed to President William McKinley and with just 4 months remaining before the opening, Congress belatedly appropriated a small amount of funding, $15,000, for an exhibit. One of the remarkable things about the stunning photographs Du Bois curated was the range of hues of the men, women, and children. More than 150 of these photographs were published by the Library of Congress in a book titled *A Small Nation of People: W. E. B. Du Bois and African American Portraits of Progress* (Lewis & Willis, 2005). The photographs, of course, are in black and white, and for many of the people depicted, one cannot readily tell if they are black or white or something else. As will be seen in the subsequent section on prisms of race, this ambiguity often also characterizes people assigned to other racial groups.

Du Bois himself was an example of racial ambiguity, as can be seen in photograph number 7 in the book, where he is standing tall and dapper in a top hat and long coattails at the 1900 Paris Exposition. Later in life, he definitively stated that racial categories along which color lines are drawn are social constructions. In writings compiled and reprinted after his death, for example, Zack (1993) noted how Du Bois critiqued race as a white construction used to support injustices against those who were defined as black. However, despite the range of hues and other considerations of ambiguity or indeterminacy within and between each ascribed racial group, people's identities have been forcibly constrained in prisons of racial identity that have taken many forms from the opening decades of the 20th century through early decades of the 21st. Maintenance of these prisons is core to the maintenance of white supremacy as reflected in its motives and methods.

To succinctly illustrate the destruction reaped by the imposition of material and mental prisons of white supremacy, I call attention to Leonardo's (2009) selective list of scholarship that identified 29 acts, laws, and decisions that characterize it with a condensed version of some of these points. First on the list was its promotion of the purity of the white race. Third was the rule of hypodescent, the one-drop-of-black-blood rule, which further reinforced the notion of the purity of whites. Sixth was white global supremacy and perceived white superiority, which is reinforced by the seventh point on cultural imperialism, through which "the other" is constructed and controlled as inferior and, in a later item, eroticized. Other key points listed the genocidal efforts against American Indians; the global enslavement of Africans; the internment of Japanese; the forced sterilization, sexualization, and rape of women of color; the creation of apartheid through Jim Crow laws, eugenics, and IQ testing; the lynching of African Americans; and the imposition of Christian religion on non-Christian peoples (2009, pp. 85–88).

To understand the motives and methods of these deplorable acts, Painter (2010) explored the white race as a concept within a history of events, a strategy that was justified because her research documented how "race is an idea, not a fact, and its questions demand answers from the conceptual rather than the factual realm" (p. ix). *Constructions of White Americans from Antiquity to the Present* was an alternative title Painter felt would also capture the broad focus of her book *The History of White People* (2010). She explored the invention of the concept of race and the social construction of the "white" race from the Greeks through contemporary times. This broad focus was needed to capture how the idea of the white race was embedded in concepts of labor, gender, and class as well as in images of beauty.

A major contribution of her work was the comprehensive description of four successive waves of enlargement of whiteness—ways that groups formerly considered to be nonwhite were designated as white and assimilated into American life against a white/black dichotomy. In addition to extending suffrage to all white men, the first wave included acceptance of the Irish as white. They were initially seen as Celts and inferior to the Anglo-Saxon English. Beliefs at this time were that there were multiple European races.

In subsequent waves the same process was extended to descendants of southern and eastern European immigrants and eventually Jews (following World War II). Brodkin (1998) also addressed this process with specific regard to the "whitening" of American Jews. She described the role of Jewish intellectuals as a driving force of this whitening process by promoting the "American characteristics" of Jewish immigrant culture. Prior to being assimilated into an expanding whiteness, each of the immigrant groups was not only considered inferior but also faced harsh discrimination. Painter (2010) discussed how the fourth enlargement was occurring currently, driven in part by greater diversification of higher-echelon jobs and by more people identifying as multiracial. From his analysis that higher classes of different groups were assuming more positions of power, Wilson (1980) also claimed a declining significance of race, but without directly questioning the issue of the racial categories themselves. In contrast, Painter's work deconstructs the very notion of race by revealing how whiteness has always been a social construct that was continually changing and enlarging over time as people in power essentially decided which groups were and were not defined as white. These carefully documented descriptions of how racial designations can be changed by political or social processes and contexts further revealed the absence of any ontological purity to whiteness or any of the other ascribed categories.

Other scholars have developed insightful analyses that go "beyond black and white," as the title of Marable's (1995) book suggested. After pondering the stagnation of a variety of pursuits for racial equality and social justice decades after the civil rights and Black Power movements, Marable argued for a strategy of radical democracy. This strategy would draw minorities into a majority of the poor and oppressed, which could significantly change power dynamics in the United States and at the same time work to deconstruct race as a social force. Except for the new ways that the pervasive power of the Internet was used, one can see how Marable's strategy was something of a harbinger of political organizing that made Barack Obama's presidential campaign successful. Despite this success, we are not in a post-race society, as many hopeful commentators rushed to proclaim. His 8 years in office and the subsequent election of Trump made it redundantly clear that race and white identity politics are as alive as ever in the United States, and the need to free ourselves from these ways of constraining identities is ever more crucial.

In this regard, the perspectives of Marable and Painter are augmented by the work of scholars who critiqued static notions of race by providing more nuanced understandings of the contexts and complexity of people's personal-cultural positioning within society and schools. Lensmire (2017), for example, examined the experiences and stories of people who identify as white in a small farming community and made a convincing case for how people "learn" to be white. Through in-depth interviews, he created a portrait of these people's complex cultures, particularly in relation to other people who are not defined as white. Insightfully, Lensmire reveals that even when white people have little or no contact with people of color, their identities as whites are still intricately dependent on how they learn to perceive people of color and blacks particularly.

Trainor (2008) also probed constructions of white identity with regard to how they are shaped in classrooms as well as communities. Essentially, she aimed to change how we think about the causes and origins of white student racism. Rather than seeing racist actions and discourses of whites as arising from a need or desire to protect white privilege or from ignorance of oppression, she argued that we must understand them as resulting from a series of "emotioned beliefs." She used the word "emotioned" to draw "our attention to interconnected but nonlinear dynamics of lived affective experiences, emotional regulation taking place through institutional and cultural practices, and language" (p. 3). Essentially, she claimed from her research on white students and teachers that their racist beliefs, acts, and discourses were affective and emotioned, rather than logical or rational, and that they are rooted in societal and schooling structures that perpetuate them. Consequently, she suggested that things like multicultural exposure to difference or critical interrogations of whiteness and privilege would be ineffective in changing these emotioned beliefs.

Lee (2003) framed a special theme issue of *Educational Researcher* (*ER*) on rethinking race and ethnicity that highlighted scholarship from a number of disciplinary perspectives. The challenge was to conceptualize "the varied struggles faced by large proportions of African American, Latinos/as, Native Americans, many Asian Americans and Pacific Islanders, and European Americans who face persistent intergenerational poverty" (p. 4). An important aspect of this challenge was to capture "the range of diversity within ethnic groups" (p. 4) in order to advance understanding of how to design more effective educational approaches.

Lee, Spencer, and Harpalani (2003) used the Phenomenological Variant of Ecology Systems Theory and the Cultural Modeling Framework to explore how youth live culturally in family systems; in peer social networks; and within larger institutional, societal, and historical systems. Focusing on African Americans, they showed how marginalized adolescents face additional sources of stress as they move across this range of settings. This article negated misconceptions regarding diversity such as notions of a normative pathway for development and learning (based on studies of white youth) and that deviance from this pathway was fundamentally pathological. It also exposed misconceptions that "racial and ethnic minorities are, on the whole, homogenous and fundamentally different from the majority" (p. 6). Further mitigation of these misconceptions, they noted, depended on better conceptual and methodological tools "that consolidate understanding how people live, learn, and develop culturally" (p. 11).

Nasir and Saxe (2003) analyzed the intersection of ethnic and academic identities in terms of how they shift as individuals position themselves in local interactions, in development over time, and in social history. In other words, identities are not located in the individual, but negotiated in social interactions and tied to cultural capital. They showed how identities also shift as individuals participate in the same practices in new ways or as they become participants in new practices (16).

Gutierrez and Rogoff (2003) cogently addressed the limits of "matching" educational strategies to the assumed cultural practices of diverse groups. They argued that these strategies distort and conflate race and culture and imply that both are static rather than dynamic identity processes and practices. Using a cultural-historical framework, they outlined how attention to specific individuals' and groups' histories of engagement in cultural practices allowed more comprehensive understanding of both similar and different forms of participation in school and society.

Orellana and Bowman (2003) also foregrounded conceptual and methodological limitations of social science researchers' tendencies "to treat race, ethnicity, culture, and social class as fixed and often essentialized categories rather than as multifaceted, situated, and socially constructed processes" (p. 26). They criticized tendencies to analyze single levels rather than looking across levels to link individual and local experiences to larger structural practices. They suggested that researchers treat culture as a dynamic set of tool kits in which people's cultural skills develop through varied experiences over time. Viewing the cultural characteristics of individuals and groups as dynamic, contextualized, and shaped by historical experiences was central to the approach of each of the studies in the 2003 special issue of ER. There have been just a handful of articles published in this journal up to the writing of this book that continued contributions to the direction of research on rethinking race that was reflected in the special issue.

A provocative approach to rethinking race is reflected in the title of a work by K. E. Fields and B. J. Fields (2012): *Racecraft*. Preceding from the fact that race has nothing to do with biology, the authors set out to explain why its folk classifications have not dissipated over time. They mount a compelling analysis of how race works as a social construct in thought and action. The trope they use as a heuristic for this analysis is to illustrate the shared irrational and rational features of witchcraft and racecraft. After establishing that there is a kind of reason in the roots of racecraft using Émile Durkheim's argument that reason is born in social life and that society can exist only by being collectively imagined, they also describe the shared features that are irrational. They note how racecraft has "such intellectual commonalities with witchcraft as circular reasoning, prevalence of confirming rituals, barriers to disconfirming factual evidence, self-fulfilling prophecies, multiple and inconsistent causal ideas, and colorful inventive folk genetics" (p. 198).

These and other shared features with witchcraft render racecraft constitutive of "a social world whose inhabitants experience (and act on) a marrow-deep certainty that racial differences are real and consequential, whether it is scientifically demonstrable or not" (p. 198). Therefore, though race is scientifically fictive in terms of categorizing humans, racism as a social practice operates through the sleight of hand of racecraft (as both action and its rationale) as if race was not just an idea but an objective reality. Consequently, they challenge us to see race as the ghastly fiction that it is and to critically question why we continue to accept and use this fictive concept to define ourselves and others. As Ta-Nehisi Coates noted in his back-cover comment on *Racecraft*, "It's not just a challenge to racists, it's a challenge to people like me, it's a challenge to African-Americans who have accepted the fact of race and define themselves by the concept of race."

If it is not a scientific fact, how do we deconstruct race as a social fact? Leonardo (2013) was right in noting we cannot simply wish race away. He was responding to Gilroy (2000), who, like Wilson (1980), had argued that there were a number of signs that race as a societal organizing principle was on the decline. Leonardo indicated that Gilroy's argument was not actually sustained empirically and that post-race thinking reflected more of an aspiration than a description of society as it actually exists. He further noted the danger in downplaying the significance of race struggles that overtly challenge the social practices of racism.

In a number of writings, Leonardo (2009, 2010, 2013) worked toward a concept of racial ambivalence and addressed post-race thinking as one of its forms. He posited race ambivalence as a third space that "exists uncomfortably alongside the first space of race-in-perpetuity and the second space of color-blindness" (2013, p. 147). He saw a concept of racial ambivalence allowing "educators some distance from the naturalness of race, its seeming permanence, which is the first step in making its familiarity appear strange" (p. 146). Despite his attempt to create a third space alongside the poles of permanent and post-race formulations, he noted that the race concept itself has been left relatively untouched in discourses like multiculturalism, critical race theory, and antiracism. As a relational concept, race is not only seldom deemed problematic; Leonardo suggested that "questioning race becomes tantamount to interrogating the very existence of racial groups, risking the very self we have come to know" (p. 150).

Perceptively, Leonardo focused on the essential challenge of deconstructing race. Despite the violent consequences of race, people in all groups resist questioning it for various reasons. Painter (2010), for example, stated categorically that she did not intend her study of the history of white people to "underestimate or ignore the overwhelming importance of black race in America" (p. x). Clearly, an important motive for resisting the deconstruction of race is risk to the self that people have come to know. But how do we circumvent the fact that some of these selves are imprisoned within their ascribed identity, while others, though also imprisoned, are permitted privileges by the identities they have been assigned? As I noted earlier, the color-coded categories ascribed by white supremacy are predicated on our subscribing to them. Instead, I argue that we can act in ways that negate the constructed racial categories and trade/transform the selves defined by them into personal-cultural identities that reflect more authentic ancestral, family, friendship, collegial, and virtual relationships, activities, and social practices. We negate race by understanding and embracing the complex, fluid micro-cultural identities and affinities that go beyond ambiguity and make the concept of race utterly indeterminate. Evidence of these ways of being and acting—the myriad ways that people's lives are not confined within prisons and prisms of racial identity—is revealed in coming chapters by the individual and collective stories of my interviewees.

PRISMS OF RACIAL IDENTITY

The way prisms disperse light into a range of colors could be seen as a metaphor for diversity. It's estimated that humans can distinguish as many as 10 million colors (Wyszecki & Stiles, 2006). However, when it's whiteness rather than white light that's refracted, the spectrum is deliberately constrained to just a few hues. Despite the reductive constructs of white, black, yellow, brown, and red that are generally used to codify human diversity in the United States, the country's population provides 325 million examples of the limitations of this scheme.

The following discussion in this chapter addresses the broader spectrum of diversity in the United States with respect to how we already exist (or can exist) beyond the color-bind. Since considerations of race and ethnicity in the United States are most often discussed with regard to the five color-coded categories ascribed to them, I framed the following sections using these categories, but as points of entry into wider considerations of diversity. Unlike with the titles of the next five chapters, which present data on the interviewees, I attempted to minimize the use of color designations by using the terms *European, African, Asian, Hispanic*, and *Native American*. Of course, there are critical problems with these terms also.

As the U.S. census evolved from 1790, it continually changed its classifications of people in grappling with the complexities of attempting to identify the country's population by race. As noted in Chapter 2, the 2010 census identified six racial categories: "white American," "black or African American," "American Indian and Alaska Native," "Asian American," "Native Hawaiian and Other Pacific Islander," and "people of two or more races" (U.S. Census Bureau, 2010). The census questionnaires indicated that these categories were not attempts to define race biologically, anthropologically, or genetically, and selection of these categories reflected self-identifications. In 2010 respondents were also allowed to select a category referred to as "Some Other Race," and it classified Hispanic or Latino as an ethnicity rather than a race. This further complicated notions of race because each of the six specified racial categories could also have "Hispanic or Latino" or "Non-Hispanic or Latino" Americans in them. All this allowed for a number of problematic and sometimes bizarre effects such as cases where some children born in the United States could be classified as of a race different from that of one of their biological parents.

Despite these problems, I used the terms noted earlier that connect a broad consideration of origin to being American in framing the following discussions in this chapter. The discussion of each group is grounded in the fact that we all came to this continent either as people who were the earliest settlers prior to European conquests, or immigrants, or people who were subjected to indentured servitude, or people who were forced into slavery. Harkening back to places and circumstances from which people came is part of the "reverse engineering" needed to understand the real diversity of this country.

European Americans

The majority of the U.S. population consists of people who can trace their ancestry to the original peoples of Europe, although soon this will not be the case, with our growing Hispanic population. Europeans came to this continent as colonizers (from Britain, France, Spain, the Netherlands, and other colonial powers) as well as immigrants and indentured servants. The term *European American* is often used interchangeably with *white* and *Caucasian* and sometimes confused with *Anglo-American* or *Anglo-Saxon*. The U.S. Census Bureau (2010) also considers people from the Middle East and North Africa as white. For many reasons, people from the Middle East and North Africa have more difficulty sustaining a white identity. For example, although Moroccans, Arabs, and Lebanese are identified as white by the U.S. census, members of these groups may be reluctant to embrace that identity in the recent and current political climate. So there are many complications to using the term *European Americans* to frame this section.

Attempting to discuss any of the peoples ascribed to various groups by forces of white supremacy is inherently problematic. Countries in Europe, the Middle East, and North Africa have a wide range of cultures, languages, and religions. The U.S. experiences of people from these countries are highly varied and intricately tied to historical and political relations with the country of origin, their religious affiliations, the number of generations that individuals and families have been in this country, as well as considerations of perceived threats from various groups. Additional considerations are circumstances surrounding immigration, connections to the heritage of the country of origin, the degree of assimilation in this country, and, of course, skin complexion. Also, it was less than a hundred years ago that "America regarded its immigrant European workers as something other than white, as biologically different" (Brodkin, 1998, p. 56). So groups like the Irish, Italians, Polish, and Jews were given a status as whites over time as whiteness expanded (Painter, 2010). As Ajrouch and Jamal (2007) argued, the positionality of these groups is not static or neutral but "fluid, situational, and emergent . . . [where] immigrants are not inherently 'White' or 'non-White,' but . . . associate or disassociate themselves with 'whiteness' in response to various situational factors" (p. 875). Clearly, the positioning of all groups in U.S. society is highly changeable and situational and usually reflects a simplified or idealized notion of histories and ancestries of individuals and groups with regard to how they came here.

Most of the people who came from different parts of Europe are known to have multiple nationality and ethnic connections. It's also well known that many people who identify as European American have some ancestors who are African or American Indian. This has come about through both interracial unions and marriages and by gradual inclusion of people with non-European ancestry into the national population. In mapping admixtures of ancestry of college students who identified as white at a university in the northeastern United States, for example, Shriver et al. (2003) estimated that approximately 30% had less than 90% European ancestry.

Despite intricate and extensive mixes of ancestry, many who identify as white connect their identity to a single European national or ethnic group, often one with which they have the most recent association (Waters, 1990). In the first census in which the option was available to choose more than one racial category* in 2000, for example, the vast majority of people still identified with only one. In the 2000 census, about 17% identified as German Americans while about 12% identified as Irish Americans, making these

---

*In 1997 the U.S Office of Management and Budget permitted respondents in the 2000 census to identify with more than one race, as reflected in its Revisions to the Standards for the Classification of Federal Data on Race and Ethnicity, available at www.whitehouse.gov/omb/fedreg/1997standards.html.

two groups the first- and second-largest self-reported ancestry groups in the country (U.S. Census Bureau, 2000). But English or British Americans are actually the largest ancestry group. However, many in this group self-identified under a new category of "American" that was also an option for the first time in the 2000 census. Those who reported their ancestry only as "American" increased from around 12 million in 1990 to over 20 million in 2000. It's been argued that the changing ethnic responses of whites to the term *American* reflect considerations by some that they have become "indigenous" based on how long their families have been here (Lieberson & Waters, 1986).

In 2010, the top countries of origin for immigrants from Europe were the United Kingdom, 14%; Germany, 13%; Poland, 10%; Russia and Italy, 8% apiece; Ukraine, 7%; and Portugal, 5%; 35% were from the rest of Europe. This partially reflects the diversity in national origins of citizens or residents of the United States who are identified as European Americans. It's important to also identify the national origins of the remaining 35% in order to more accurately specify the full range of groups that are left invisible in the cloud of whiteness. A major issue affecting European Americans is what Reason and Evans (2007) referred to as "white transparency," the widespread reality that they can move through life without the need to examine their own racialized identity beyond being simply white. One problem with this is that the cultural markers of whiteness are actively maintained and propagated in hegemonic narratives as normative for all groups. Lewis (2004) noted that people who accept and are accepted into whiteness as an identity tend to racialize other groups in society without racializing themselves. The acceptance and privileging of whiteness further reinforces feelings of superiority for those associated with it (Hernández Sheets, Howard, Dilg, & McIntyre, 2000).

The superiority/inferiority binary extends to ways that people's diverse identities are intentionally structured to maintain division and mitigate productive, sustainable human interactions and relationships. Those who identify as European American will benefit by disaggregating whiteness just as the U.S. census has increasingly disaggregated the designations of other groups that make up the population. In the 2010 census, there were 57 possible multiple-race citations based on the five race categories and the "Some Other Race" category authorized by the U.S. Office of Management and Budget (OMB) (Rastogi et al., 2011). These myriad designations for racial positioning actually reflect the weaknesses of attempting to use the idea of race to identify people. Fifty-seven combinations do not nearly exhaust the full range of self-selected possibilities, and ultimately the hyperdiversity of citizens and residents of the United States makes the idea of race essentially meaningless as a framework for identity. What is affirmed, however, is a better sense of the distinct histories and heritages that constitute this country's population. European Americans as individuals, families, and communities also reflect diverse histories and positionalities that intersect in numerous ways with other individuals and groups. Just as Hispanic/Latino has been defined by the U.S. census as an ethnicity and not a race, so too can the designation of people as white. Lifting the veil of whiteness allows us to see and appreciate essential human connections and differences without racialized structures that amalgamate or decimate them.

African Americans

In addition to the term *white*, *black*—often used interchangeably with *African American*—is the only other color term used in the U.S. census to identity certain citizens and residents. This use contributes to sustaining the idea of a white/black racial binary in this country. The Census Brief "The Black Population: 2010" by Rastogi et al. (2011) noted that "according to OMB, 'Black or African American' refers to a person having origins in any of the Black racial groups of Africa" (p. 2). Since racial identity is self-selected in the census, this report further described this category as including "people who marked the 'Black, African Am., or Negro' checkbox. It also includes respondents who made written entries such as African American; Sub-Saharan African entries, such as Kenyan and Nigerian; and Afro-Caribbean entries, such as Haitian and Jamaican" (p. 2).

Most African Americans are direct descendants of people in regions of West Africa. The first West Africans were brought to Jamestown, Virginia, in 1619, and these early captives were initially treated as indentured servants. However, this practice was soon replaced by the same system of race-based slavery used in the Caribbean. Although there were far fewer in the North, all the American colonies had slavery; up to 25% of the population of the South were enslaved (Gomez, 1998). Northern states abolished slavery by the turn of the 19th century, but southern states continued the practice until the passage of the 13th Amendment at the end of the Civil War. Disenfranchisement, stigmatization, and inequitable treatment continued for African Americans through the Reconstruction era, the Jim Crow era, and the civil rights era and into the present day. The majority of African Americans, approximately 55%, still live in the South; 18% live in the Midwest, 17% in the Northeast, and 10% in the West. Having large concentrations in urban areas, this population grew in every state between 2000 and 2010. However, nearly 60% live in 10 states: New York, Florida, Texas, Georgia, California, North Carolina, Illinois, Maryland, Virginia, and Ohio (Rastogi et al., 2011).

In 2010 the African American population, including those who identified as multiracial (African American in combination), was just over 42 million, or approximately 14% of the total population of the United States. This was more than a 15% increase over the 36.4 million reported in the 2000 census. Also between 2000 and 2010, people who reported they were African American in combination with another racial group increased by

75%, from approximately 1.7 million to 3.1 million. The largest number of African Americans in combination with other groups was of those who reported the category of "white" as their other race. This group increased by 134% from 2000 to 2010 (Rastogi et al., 2011). So African Americans who reported more than one race grew at a much higher rate than that of those who reported themselves as African American alone.

One contradictory aspect of using the term *black* as a racial designation, essentially synonymous with *African American*, is that it is also used to refer to some people who identify as Hispanics, most people from the Caribbean, and many people from sub-Saharan African countries. These people have very different histories, languages, and cultures. For example, aided by the Refugee Act of 1980, voluntary migration from Africa has increased significantly, especially from countries experiencing high levels of violence. Sub-Saharan African immigrants are one of the fastest-growing populations in the United States, especially in the cities (Knight et al., 2014). The census included these diverse groups in the category of "black or African American" even when people write in entries like "Kenyan and Nigerian," or "Haitian and Jamaican." Yet the census data also indicated that the vast majority of African immigrants did not self-identify as African American and instead identified with their respective countries of origin. Many members of these groups don't integrate or interact at high levels with African Americans, and there also have been experiences of various kinds of cultural conflicts (Mwakikagile, 2007). They may not suffer the level of injustices visited on African Americans such as being targeted in ways that ultimately result in higher rates of incarceration and all the problematic consequences of imprisonment (Alexander, 2012; Stevenson, 2015).

Asian Americans

Awkwardly positioned between the poles of white and black, the construction of Asian Americans as a race further demonstrates the inadequacy of this idea for classifying people. The color codes also break down in that people identified as members of this group range in hues that can be as light as any European American and as dark as any African American in what one of my Asian interviewees called the "pigmentocracy."

The Census Brief "The Asian Population: 2010" by Hoeffel, Rastogi, Kim, & Shahid (2012) provided the OMB definition that "Asian refers to a person having origins in any of the original peoples of the Far East, Southeast Asia, or the Indian subcontinent, including, for example, Cambodia, China, India, Japan, Korea, Malaysia, Pakistan, the Philippine Islands, Thailand, and Vietnam" (p. 2). People self-reported Asian identities by checking a box for one of 11 designations. Two of these designations allowed for additional categories to be written in, such as "Hmong" or "Pakistani" under "Other Asian" or "Fijian" or "Tongan" under "Other Pacific Islander." Pang, Han, and Pang (2011) noted that the range of possible census designations for Asians encompassed 67 distinct cultural and ethnic national groups, with many of these having a number of subgroups within them.

There were just over 17 million Asian American/Pacific Islanders counted in the 2010 census, about 6% of the U.S. population. This number included Asians alone or in combination with other groups. The self-identified nations of origin for the largest groups were China, the Philippines, India, Vietnam, Korea, and Japan. Between 2000 and 2010, the Asian population grew more than four times faster than the total U.S. population. This was also a faster rate than every other race group in the country (Hoeffel et al., 2012). Additionally, Asians who reported multiple races grew at a faster rate than Asians alone, and the combination of Asian and white contributed the most to the growth of their multiple-race category (Hoeffel et al., 2012). Asian Americans in combination with other non-Asian groups can be perceived as nonauthentic, alienated, and "fixed to an insider/outsider racial status" (Kina & Dariotis, 2013).

In the 19th century, the first major wave of Asian immigration consisted mainly of Chinese and Japanese laborers, but also included Koreans as well as people from South Asia. Many Filipinos also came during and after this period. The Philippines was a colony of the United States from 1898 to 1946. Changes in exclusion laws and policies during the 1940s to the 1960s precipitated a new and larger wave of Asian immigration. In 2010 nearly three-fourths of all Asians in America lived in 10 states: "California (5.6 million), New York (1.6 million), Texas (1.1 million), New Jersey (0.8 million), Hawaii (0.8 million), Illinois (0.7 million), Washington (0.6 million), Florida (0.6 million), Virginia (0.5 million), and Pennsylvania (0.4 million)" (Hoeffel et al., 2012: 8). However, the counties now experiencing the fastest growth of this population are in the South and Midwest.

Despite greatly varying histories, cultures, and languages as well as wide-ranging economic conditions and academic achievements, Asians are usually seen as a relatively homogeneous group in U.S. society. Perhaps the most pervasive aspect of homogenization is the stereotype of Asians as the model minority. Wu (2002) described how this stereotype is a myth used to elevate Asian Americans as a "trophy population" who reflect a great success story of achievement and assimilation—a model for other people of color, especially African Americans. Wu discussed how his myth derived from glorification of Chinese laborers who came to work on southern plantations after the Civil War. These plantation owners went to great lengths to avoid hiring African Americans who had been recently freed. Eventually, other minority groups were asked to look to Asian Americans as a model for how to behave, diverting attention away from other racial inequalities (Lee, 2015) and other issues such as developing English abilities and cultural dissonance with regard to both mainstream American culture and the cultures of national origin (Purkayastha, 2005).

Wu (2002) argued that the model-minority myth is also used to deny Asian Americans' diverse experiences in this country, including their own differential experiences of racial discrimination. One aspect of their diverse experiences is that many Asian groups do not perform academically as the stereotype suggests. For example, Pang et al. (2011) found that although Asian Americans as a whole group achieved at higher levels than whites, when scores were disaggregated the majority of Asian racial/ethnic groups performed at significantly lower levels in reading and math (p. 384). Even when Asian educational attainment and achievements are higher than those of whites, the incomes and professional status of Asians are not commensurate (Lew, 2006).

While used as evidence of meritocracy, the model-minority myth creates a double-bind mask that hides differential experiences of both success and oppression, with little mention of injustices past and present. While celebrating Asian achievements, it also aggregates and stigmatizes them. According to Wu (2002), every attractive trait has its problematic complement. He noted that as a group Asians are seen as gifted in math and science but mechanical and uncreative; polite but submissive; hardworking but not well rounded; family oriented but clannish or too ethnic; law abiding but rigidly rule bound; a trophy race but tarnished (p. 67).

Filipinos, the second-largest group of Asians in the United States behind Chinese, clearly illustrate how the rules of race are broken. This is the focus of Ocampo's (2016) book *The Latinos of Asia*. The Republic of the Philippines, named in honor of King Philip II of Spain, consists of 7,641 islands near the equator in the Western Pacific. In 2014 its population surpassed 100 million, making it the 12th-most-populous country in the world. It also has about 10 million people living in other countries, constituting one of the largest diasporas. In its attempt to increase nonagricultural growth, it might be seen as a microcosm of the developing world. There are numerous ethnicities and cultures throughout the Philippine Islands, and it has 182 individual living languages. From the original Negritos; to successive waves of Taiwanese aborigines; to influxes of people from China, Indonesia, Malaysia, Singapore, and some Islamic states; to conquest and colonization by Spain (for over 300 years), Japan, and the United States (for almost 50 years until after World War II), the Philippines exemplify the inherent contradictions of collapsing the diverse histories, cultures, and languages of people into a nebulous category of race.

Ocampo (2016) noted, "The term *Asian American* did not even exist until the late 1960s, when Chinese, Japanese, and Filipino activists coined the identity as an ideological strategy to advocate for civil rights" (p. 2). He discussed how the historical connections Filipinos have with Latinos is at least as influential on their culture(s) as are connections to Asia. According to Ocampo, "Filipinos understand that nearly four centuries of Western colonization (by the Spanish and the Americans) have influenced their country in ways unparalleled in other Asian societies" and that "some Filipinos feel that their categorization as Asian American is little more than a 'geographical accident'" (p. 9). Additionally, citing Guevarra (2012), Ocampo noted that many Filipino males who made up the vast majority of early waves of immigration to the United States married Mexican women and formed "Mexipino" families and communities (p. 10). Ocampo concluded that despite the shared history, Filipinos do not generally identify as Latino. Yet their complex, variegated experiences before and after coming to the United States make it difficult to justify racializing them simply as Asian Americans.

Hispanic Americans

According to the 2010 Census Brief on the Hispanic population authored by Ennis, Rios-Vargas, and Albert (2011), the U.S. census defined "Hispanic or Latino" as of "Cuban, Mexican, Puerto Rican, South or Central American, or other Spanish culture or origin regardless of race" (p. 2). This report further noted, "Hispanic origin can be viewed as the heritage, nationality group, lineage, or country of birth of the person or the person's parents or ancestors before their arrival in the United States (p. 2). Although the census indicated that people who identify themselves as Hispanic, Latino, or Spanish can be of any race, the more descriptive identification of people's ancestry, including ethnic and geographic origins, obviates any additional imposition of a racial identity. That more than half this group also indicated they were white (Ennis et al., 2011, p. 15) makes racial classifications all the more contradictory and confusing.

Just over 50 million people, or about 16% of the U.S. population, identified themselves as Hispanic or Latino in the 2010 census. Up from approximately 35 million in 2000, this group reflected more than half the growth of the total population during this period. Mexicans accounted for about three-quarters of this increase, while the number of Cubans and Puerto Ricans also grew substantially, by 44% and 36% respectively (Ennis et al., 2011, p. 2). Also, more than 12 million people self-identified as "Other Hispanic" in 2010, with the highest numbers (and largest increases) citing Dominican, Salvadoran, Guatemalan, Honduran, Uruguayan, Colombian, Bolivian, Venezuelan, Ecuadoran, Argentinean, Paraguayan, or Peruvian origins. Additionally, the Spaniard population increased by more than 6 times during this decade, from 100,000 to 635,000 (Ennis et al., 2011, p. 3). Interestingly, more than three-quarters of the Hispanic population lived in the West or the South, with more than half living in three states: California, Texas, and Florida.

Although the U.S. government mandated the terms *Hispanic* and *Latino* for citizens and residents with ancestry in Spanish-speaking countries more than 40 years ago, results of a Pew National Survey of Latinos in 2011 found that neither term has been fully embraced. Fifty-one percent of those surveyed indicated that they had no preference for either term though

Hispanic was chosen more than *Latino* * when a preference was expressed. The majority (51%) preferred to identify themselves by their family's country of origin, and 69% indicated that Hispanics or Latinos in the United States have many different cultures rather than a common culture (Taylor, Lopez, Martínez, & Velasco, 2012).

It's a frequently held misconception that most Spanish speakers in the United States are foreign born. In fact, there have been Spanish-speaking communities in this country for centuries. García and Kleifgen (2010) noted that although 50% of Spanish-speaking emergent bilinguals are foreign born, the rest were born in the United States. Additionally, more than 60% of Hispanic adults are bilingual. One of the challenges Hispanics face is the devaluation of Spanish language and culture (Fraga & Garcia, 2010) as well as the increasing criminalization of Hispanic youth (Morín, 2008; Pantoja, 2013; Rios and Galicia, 2013). Recent economic and political conditions have contributed to a significant increase in Hispanic immigrants to the United States and the problematizing of them in public discourse (Santa, 2002; Yosso, 2005). But it's important to recognize their distinct trajectories and the critical differences in histories, languages, and cultures in conjunction with the fact that many generations have resided in this country, going back hundreds of years.

Clearly, Hispanic Americans reflect tremendous diversity in ethnic and geographic origins as well as in their social, political, and economic positioning in the United States. Like members of each of the other groups, they reflect a wide range of skin colors. Intricacies of their identities are too complex to be contained within the idea of race as it is defined and assigned in the United States. As I described in previous sections of this chapter, intricacies of European American, African American, and Asia American identities are equally complex. Despite the insurmountable inadequacies of *race* as a descriptor for different groups within this country's population, it continues to be used to extend political, economic, and ideological interests of white supremacy.

American Indians and Alaskan Natives

The term *Indian* resulted from Columbus's mistaken assumption that he had arrived in India after crossing the Atlantic Ocean. Controversy remains over an appropriate name after individuals being referred to as "Indians," "American Indians," "Native Americans," First Nations Peoples," and "indigenous peoples." In 1995 a census poll asked members of these groups which term they preferred, and about 50% selected *American Indian*, while about 37% selected *Native American*. Walbert (2009) noted that some preferred the former term as an explicit marker of the historic oppression that "Indians" have experienced in this country.

The term *Latinx* also has been used, in order to include all gendered individuals.

The 2010 Census Brief on the American Indian and Alaskan Native population authored by Norris, Vines, and Hoeffel (2012) cited the following OMB definition used in the 2010 U.S. census for a member of this group: "A person having origins in any of the original peoples of North and South America (including Central America) and who maintains tribal affiliation or community attachment. This category includes people who indicate their race as 'American Indian or Alaska Native' or report entries such as Navajo, Blackfeet, Inupiat, Yup'ik, or Central American Indian groups or South American Indian groups" (p. 2).

Either alone or in combination with one or more other races, 5.2 million people identified as American Indian and Alaskan Native in 2010. The Cherokee were the largest tribal group, with almost one-fifth of this population's total. The entire group constituted 1.7% of the U.S. population in 2010. This reflected considerable growth of 39% since the 2000 census and counters the myth that this group might be facing extinction (Fleming & Juneau, 2006). Interestingly, nearly half this population (2.3 million) reported being American Indian or Alaskan Native in combination with one or more other races. Sixty-three percent identified the other race as white, while their combination with blacks actually grew at the fastest rate since 2000. By 2010 the three combinations of white, black, or white and black represented about 84% of all American Indians and Alaskan Natives who reported multiple race combinations.

The different racial combinations of this group are overshadowed by the diversity of tribes and languages. Although they are grouped together under the term *American Indian and Alaskan Native*, there are 567 ethnically, culturally, and linguistically diverse nations, tribes, or bands recognized by the federal government. More than 200 of these groups are in Alaska, with the others located across 33 states. However, the majority of American Indians and Alaskan Natives live in 10 states: California, Oklahoma, Arizona, Texas, New York, New Mexico, Washington, North Carolina, Florida, and Michigan (Norris et al., 2012, p. 6). Additionally, there are over 325 Native American reservations in the United States, and each one is associated with and managed by a particular tribe or group of tribes.

Historically, these nations and tribes have spoken more than 100 distinct languages, with over 300 different dialects (Diversity of Native American Groups, 2014). Unfortunately, since the conquests of the Americas by Europeans, many of these languages have been lost. Children are not learning tribal languages from the remaining speakers, so the languages continue to die out (McCarty, Romero, & Zepeda, 2006). Currently, there are only eight American Indian and Alaskan Native indigenous languages that have more than 9,000 fluent speakers in the United States and Canada (Diversity of Native American Groups, 2014).

Other issues facing many American Indians and Native Alaskans include disproportionately high incarceration rates (NoiseCat, 2015); high levels of unemployment and poverty, especially on reservations or trust lands; and stereotypical and derogatory portrayals in literature, textbooks, movies, television, sports mascots, and children's toys (Fryberg, Markus, Oyserman, & Stone, 2008; Johnson & Eck, 1995). In schools, in addition to disproportionately high suspension rates and enrollment in special classes, American Indian and Alaskan Native children encounter pedagogical approaches and expectations that can be in conflict with their cultural perspectives and practices (Castagno & Brayboy, 2008). For example, appreciation for community and the wisdom of elders can present obstacles to school emphases on individual performances and one adult as the primary assessor and authority in the learning environment (Cleary, 2008; McCarty et al., 2006). Although the Indian Self-Determination and Education Assistance Act of 1975 gave this group more opportunities to plan and implement a wide range of educational, health, and social services for its members (Gross, 1979), disturbing disparities persist.

During hundreds of years of oppression, the U.S. government also tried to assimilate American Indians and Alaskan Natives. At the same time, the federal government instituted laws that limited their rights and access to their lands. Beginning with the earliest instances of oppression and plunder by European colonists, control and use of land has been central to these peoples' struggles on this continent. After the principle of tribal sovereignty became legal through the U.S. Supreme Court's interpretation of the Trust Document in the case of *Worcester v. Georgia* in 1832, American Indian and Alaskan Native tribes developed different treaty agreements with the federal government (Wood, 1994). Ultimately, each tribe ended up with differing rights and access to various lands. Yet the Trust Document's affirmation of tribal sovereignty was critical to modern-day land rights and use disputes. And tribes must continue to fight to protect their lands—such as in the current Standing Rock battle against the Dakota Access oil pipeline—from "black snakes" of resource exploitation by private industries and the U.S. government.

325 MILLION STORIES

In this chapter I probed the diversity of peoples' identities in the United States to reveal how they are constrained in color-coded categories within a hierarchy of white supremacy that clouds rather than clarifies how we actually exist in the world. I discussed scholarship that critiqued the false premises and contradictions underlying the severely limited spectrum of positionalities that are allowed by the idea of race. This scholarship also illuminated something of the complexity and fluidity of peoples' lives beyond the color-bind. Although I argued that the U.S. census perpetuates the idea of race by framing it within a white/black binary, I also used data from the most recent census to illustrate the wide-ranging ways that people actually identify themselves within and beyond essentialized groups.

The ancestry of the people in the United States is extremely varied and includes descendants of populations from every place in the world. European Americans come from many countries in Europe, the Middle East, and North Africa that have numerous ethnicities, cultures, languages, and religions. African Americans come from any of the numerous ethnic or tribal groups of Africa, and their identifications in combination with other groups increased by 75% between 2000 and 2010. American Indian and Alaskan Natives reflect 567 ethnically, culturally, and linguistically diverse nations or tribes and have spoken over 100 distinct languages, so why are they identified as a single race? Asian Americans come from many countries, and the diversity noted within just one of its groups, Filipinos, is a prime example of how all the groups discussed break the rules of race. Filipinos can come from 7,641 islands that have 182 individual living languages and draw as much from Hispanic cultures as they do from Asian. Hispanic Americans come from any of the numerous countries of South or Central America as well as Spain, and though over half of them identified as white, the census does not include them in the white category. I made the case that similar to how the census identified Hispanics as not a race, everyone else should also identify themselves in connection with their ancestors and the origins of their heritage, including considerations of lineage, nationality groups, and prior countries of birth.

In addition to the limitless diversity and the situational and changeable positioning of different ethnic group identities, we must understand how this plays out in people's everyday lives. In the United States, there are as many stories of personal-cultural identities and affinities as there are people. The next five chapters tell some of these stories to offer particular ways that the interviewees' positioning, practices, life choices, and evolving perspectives are deconstructing race. As Salman Rushdie (2016) said in a magazine interview, "There's something so very beautiful and metaphorical about human life. . . . We are ourselves unfinished stories living inside many other unfinished stories which could expand to the story of our country, to the story of the human race, to the story of the universe."

CHAPTER 4

Pretending to Be White

> So passing sounds like something less active, like something that just happens. Like I pass as a white American because of how I look. But if I'm pretending, it's like I have a role in it. To some extent, I think any immigrant who's assimilating into a culture is pretending.
>
> —Sasha (March 16, 2015)

Sasha is one of the 20 interviewees whose stories and perspectives will be heard in this and coming chapters, often in their own words. Her statement captures an important aspect of race. People can be socially constructed to pass for a racial, ethnic, or gender category, but they must also play an active role of pretending—performance of certain cultural practices (language among them) that are consistent with understood or internalized codes identified with an assigned racial or ethnic category—in order for the idea of race to work.

Pretense and performance are connected to how Gee (1991) defined being identified with a specific discourse community. He noted that we should "think of a discourse as an 'identity kit' which comes complete with the appropriate costume and instructions on how to act and talk so as to take on a particular role that others will recognize" (p. 3). More recently, Gee (2013, 2015) delineated a related concept of "activity-based identities" as freely chosen identities. He contrasted these to "relational identities," classificatory labels that usually are not freely chosen. The latter work more to efface than reflect diversity, but when accepted and owned they can be like activity-based identities. Relational identities also connect to Steele's (2010) concept of "identity contingencies" that can be the focus of stereotyping and "stereotype threats." These ideas and others that will be discussed are grounded in the interview data and used to further explore the extensive diversity illustrated in the scholarship and U.S. census data in the previous chapter. The point is to demonstrate the spectrum of differences within and between constructed racial groups to clarify how people actually exist and engage in the world. This and coming chapters, like the narrator in Ellison's (1947) prologue, discussed in Chapter 2, attempt to "slip between the notes" to drill down to the level of individuals and their families and reveal the rich diversity in their lives that is already working to deconstruct race.

The four interviewees focused on in this chapter are Samantha, Sasha (whose quote began the chapter), James, and Ryan. Samantha, an associate professor at a university in the Northeast, is 5'9" tall, has very light complexion, blue eyes, and blond hair. She was 45 years old when interviewed and is married to a man identified as white, and they have two children. She accepts that she is identified "as white, female, probably upper middle class, academic professional." But she also talked about many influences on her identity that go unseen, such as the fact that her mother is Armenian. Sasha is a U.S. citizen who was born and lived in Russia until she was 5, when her family came to the United States. She identifies herself as middle class, Russian American, and Jewish. She is 5'8" tall, has very light complexion, red hair, and green eyes. She is married to a man from Spain. She was a 29-year-old graduate student when interviewed. James was 37 and single when interviewed and teaches at an urban high school with mostly Hispanic students. He is 6'1", has a very light complexion and black hair, and said that people see him as a white male. He also noted how other identities he has are important to him such as coming from a working-class background and being a musician. Ryan was 28 and single when interviewed and teaches at an urban continuation high school with nearly all African American students. Ryan is 6', has a very light complexion and brown hair and also accepts that he is seen "first and foremost" as a white male by people in this country, and probably as one with education and class privilege. He also identifies as a queer, cisgender man.

The other interviewees who will be discussed in subsequent chapters are Relene, introduced in Chapter 2, who identifies as African American, along with Joshua and Ethan. Ingrid is discussed in conjunction with the African American category too, although she doesn't necessarily assert that identity. Chloe, Halle, Phil, and Felix identify as Asian Americans, while Carmen, Suzana, Anton, and Javier identify as Hispanic or Latino Americans. The final four—Lily, Alexandra, Mila, and Darien—identify with the category of "American Indian." These pseudonyms for the interviewees have similarities to their real names in terms of ethnic, linguistic, national, or religious origins.

An overview of the qualitative methods used for analyzing the interview and field note data was provided in Chapter 2. To add to that description, I want to indicate that I coded across all data sources to capture recurring patterns, then organized these patterns into meaningful categories that I grouped with respect to overarching themes. I briefly describe these major themes and categories before presenting findings from the perspectives and stories of the interviewees. Thirteen key categories were identified in the analysis. Three of these categories—"hyperdiversity," "stereotyping," and "identity constructions"—became major themes for organizing the other ten categories.

The theme of hyperdiversity reflected the highly diverse personal-cultural positioning and family/community networks interviewees described that indexed the complexity and uniqueness of individual lives across all the groups. Two additional categories—"within-group distinctions" and "indeterminacy" (of race/ethnicity)—were connected to this theme. Within-group distinctions that interviewees discussed uncovered specific differences that often are not seen at the group level, both by people outside and by those within the group. Indeterminacy was reflected in how some interviewees' diverse physical, cultural, or linguistic representations made identifying them in connection with their actual ancestral group or in some cases even within a specific racial group highly ambiguous or completely indeterminate.

Stereotyping was another major theme where interviewees felt they were responded to either pejoratively or with privilege based on how they were seen by others. Five categories were connected to this theme. One was "relational identities." Consistent with Gee (2013, 2015), these are classificatory labels placed on people that are not freely chosen. Relational identities can also be linked to identity contingencies (Steele, 2010). Additionally, interviewees talked about "homogenization"—the boxing in and erasing of distinctions within racial, gender, and sexual orientation categories. "Invisibility" was another category connected to stereotyping. It reflected experiences in which pertinent aspects of interviewees' identities were either not seen or not seen as important. Experiences of "discrimination," inequities and microaggressions based on external perceptions of the interviewee's identities, were also connected to stereotyping. Finally, some of the male interviewees discussed being perceived or responded to as "hypermasculine," or prominently reflecting heightened characteristics stereotypically associated with masculinity.

The third major theme of "identity constructions" involved creating and negotiating identities through practices and choices enacted in different social contexts such as work affiliations; affinity groups; media, sports, and popular culture; or language, heritage, or religious communities. "Activity-based identities" was one category of these kinds of identity constructions. A key aspect of the activities of all the interviewees was their use of digital texts and tools. So "digital identities" was another related category of identity constructions. "Identity rejections" revealed how some interviewees consciously declined or expressed ambivalence about identification of themselves by race, or gender, or sexual orientation. A related category of "challenging binaries" addressed how some interviewees actively worked to disrupt conceptions of themselves and others being defined within reductive frameworks. Importantly, the practices, choices, and perspectives that resulted in identity constructions also worked against stereotyping.

Numerous examples of hyperdiversity, stereotyping, and identity constructions were revealed in the lives of the interviewees. This chapter is structured to address these three major themes along with their associated categories in succession. Evidence is provided for each interviewee in the succession of Samantha, Sasha, James, and Ryan with respect to each theme and its associated categories. In this approach, it was necessary to shift back and forth between the stories of each interviewee, and, of course, there is some overlap among categories because aspects of the positioning, practices, choices, and perspectives of the interviewees can provide evidence for more than 1 of the 13 categories.

HYPERDIVERSITY

I begin discussion of hyperdiversity, the myriad personal-cultural positions and family/community networks within the group identified as white, with a vignette about Samantha. During April 2015, I met with her in a downtown Chicago restaurant for a post-interview conversation. We both were keenly aware of frequent stares from people at other tables. Although she recognized that people identify her as a white woman, she constructs her own identity "in multiple ways" in different contexts. Some of her identity contingencies are that she is tall, looks athletic, and has blue eyes and blond hair. Because of how she talks, students in her university classes think she's a "Valley Girl" from Southern California, but she grew up in Washington, DC. In 1991, she completed an undergraduate degree at a prestigious university in the Chicago area, and Chicago is also the city where I grew up. So we understood what motivated the stares from other tables. Yet Samantha's life is quite different from what these diners might have assumed. As the following events that she shared with me illustrates, it's one of the many examples of hyperdiversity in the lives of the interviewees, and arguably in the lives of most people in the United States.

Last summer, Samantha's mother, a first-generation Armenian American, organized a family hiking trip in the White Mountains of New Hampshire. Samantha is married and has two children, a teenage girl and a boy three years younger. Two first cousins and 10 second cousins ranging in age from 10 to 18 were also on this hike up to a peak to spend the night, then back down the next day. At one point her 11-year-old son asked, "People keep asking us if we are a camp group or a church group. Why don't they think we're a family?" She explained that some people aren't used to the idea that a family can include people from a range of countries with a range of skin tones who speak various languages. "We're a 21st-century family," she told him.

After hiking, the group convened at Samantha's mother's house for a family dinner where other adult first and second cousins joined them. One cousin is Armenian American, and his wife is Chinese and Austrian. Their three children identify with all three cultures. Of the two other cousins who joined, one is Armenian and was raised in Lebanon. He came to the United States in his late teens and speaks multiple languages, as is common in Beirut. His wife is Russian and came to the United States when she was in her 30s with her daughter. Both speak English and Russian. Emblematic of this family's hyperdiversity, the couple's younger daughter is Armenian, Russian, Lebanese, and American.

An important part of her family's memory is the Armenian genocide in Turkey and Syria that her grandparents fled to the United States to escape. The 100th anniversary was coming approximately 2 months after our interview took place in February 2015. Samantha noted that she was closely following articles in the media about the current political climate in Turkey and thinking a lot about what she and her children would do on April 24. She doesn't respond as strongly as some Armenians. "For me, an Armenian identity does not go as far as hatred against Turks," she said. "I certainly know Armenians who feel that way and won't be friends with anyone Turkish and won't buy any products made in Turkey." But she sees a shared historical background with Armenians, partially expressed through arts and culture—the music, dancing, and aesthetics—as central to her personal identity.

The hyperdiversity described for Samantha and her family is also present for Sasha, James, and Ryan. Sasha, for example, identifies as Russian, American, Jewish, and a woman, but said she needed to "break that down a little." She indicated that people see her as "a middle- to upper-middle-class white woman, and they probably don't go further from that." However, she added, "I would never say I feel truly American." Both of her parents are from Russia, where she was born and lived until the family came to the United States when she was 5. Russian culture permeated her home life while she was growing up in Southern California, including the food and the mix of Russian and English that was always spoken.

Sasha goes back to Russia every couple of years to stay connected to family living there, including a younger sister, who is her only sibling. She had just returned from there 2 weeks prior to being interviewed. Interestingly, when she goes to Russia, she is immediately identified as an American. "Here, nobody thinks I'm an immigrant. But when I go there, I have an accent when I speak Russian. But it's more my mannerisms. So people completely read me as American there because I smile a lot, and I'm kind of open, and there's just these American things I do that I'm not even conscious of that people get right away there." Living between cultures, languages, and geographies, Sasha always felt she had a hybrid identity. In the United States, she said, "I would pretend that I wasn't Russian until I was like in high school, and then it became something I was proud of and wanted to explore more."

Then, there's the whole Jewish element in Sasha's background that she said she did not fully understand. Three of her grandparents are Jewish, and one is Russian with blond hair and blue eyes. When her Russian grandmother married her Jewish grandfather, it was considered an interracial marriage. Sasha would tell her parents, "'I'm Russian,' and they're like, 'No you're not. You're Jewish. What are you talking about?' And I'm like, 'What do you mean? I'm from Russia.' And they're like, 'Yeah, but, we're

Jewish. Our ancestors are Jewish.'" Her family is not religious, so she came to see their Jewish connections (as well as her own) being more ethno-cultural than religious. Her parents tried to explain what being Jewish meant to them and what it should mean to her. It turned out that the whole reason her family was in the United States was because they were able to immigrate on refugee visas to escape persecution as Jews. Although her dad is readily identified as Jewish, Sasha is not, and her mother tells her she would not be identified as Jewish in Russia either.

The multiple layers of diversity in Sasha's life are accentuated by her having lived in Spain for 2 years, becoming fluent in Spanish, and eventually marrying a man from there. They would have conversations in which he challenged her claim to feeling "very Russian," while she challenged his claim of being Latino. She said, "I don't think he's Latino because I think he's white. Everywhere we go, he's perceived as white. We lived in the Mission where many people speak Spanish. He would try to order churros in Spanish, and they would always answer him in English even though Spanish is his first language. So, it's like, your skin is white. People perceive you as white. We totally pass as white."

In contrast to Sasha's sense that her husband is not really Latino, he argues that she is not really Russian based on things like her not being "hard and tough" like he perceives her mom to be. They both realize the stereotypical underpinnings of their disagreements, and she admitted, "We probably shouldn't do that—like try to label each other." For one thing, they both feel comfortable traveling to all kinds of different places regardless of how they are perceived. "I'm so attracted to cultures that are different than mine and people that are different than mine," she said. "I feel like that has a lot to do with immigrating and how I was raised. I never really felt fully a part of, like, the dominant American society. Even if other people perceive me as part of that, I didn't feel that way." Sasha's Russian/Jewish parents and grandparents and the linguistic and cultural practices and perspectives of her home life, her sense of being an immigrant with strong connections to her younger sister and other family members living in Russia, and her development of fluency in Russian and Spanish and other life choices such as marrying a Spaniard and loving to travel all contribute to her hyperdiverse personal-cultural positioning and sense of hybridity.

For James, hyperdiversity was manifested quite differently from how it was with Sasha, yet it also stemmed from positioning, practices, and unique life choices. Unlike Sasha, James was born in the United States. Both his grandfathers are German, and through genealogical research he found out that his family is primarily German with French, Irish, and other nationalities mixed in. He's traced his ancestors in this country to the 1650s and accepts that he is identified as a white male. However, when asked what group he connected to with regard to his ethnic or national identity, he said, "Growing up in our family there was nothing. No indicator, no residual cultural practices. None that I can remember."

James's parents divorced when he was 3, and his mother was pretty much not present in his life, especially after she remarried and started a second family. James felt he had significantly distanced himself from his upbringing, not through formal education initially, but by becoming an autodidact, reading voraciously, viewing films, and exploring various kinds of music and art. The Saint Paul, Minneapolis, neighborhood that James and his siblings grew up in had a mixture of Vietnamese, African American, and white residents. From about 8 to 14, he noted that all of his friends were black and that there were lots of youths from this neighborhood "who got into trouble, got arrested, and went to prison." After attending his neighborhood elementary school, he was bused to a mainly white high school and started hanging out with kids from middle- and upper-middle-class homes. He found he could connect with them by talking about music, movies, books, and art. Still, he dropped out of high school and eventually went to a continuation high school to get his diploma.

When James was 21, he left the United States and after spending 6 months in Mexico and Central America, he moved to Taiwan to live for the next 8 years. In addition to becoming fluent in Mandarin while there, he played music in many different parts of that country with a variety of bands. At one point he made a hip-hop album using samples from old Taiwanese music from the 1960s and 1970s. When he returned to the United States, he was almost 30. He enrolled in a community college, then transferred to and graduated from the University of Minnesota. "That was the cheapest; I mean it was the only place I could go because I really didn't have any money when I moved back." He ultimately wanted to continue for a PhD and become a college professor in Chinese language and Asian studies. Eventually, however, he was pulled aside by the department head and told that the university was seriously cutting funding for East Asian studies programs and that it would be extremely difficult to get any financial support. So he became a high school English teacher.

As with Samantha and Sasha, the complexity of James's personal-cultural positioning revealed something of the diversity reflected in his life. Beyond being identified as a white male, other aspects of his German, French, Irish, and other group ancestry were not visible or not emphasized in his family and home context, causing him to feel an absence of a specific cultural heritage to connect to. However, his sense of who he is comes from unique activity-based identities and selective identity affinities. As he said, "I also have another identity which is kind of being a musician and that lifestyle that I've been in for 25 years."

Clearly, distinctive aspects of James's positioning, practices, choices, and even serendipity are drivers of significant diversity in his life. Being raised with two siblings by a single father who struggled financially, growing up in a poor mixed-race neighborhood, dropping out of high school, becoming a musician, eventually becoming fluent in Mandarin, and leaving the United States for 8 years during his 20s to experience different cultures in other countries all contributed to shaping a personal identity that is much more nuanced than the label "white male."

This label is also applied to Ryan. Like James, he is over 6 feet tall, teaches high school, and acknowledges a white male identity, but as a way to make visible the privilege that comes with it. However, he gave many more dimensions to how he identifies himself. His father and grandfather were born in New York City, but both of his grandfather's parents came to the United States as immigrants from Ireland in the 1860s. Also, his grandfather's wife was an immigrant from Germany. Although one of his dad's parents is Irish and the other is German, according to Ryan, his father "holds tight to his Irish roots." The family's last name is very Irish, as is Ryan's first name, given to him by his dad. "His Irish heritage feels really important to him, and I think that's because of the very close relationship he had to his father," Ryan said. On further reflection he added, "My dad grew up in the 40s, during World War II, and I think that he very consciously, and even as an adult, turned away from his German heritage because of the connection to the Nazis, Nazi Germany, the Holocaust, and all that. So he's never vocalized any sort of pride in his German heritage. He has definitely always had pride for his Irish heritage like the family crest on the wall and passing on Gaelic names to his children." Ryan knows much less about his mother's background, except that she is eclectic in describing it. She was born in Philadelphia and met his father in New York. She identifies as American, and unlike his dad, "her roots have never been very important to her." Instead, she *pretends* to have identity connections to all kinds of groups, as will be described in coming sections.

Ryan is the youngest child in a family of seven sisters and one brother. "It's a big mixed family," he said, in which five of his sisters are half sisters, one is his full sister, and one is "unofficially kind of adopted." When his father and mother married, his dad brought two kids from his prior marriage, and his mom brought four daughters from hers. All these children were very young at the time and grew up together in the same household. The bond between his mom's daughters and his dad was such that when his mother decided to leave the family, her daughters stayed with his father along with the other children. Yet these four daughters have their biological father's last name and, of course, a different ancestral line that they feel is very important to them. "They are European folks of Jewish heritage," Ryan said. "They carry with them a really strong, um, Jewish identity. Jewish, not as religious, but as hereditary, as genetics, as ethnicity." In characterizing this group of sisters, Ryan noted, "Uh, there was a lot of noise. They're very loud. They have big hair and big voices." Ryan continued, "So they have these two dads who are very close with each other. On family occasions, all family occasions, our mom's not in the picture, but our two dads are, and we have this big family together."

This modern family that Ryan grew up in is like the families of Samantha, Sasha, and James mainly in terms of nearly limitless and unpredictable variability. The hyperdiversity of the interviewees' unique positioning in families, communities, and society as well as the endless range of their practices, choices, and perspectives reveal the vacuous pretense of societal forces that attempt to define them simply as white. Their stories illustrate that hyperdiversity is in essence human diversity when it is not restrained by the idea of race.

Within-Group Distinctions

Differences that often are not seen at the group level by people outside as well as within a group are aspects of hyperdiversity extending from the variable social positioning and distinct identities of individuals. Like Conrad's "secret sharer," alluded to in Chapter 2, people across as well as within groups can be limited to engaging surface levels of each other's identities. Knowledge of the activities and perspectives of Conrad's captain *below deck* would have given his crew a very different understanding of the complexities of his identity. To the captain, it was necessary for hidden aspects of his identity to remain secret. In deconstructing race, it's necessary to make hidden aspects of people's identities visible.

Recognition of within-group distinctions also works against stereotyping, relational identities, homogenization, and ultimately discrimination. Samantha's heritage and language connections to Armenian people through her mother; Sasha's familial and language connections to Russian and Jewish and Spanish cultures through her parents and her husband; James's German, French, and Irish connections through his parents; and, Ryan's Irish/Gaelic and German connections through his dad represent ways these women and men are uniquely positioned that are obscured by whiteness.

April 24 is an important date for Samantha and her children as they decide each year how to observe the anniversary of the Armenian genocide. Her family appreciates and participates in specific kinds of music, dance, and other aesthetic and cultural practices that would be foreign to the others broadly identified as white, and, of course, the same can be said for them. Samantha is fluent in Spanish, as is Sasha, but as will be seen later in this chapter, Samantha's links to this language are through extensive travels and social networks she had in Argentina that are quite different from Sasha's travels and social connections (including with her husband) in Spain. Although Sasha's links to Russia might have parallels to Samantha's Armenian connection, the content of their experiences through these connections are dramatically different.

Sasha's husband's life in the United States is another example of within-group distinctions. They have lived in this country for years but she said, "He never feels like he's part of American society." There are no outward distinctions between how he and his engineer colleagues look, yet "he doesn't have any friends among his co-workers who are white Americans." He feels distanced from them and tells her that nobody travels, nobody talks about or is interested in cultural events. He sees them being almost exclusively interested in and incessantly talking about their work.

Sasha and James both came from working-class backgrounds, but Sasha's early experiences as a Russian Jewish immigrant were starkly different from James's growing up in what he called a poor, urban neighborhood. Both changed dramatically by the time they were in high school, where Sasha actively embraced her Russian background, while James worked to negate his. Now James and Ryan are high school teachers themselves. Although both have part-German ancestry, they reflect many within-group distinctions beyond these similarities. James's family simple didn't acknowledge this lineage, while Ryan's family actively sought to suppress it and instead embrace their Irish side. Identifying as queer is core to Ryan's identity. A key part of James's sense of himself is tied to his fluency in Mandarin and the fact that he spent almost a third of his life up to the age of 30 mainly in countries in Asia.

These and other within-group distinctions are some of the constituents of people's identities that shape and are shaped by their choices and practices. Embracing and making these distinctions more visible is the beginning of the process of disaggregating broad identifications with racial categories that eventually can be drilled down to the micro-cultural level of each individual. People have to actively work to do this in their lives, personally and publicly. Publicly, more efforts are needed to change how race is reductively coded in institutional structures and processes such as the census, job and school applications and records, media representations, and general public discourse. Personally, taking stances and not accepting identity constructions based on ascribed racial categories is needed while also exploring and promoting identities directly connected to one's positioning, practices, and choices.

Indeterminacy

There were instances in the stories of some of the interviewees when it was clear that their (or their families') diverse physical, cultural, or linguistic representations made identifying them as a specific ethnic/ancestral group or racial group highly ambiguous or completely indeterminate. For example, because of how Samantha looks and talks no one perceives that, in part, she has Armenian roots connecting her to people who are generally darker in complexion. Instead, many type her as a Valley Girl. Her daughter, on the other hand, has been seen as biracial, Asian and white, despite her mom and dad being seen as white. "There's something about her that makes people think she's half Asian." Some of her daughter's diverse group of friends not only recognize but also embrace the fact that people can't identify them by race. They are either misread with regard to racial categories or they confound assumptions associated with these categories. For example, her daughter's best friend talks openly about how she is always read as white, but *chooses* to identify as African American. Another of her daughter's close friends, who is southern Indian and has darker skin than most of the African American students, is also always misread, as is another friend who is seen as African American. But her mother is Peruvian and the girl identifies as Latina. From these observations of her daughter's friendship group Samantha surmised, "I don't really know yet how this is going to shape my daughter's perception of who she is racially, but I do feel like it's not a pipe dream that she's gonna think of racial categories and racial identity in a much more complex way than my generation has."

Sasha is also completely misread. Based on her last name and how she looks, she said, "no one in the U.S. ever saw me and said, 'Oh are you Jewish?'" She is not seen as Jewish in Russia or Spain either. "How I look, you can't tell I'm Jewish that much," she said. "It's like my body structure and my height. . . . I have light green eyes and red hair." Her Spanish husband, on the other hand, is identified as a white man not only in the United States; when he's with her in his own country, people see him as a white foreigner there too.

Starting in high school, James made aspects of his life indeterminate to others by actively hiding them. He ended up being bused to school with students who were mainly from affluent backgrounds. In making new friends in this setting, James decided to never bring these kids home, and never talk about his family, or never indicate what his dad did for a living, which was mainly odd jobs. "It was hard," he said. "There's a lot of shame coming from a very poor family when you want to fit in." Ironically, his own ethnocultural background was hidden from him through its dis-acknowledgment by both of his parents, and, as noted earlier, he talked about having no sense of connectedness to any ethnicity or nationality.

For Ryan, indeterminacy was associated with sexual orientation as well as nationality and ethnicity. Both will be addressed further in the coming sections, but they also reflect indeterminacy in interesting ways. He is a cisgender man, which to him means "someone who identifies with a gender that was given to them at birth," and he also affirms an identity as "queer." He feels "this word has a bit of ambiguity around it, and intentionally so. So folks who just don't necessarily subscribe to kind of rigid gender and sexuality identities get to take this term on, or can choose to take this term on, if it feels appropriate and applicable to who they are and how they express themselves." Yet he does not project himself in ways that would cause people to assume he is queer. Instead, he uses his queer identification to push back on rigidly defined sexual orientation categories. For example, he purposefully leaves his own sexual orientation totally ambiguous to his mostly African American male high school students as a politically determined stance.

Regarding the other aspect of indeterminacy of ethnicity or nationality noted for Ryan, although his father made conscious decisions to embrace the family's Irish rather than German heritage, his mother was always intentionally unclear about her own ethnic or national background. According to Ryan, "My mom's side has always been kind of obscure and ambiguous as far as where her family comes from. Um, and that's mainly because we can't ever get straight answers out of anyone. . . . I have no clue, but according to her there's just a big mix of all kinds of European folks. . . . It's complicated because she's complicated. She seems to have, uh, genetic connection to whomever it's cool in the moment to have genetic connection to."

In addition to within-group distinctions, indeterminacy is a manifestation of hyperdiversity that's rooted in Ryan's life and family. The same can be said for the lives and families of Samantha, Sasha, and James. The Armenian influences on aspects of Samantha's identity for the most part remain veiled, while her daughter and some of her friends defy racial labels. Although the 2010 census indicated that about 8% of immigrants in the United States are from Russia, that part of Sasha's background is similarly veiled, while she and her husband's identities are mutable depending on the contexts they happen to be in. When the 2000 census first allowed respondents to choose more than one racial category, approximately 17% identified as German Americans, while 12% identified as Irish Americans, making these the first- and second-largest reported categories. Yet these aspects of James's identity were opaque during his development into adulthood.

Indeterminacy is a stake in the heart of white supremacy. Both physical and ethno-cultural indeterminacy disrupt simple binaries and make visible how human proclivities and practices refute ascribed categories of race. I have a colleague who I think looks exactly like Rashida Jones, who played Ann in the political comedy sitcom *Parks and Recreation*. My colleague identifies as Italian and talks about how people are disconcerted by not being able to place her in a specific ethnic/racial category. Now people are further confused about her identity after she married and took on a Latin last name.

Rather than being uncomfortable with indeterminacy, we should see and celebrate it as an instantiation of human diversity. As a pop culture aside, I feel this is what Amy Poehler's character, Leslie, is doing throughout the *Parks and Recreation* series when she responds to Rashida Jones's character, Ann. With hyperbolic humor, Leslie says things like "Ann, you beautiful tropical fish. . . . You resuscitated a human heart in your bare hands . . . [or, if not] you will. You're just that good" (Season 4, Episode 11); or "Look at Ann. She's a perfect human specimen . . . the greatest human being ever invented" (Season 4, Episode 14); or "Oh Ann. . . . I've said this to you before, and I know it makes you uncomfortable, but you're thoughtful, and you're brilliant, and your ambiguous ethnic blend perfectly represents the dream of the American melting pot" (Season 4, Episode 22). A pop culture example might seem like a stretch, but it captures how indeterminacy also reveals the limits of the idea of race.

STEREOTYPING

Pejorative or privileging responses to various stereotypes associated with the four interviewees discussed in this chapter were revealed through relational identities, or being homogenized, or invisibilized, or discriminated against, or in the cases of the males being perceived as hypermasculine. Samantha, Sasha, James, and Ryan are seen as white women and men who are tall, relatively young, and middle to upper middle class. Stereotypes associated with these aspects of their positionalities were usually responded to with privilege, and each person was conscious of this. However, they also worked in various ways to actively resist these stereotypes or to make their privilege in connection with them visible.

Relational Identities

Since relational identities are classificatory labels that are not usually freely chosen by the people on whom they are placed, they can be accepted and owned, or attempts can be made to circumvent or diminish their defining influences. Stereotyped relational identities of the other 16 interviewees were almost always negative. However, the relational identities of those discussed in this chapter are usually responded to with unearned privileges, although they are still reductive.

Despite the richness and diversity of her background, for example, Samantha feels she is most often seen mainly as a white woman. This is a conflict for her, and she talked about ways that she acknowledges unearned privilege to make it transparent. She also does this with her children by making them aware of their privilege. "They're starting off with a pot of money that they inherited from their grandparents," she said. "I mean it's not a huge pot, but it's something." As an illustration of how certain relational identities are privileged, Samantha related a story about a former colleague with whom she traveled to conferences a lot. This colleague often forgot to bring her driver's license but is privileged based on particular identity contingencies. "[She] looks somewhat like me, blond, blue eyed, light skinned, white woman. . . . A hundred percent of the time she was allowed to go through FAA security without a photo ID. People just read her as not someone you have to worry about because of, I'm sure, her race, her gender, appearing to be a professional. . . . How people position you or read you in terms of racial/ethnic group and gender is really important."

Sasha is keenly aware of how she and her husband are stereotypically read, and in addition to struggling with this personally, she tries to get him "to acknowledge all the privileges they have being identified as white." Sometimes he pushes back, saying, "You need to, like, tone it down a bit," but her experiences as an immigrant have helped her see the problematic aspects of being socially constructed as white. In terms of the males, James noted, "I think in terms of race, definitely I'm seen, you know, I'm a white male and that's what people see. . . . Growing up you know that was just what we were, that was what you were told you are." Interestingly, during his long stay in Taiwan, James was sometimes responded to negatively because of identity contingencies that had been privileged in the United States. Ryan used being read as a white male to challenge the very construction of this stereotype, and reminiscent of Samantha, he noted, "If I'm identifying myself to the world, I think it's important that I identify my whiteness because of all of that brings with it—all of the privileges that I carry on account of that."

Homogenization

Sasha's early experiences growing up provide insights into forces at work to erase distinctions within categories. When her family first came to the United States, they moved into subsidized housing that, according to her, was in a "lower-middle-class, like poor, white suburb." She remembered thinking how "everyone seemed Christian and white." They called the area "Santy" because of its proximity to San Diego, California, but she called it "'Klanty' because there's like actually Klan there." At a young age, she realized that being different from the expectations and conventions of this group was not accepted, so she pretended to be American to fit in. "It upsets me to think about that now," she continued, "because I don't feel that way now. But when you're a kid, you're like that. . . . I wonder how my experience maybe would have been different if I hadn't been dropped into such a, like, homogeneous place, if I already had that system for acceptance, or if it was somehow built into the curriculum or something."

So Sasha also felt boxed in by her Russian background with regard to her elementary and middle school teachers. She recalled "several definitive memories of like, being asked in front of everybody where I was born, or in 7th grade a teacher trying to make me be friends with this Russian kid who just moved in. And I wanted nothing else than to not be associated with him." An ironic side note is that now her husband doesn't accept her sense of connectedness to her Russian background. By the time she was in high school, she noted, "I just felt like a repulsion to white, American people." Although she felt early on that she was pretending to be white American, her experiences with other languages, cultures, and places eventually allowed her to see herself in ways that did not fit within this constructed positionality in her school and neighborhood context.

Samantha, James, and Ryan also feel boxed into homogenized whiteness. All began their interviews by acknowledging that most people in U.S. society identified them simply as white. The only differentiation Samantha seemed to get was the label of Valley Girl, which essentially is a culture/class stereotype within the category of "white woman." James noted that he's definitely identified as a white male—"that's what people see." Yet he's offended by being reduced to that identity and all the signals he's expected to give to affirm it. He said, "I feel like when I walk on the street I want people to understand intuitively, okay, yeah, I get where you're coming from. I can understand that you are not going to be straightforward, or you're not going to be part of that mainstream culture." But since returning from Taiwan, he hasn't found it easy to project the person he feels he really is.

In a different way, Ryan feels he also has to make conscious efforts to project who he really is beyond the restrictive categories of white and male. Admitting that "society primarily identifies me as a white male—and that's like mostly as a white, straight male, because I don't have many indicators of queerness or of gayness," Ryan also talked about how his whiteness and his man-ness in and of themselves are not that important to him. As noted earlier in this chapter, he definitely thinks it's important to acknowledge the privilege that comes with being white and male, but he also wants to project "non-normativity or nonhetero normativity without placing oneself into kind of a rather rigid role or label." He went on to say, "when it comes down to what is most important to me, my gender is not very important to me. Being a man is not important to me at all."

In their own ways, Sasha, Samantha, James, and Ryan struggle with how the idea of whiteness is homogenized into rigid roles and labels. They realize that through one's accepting the labels and playing the roles, privileges are also bestowed. Sasha became repulsed by experiences growing up that simultaneously pulled her into and pushed her out of white America. Samantha also understands the unearned privileges of being reductively defined as white, and she consciously works with her children to help them see these inequities. Being outside America for so long, as James was, and being outside of heteronormativity, as Ryan is, these two also understand and resist homogenization into whiteness—a process that is facilitated by ongoing ways to make whiteness invisible.

Invisibility

"I just had a conversation recently about whiteness and how it is often invisibilized," Ryan noted. Invisibility occurs when pertinent aspects of the interviewees' identities were either not seen or not seen as important. "Often times, white folks kind of don't hold their whiteness as a primary piece of their identity." He continued, "Though my whiteness is not kind of important to who I am as a person, I think it is important to be very conscious of my whiteness and not let it become invisibilized." Trainor (2008) offered a way of thinking about the normalization of whiteness that contributes to its becoming an invisible component of identity for many people identified as white. Her work on rethinking racism, discussed in Chapter 3, called attention to the continual, interconnected, nonlinear dynamics of institutional, cultural, and language practices that shape affective and emotioned beliefs about race, rather than logical and rational ones. The inculcation of emotioned beliefs instead of rational interrogations of whiteness works to render it invisible. In addition to these forces at work to make whiteness invisible, important aspects of the interviewees' personal identities were not seen. For example, being an athlete is core to Samantha's sense of self, while being an artist is core for Sasha's. For James, being a musician is an essential part of his identity as a person, while being queer is core to who Ryan is.

In Samantha's case, she has played sports her entire life. From middle through high school, she played field hockey, lacrosse, and basketball. The midwestern university she attended did not have these sports for women, so although she had never played soccer in her life, she tried out for and played on the varsity for all 4 years of college. Now in her 40s, Samantha said, "The social group I closely identify with and feel the most strongly about is the group of women I play soccer with." They are all in their 30s and 40s, and she feels they are the most interesting and fun women she has met since she moved to take her current faculty position more than a decade ago. Sasha became impassioned about art after seeing amazing digital art and other multimedia productions by young people. "It was really cool to see the things that they were able to do and the voice they were able to have," she said, and she decided the best way to understand the creative things people make and what it means was to begin doing it herself. After describing one of her recent digital art projects, she said, "It gives me a lot of confidence. . . . I'm addicted to it. I just want to do that all the time now."

James is just as addicted to his music that he's been into for more than 25 years of his life. He talked about always having a strong connection to playing music. In Taiwan he was playing professionally and had his own band, and it basically became his life. Additionally, though he came from a "low-income family and neighborhood background," that element of his identity remains hidden also, in part, because, as he noted, "It's not necessarily evident in my speech or mannerisms." There are subtle and overt ways of making identity invisible through hidings.

Invisibility of and within whiteness are two sides of the same coin. Political, cultural, economic, and educational institutions in U.S. society work to normalize whiteness as a system of emotioned beliefs that become impervious to rational critique. At the same time, personal, micro-cultural identities and affinities are not as visible or valuable—small change in the currency of whiteness.

Discrimination

Unlike the other 16 interviewees, Samantha, Sasha, James, and Ryan did not talk much about experiences of inequities or micro-aggressions linked to external and often stereotypical perceptions of their identities. This is probably the result of their being identified as white. The few exceptions noted were connected to the immigrant or working-class experiences of Sasha and James, or they occurred during travels abroad.

As an immigrant family living just outside of San Diego in a neighborhood she called Klanty, as mentioned earlier, Sasha remembers things like Easters, when the local tradition was for neighbors to draw little bunny footsteps on the walkways to people's houses. "Like everyone's house had bunny footsteps except for ours. So I definitely, even as a 7-year-old, felt outside of something." She was also made to feel like an outsider in school by being called out in front of the class by her teachers and made to talk about the country she was from. "And then," she went on, "that same year, I think it was like 7th grade, when you're at your most awkward and insecure, I remember a kid, um, like called me a communist. And neither of us, I'm pretty sure, knew what that meant at all, or I would have come up with a really good comeback. But I just remember feeling really identified." She also recalled "othering" experiences at times when she traveled, even in places where she could speak the language, such as Spain and all through Central America. She noted, "People would just stare, and you go to talk to them and they start straining their eyes and you see in their face that they're like, 'I'm not going to understand you.' It's like, that's such a thick barrier, and you perceive them perceiving you like that."

There were times when James too was made to feel like an outsider as a foreigner living in Taiwan or because of his working-class background. One example was when he wanted to work with the Taiwanese on a music album. "Those guys saw us as foreigners, as white American or British nationals. That was not cool with them." Even so, James was able to blunt negative responses in other ways tied to whiteness. He could circumvent people's perceiving his class background, for example, through how he learned to speak and what he learned to speak about such as literature, philosophy, and art. But for the most part, this group of interviewees did not talk a lot about experiences of inequities or microaggressions linked to perceptions of their identities.

Hypermasculinity

Some of the male interviewees discussed being perceived and responded to in ways that can be defined as "hypermasculine." There are multiple dimensions of masculinity, and the form often seen as normative in the United States is hegemonic masculinity, which was initially characterized as patterns of practices and power relationships that reflected men's power over women. As fixed notions of gender changed, these practices and power relationships came to be seen as more interactionally and positionally defined within a fluid range of masculinities and femininities that contained multiple hierarchies. Hypermasculinity is a dominant masculinity associated with violence or the threat of violence that embraces heteronormativity in conjunction with the subordination of women and perceived femininities as well as the subordination of men who exhibit alternative masculinities. It is characterized by the performance of hardness, including aggression, daring, physical prowess, authority, and a projection of compulsory het-erosexuality. In different ways, James and Ryan both revealed and resisted hypermasculinity.

In addition to long-distance running and road biking, James is an avid participant in other sports that are extremely challenging. "I usually have phases," he said. "I was into surfing culture for years, you know, where I went surfing every weekend. Now I'm rock climbing . . . so basically every day I'm either rock climbing or running." I inquired if cuts I saw on his hands were from climbing, and he said, "Yeah, and my legs are covered with cuts." When school isn't in session or when he otherwise has a free week or two, he said he liked to "thru-hike" which is long-distance backpacking. "I'm a very active person. And, you know, I'm very conscientious to use my body all the time, you know, as much as I can."

James also talked about times in his life when he could be or had to be physically aggressive. "Growing up in my neighborhood, it was violent. And you settled things; you didn't get punked. . . . Through high school, or until I was 18 or 19, if somebody did something that offended me or tried to insult me, violence was the first thing I thought of. . . . It's still something I think about, but after 25 years it's not that strong anymore." At the high school he was bused to, he initially had the reputation of being a bit crazy, kind of a loose cannon. "Upper-middle-class white kids who were listening to hip-hop music would say something to me that I didn't like, and I would legitimately get in their face, like this is gonna happen now. And, you know, it would scare the shit out of them."

James says he "learned" not to be violent, partially through under-standing the economic and political dynamics affecting his neighborhood that contributed to violence, in contrast to dynamics that made the affluent high school he attended safe. He also learned to be more nonviolent by living for significant periods of time in countries with non-Western cultures and traditions. Additionally he said, "I got involved later with people who were like hippies, and then I became a hippie. Then it was just like, oh yeah, that doesn't matter anymore! I don't have to fight anybody. Nobody's trying to hurt me. . . . If I can think of the one value that I really embraced it would be kind of a nonviolent existence."

Ryan believes that the way boys are socialized into masculinity and hy-permasculinity is a highly problematic aspect of U.S. society. In describing himself he said, "I have a beard. My voice is low. I'm 6 feet tall. . . . I've biked across the country. . . . I drive a truck." On the surface he is not ques-tioned regarding masculinity. However, he feels it is necessary to actively work to challenge and disrupt the dominance, psychological and physical violence, and heteronormativity of hypermasculinity. He takes this on per-sonally and publicly, especially as a teacher at a continuation high school where the culture of hypermasculinity is palpable. He engages his students and teaching colleagues in ways that encourage them to question normative notions of hypermasculinity. This will be discussed in more detail later in this chapter with regard to resisting binaries. But it's another aspect of the problem of stereotyping in our society.

IDENTITY CONSTRUCTIONS

Recognition and acceptance of multiple constructed identities make the range of human diversity more visible. The interviewees' personal and familial identities were reflected in a number of ways, including activity-based and digital identities as well as through identity rejections and challenging binary ways of seeing and being in the world. Interviewees' unique constructions of identity were enacted across interpersonal, social, and professional contexts. Beyond whiteness, for example, Samantha had multiple identity constructions that varied depending on contexts—as an academic, as a writer, as an athlete, as a parent and wife, and as a multilingual person. There are also Armenian connections to her identity because her mother is Armenian and that culture was always present in her home while she was growing up.

Sasha and James talked about ways they constructed identities when they were young. As noted at the beginning of this chapter, one method of constructing identity for Sasha early on was to pretend to be white and American. "I think my entire childhood I was probably pretending to be, like a person born in the United States because I didn't want to be a person—a foreigner. So I'd pretend about, you know that my family was from here, and that I was born here. . . . I tried to very actively hide, which is a form of pretending, that I had been born outside of the country. . . . My whole life I passed for somebody who's born in the U.S." Sasha also described selective constructed identities in relation to her parents, her sister who lives in Russia, her husband, her co-workers, her graduate student cohort, and her students when she was a teacher. James constructed an identity as a middle-class white kid in part through a pretense that his mostly African American friends and his upbringing in a working-class neighborhood didn't exist. With his neighborhood friends, he would work to not disclose his friendships with affluent kids at the high school he was bused to, and with these high school kids he would pretend he did not have friendships and connections to the neighborhood he was from.

Beyond consciously visibilizing whiteness, Ryan identified himself as an educator, a caretaker, an adventurer, a creative, a bit of an idealist, a radical, a queer person, a friend, and someone who is passionate. I will discuss some of these identities later in this chapter, but I have also discussed how family contexts have shaped aspects of individuals' identities. Ryan's family provides an interesting example of this. Although his father actively defined the family as Irish, his mother had very different ideas about how she and her family could be identified, and she is able to shape-shift into a nationality she wants to associate with. She was born in Philadelphia, but as Ryan recalled, "It seems like if it's hip in the moment to be Russian, somehow we have some Russian in us. Uh, if it's hip in the moment to have Irish, okay now we're Irish. And, it looks like we also have Dutch or Belgian in us, and maybe there's French in us. Like it all kind of depends on whatever moment we're in, and she somehow pulls up some sort of deep family roots there." Although these examples of identity constructions may also include aspects of "rejecting identities" that will be addressed in more detail later in this chapter, they also are active choices to construct alternative identities to those being negated.

Additionally, all the interviewees talked about how hip-hop music and culture had varying influences on their identities and activities. The rise of hip-hop culture has been collateral with the increasing pervasiveness of digital media in most people's lives. More than 45 years after its birth during the early 1970s in New York City's South Bronx, hip-hop culture continues to leverage and be leveraged by digital media to significantly influence the cultural practices, choices, and perspectives of people who become dedicated hip-hop heads to less devoted youth and adults. These influences on people's identities and affinities rhizomatically flow across the United States and the globe, connecting diverse cultural positions and activities.

Activity-Based Identities

Gee's (2013) concept of activity-based identities focuses on the freely chosen practices of an individual that contribute to grounding and delineating a sense of self. These practices can reflect resident and emerging forms of social organization or what Gee earlier referred to as discourse communities. He described how discourse communities come with "identity kits" that include how to act, talk, and take on specific roles that others in the community recognize (Gee, 2003). Activity-based identities also can be digitally mediated, and this aspect will be taken up in the next section.

Identity constructions extend from selective practices and choices people make to engage in specific activities. Samantha engages in multiple activities as an academic and enacts behaviors and other elements of that identity kit such that the "academic" identity is real for her. These are quite different from her identity and activities as an athlete or as a parent. She said, for example, "I feel a strong identity as, um, a parent at my children's school, and I am active in my school programs, and I socialize with a lot of other parents from the same school, but I'm active in programs at the school." Although her multiple identities cross over into social and interpersonal connections, there usually is not crossover among her different affinity groups.

The main music Samantha listened to growing up was go-go, which she feels was one of the precursors that influenced hip-hop. "I still listen to go-go even though people make fun of me," she said. But now she's influenced by hip-hop, mainly through her children. They listen to the music in the car together and find it enjoyable but laughable when her son, who has taken hip-hop dance for 2 years in Christian dance academy, tries to teach her a few moves. "He was the only non–African American child out of about 250 kids in the academy," she said, "and in their big performance, he did a number of hip-hop dances with the crew." Additionally, Samantha has a couple of African American colleagues who often send her new articles or songs and videos that they either think are really good or that could be used in teaching. Clearly, Samantha is not a hip-hop head, but unique identifications with and through this music and culture are woven into activities and interactions she has with family, colleagues, and friends.

Connections to hip-hop and, more so, activities surrounding being a musician are core to James's identity. He grew up playing punk rock and rock and roll, then got into jazz, but his true loves are funk and reggae. He was into hip-hop. "From 8 to 14 all my close friends were black," he said, "and so I knew about, you know, hip-hop music and culture. . . . Like I think my first record was 'Rapper's Delight.' . . . When I was probably 11 or 12, me and my friend would go to the malls and we would shoplift the clothes—Cross Colors and things like that." Around 14 when he was bused out of his neighborhood, he "kind of moved away from hip-hop." In his new school environment, he noted, "When white kids would listen to it, I kind of was like, that's not who you are. And I really did feel kind of affronted by that. And I think listening to punk rock music felt authentic to me. Like this is legitimate."

When Sasha was in high school, she did not feel that the activity-based identity she constructed, which was heavily influenced by hip-hop, was inauthentic. Her primary friendship and affinity group was Filipino/a students with whom she participated in many aspects of hip-hop culture such as particular styles of dance, dress, and talk. "I had like a B-girl name," she said. "It was like B-girl Trinity. We had like a crew. . . . I wore like one glove to school for a while. . . . And I wore like warm-up pants. . . . I wrote, like, 'dis' instead of 'this.' You know, like things that you would never associate with being like a Russian, white girl." Pulling from her artistic inclinations, she developed a much-admired graffiti writing style. She wouldn't tag buildings, but her friends wanted her to do their party fliers and would ask her to write their names in graffiti style. She recognized that her friendship group was actually pretty removed from the centers of hip-hop, and noted, "Maybe they were pretending at certain levels. . . . And then I went to college and it just went away."

Some of the multiple identities noted for Ryan, such as being an educator, an adventurer, a creative, a radical, and queer, were inhabited and in some cases intertwined through selective activities. He considers himself a DIY (do it yourself) person or someone who likes to create things collectively in a community. "I'm really into being able to actually self-determine things in this way, where we actually get to have our hands on the mechanisms from start to finish and really create something as opposed to pushing a few buttons." About 10 years ago, he did graphic design as an extension of his creative, DIY identity, and in the next section we will see how this contributed to his digital identity in an unexpected way. Specific activities that constitute his intersecting identities as a radical, queer educator will also be taken up in the sections on identity rejections and challenging binaries.

Digital Identities

There were unique ways that identity constructions linked to variable uses of digital texts and tools. The Internet and other digitally mediated practices have significantly transformed how adults and youth leverage online communities and tools for exploring and expressing personal identities and affinities. They permit multisensory, multidimensional, interactive cyber experiences with nearly an infinite range of written, audio, visual, and animated texts. In other words, people don't just consume and respond to digitally accessed messages and images; they also produce and propagate meanings and representations of their own that can challenge or counter the defining power of other societal representations. The remixing practices characteristic of digital production lend themselves to experimenting, analyzing, and performing different realities and selves (Mahiri, 2011), and the use of online spaces and tools for identity exploration, formulation, and expression are now pervasive throughout the world.

In outlining enabling aspects of digital media, Gee (2003) indicated the significance of identity affinities. This idea is that people use digital texts and tools to develop individual identities and selective affinities with chosen groups. Gee noted that membership or participation in affinity groups or affinity spaces (the virtual sites of interaction) is defined primarily by shared endeavors, goals, and practices, rather than shared race, gender, nation, ethnicity, or culture.

Samantha talked about her identity being anchored in how she was positioned in the world with part of that being how she is positioned digitally. She prides herself on being open to new technologies, but her digital identity begins with email as a main mode of communication both professionally and personally. She saves every email that she sends, and in the year prior to being interviewed, she sent on average over 100 emails a day. In addition to mentioning email, she noted, "I've become more aware of how my Internet profile is really the main way that people get to know me. . . . I don't know if it's identity or relationships, but a lot of the primary contact, and sometimes the only contact, I have with others is through the Internet." She also uses the Internet constantly to research things for her work and personal life, and she finds herself using digital texts and tools more and more in her teaching.

Samantha doesn't feel she has time to be a big social media user, but she does go on Instagram to monitor what her children are posting. She's also cautious about what she posts in social media. She experienced something with Instagram that she had not anticipated. When she started following her children, she instantly received requests from their 11- and 13-year-old friends to follow her. Rather than seeing the parents' presence as just sur-veillance, Samantha reflected the way that kids and parents were commu-nicating by saying, "I don't know if it's in this particular generation or in my social group, but children and parents don't feel like they're at odds and have really different interests." Interestingly, she is not as welcomed on Snapchat, where her daughter and friends do things like post satirical videos of teachers whose classes they find boring.

Samantha gave other examples of how she uses digital media to sustain interpersonal relationships and how these activities in turn shape her identi-ty, perspectives, choices, and actions. She joined Facebook "as a way to stay in touch with people across cultures and across huge geographic expanses," but she also found it to be a good way to project her identity as a parent by posting about things that were going on with her children. Joining was ini-tially motivated by the desire to stay connected to a friend she met while she was living in Argentina. They select different media for different kinds of discussions; for instance, email is used when they talk about their children.

"Her different cultural perspectives on adolescents has been very infor-mative to me," Samantha said, "and that's helped me change my expecta-tions for what happens with my own kids." For example, Samantha shared how her son would easily cry over something that was sad, or really burst out laughing when something was funny, and how he has had struggles at school with these behaviors. "If he were living in Argentina," her friend often told her, "no one would think this is abnormal behavior. He's a pas-sionate kid. He's interested in the arts. This is how it should be." Having this cultural lens from outside the United States that showed her that her son's personality did not need to be fixed was reassuring, and it also gave Samantha new perspectives on how to talk to her son's teachers that she would not have had access to without her digital identities and activities.

"In my lifetime, I saw the Internet develop," Sasha said. " So that was huge when I was younger, and one of the first ways I participated in digital culture was I taught myself how to make websites." At 12, she figured out HTML on her own. "I had a website with my friends and a blog with my friends, so all through high school I would write [in these mediums]. And, you know, digital culture is so expansive, like chatting online, that my mom would hide the Internet cord. I would find her hiding places when she was at work and just be online for the entire day talking to people, talking to friends. This is, like, AOL chat or something. Then I'd like put the cord back in her hiding spot. She never knew."

Sasha wanted to stay connected to her friends all the time. "And then," she said, "the Internet just kind of became part of my life." Her digital ac-tivities continued to evolve and expand. She took photographs and created little online galleries to show them way before social media websites took off. "It gave me confidence," she said. After a relatively dormant period, she has really gotten back into photography and digital media production and uses them as a form of expression generally as well as a way to communicate specifically to significant people in her life; for instance, she intertwined some of her drawings, photographs, and audio recordings of her grandmother to make a little animated film as a gift for her birthday. "Like 5 years ago, I recorded her stories because she's an amazing storyteller, and she was an actress. And then I kept them, and then I took little clips, and then I illustrated it kind of symbolically. Then I threw everything into iMovie, sped it up in a way that, you know it looks like an animation. I'm addicted to it. I just want to do that all the time now."

Sasha tries to avoid using Facebook, however, because she feels she will waste too much time and still not meaningfully engage with people. "I almost never post on Facebook. . . . I just like delete it every other week, and then it comes back," she said. "It's just like a time sucker." But she feels differently about her current photography website. "That's something I tie my identity to. It's not necessarily my goal to be a professional photographer. But there's something about making art and then posting it. It's kind of like your parent putting it up on their refrigerator or something. It just feels more real."

James uses digital technology a lot, but mostly as tools. He takes advantage of complex software programs for his music production and recording, for movie editing, and for his Chinese-language learning. "I'm good at using that stuff," he said, "and I'm really fascinated . . . [by] the sheer amount of just amazing technology that it provides in our hands." But he tries to avoid using digital technology for social things. He noted, "I really just think it's just not good for us." He does use Facebook as a convenience, however, because he has so many friends living in other countries. "It's not that we really communicate that much . . . and we don't really talk on the phone or write letters . . . so [with Facebook] I know a little bit about what's going on with them. But I don't really participate in it, and I don't use any other forms of social media."

James decidedly does not use Instagram, Snapchat, or Twitter. Although he's in the millennial generation, he takes pride in his minimal use of digital tools for social purposes. It was 2001 before he got his first cell phone, and that was because he moved to Asia and basically had to have one there. After returning to the United States, he lived for more than a year without a phone. "All my friends got really mad at me," he said, "but I thought it was fantastic. You know, it would be like you hear the phantom ring of a phone . . . and we are not giving ourselves peace and time, and this is a really unhealthy thing that we're doing to ourselves." Essentially, James feels that human interactions should not be so heavily dependent on digital devices, yet he loves their power and convenience as tools of production.

Ryan appreciates some of the affordances of digital media, but he does not want to be overly dependent on it. This may stem from an unfortunate experience he had when he used to do graphic design. He was designing a big website project that he hoped would give him enough money to settle in Argentina and live abroad for an extended period of time. As he was wrapping up the project, his computer crashed, and nothing was backed up on external drives; nothing was saved. Not only did he lose all of his creative work, he also lost the hope of financial security he had been anticipating. "It kind of destroyed me," he recalled, "and after that moment, I wanted to be intentional about keeping my distance—being careful not to put too much of myself into this kind of immaterial realm over which I don't have much control."

Ryan noted, "This definitely is a piece, a big piece, of how I approach digital media that connects to how I identify in the world. [It's] more around my own kind of personal ideologies of how I like to cultivate myself and my relationships." He appreciates digital technology and culture, but he's also very intentional about keeping his distance and not getting too wrapped up in it. "I don't have a smartphone, and that's intentional because I don't want to be constantly connected to it." He feels that other people have developed so much connection to social media that they stress out when they're not connected. He said he loves it when his phone dies or when he travels and doesn't have access to the Internet; he breathes a sigh of relief. "There's something liberating about that," he said. "I don't want my daily life to shift from being in the kind of tangible material world, to being in this more digital, kind of, immaterial world because it scares me a little and because I don't totally trust it, and this may have come out of that rather traumatic experience."

The digital identities of Samantha, Sasha, James, and Ryan vary considerably based on the kinds of practices and choices they enact that extend from their positioning and perspectives. Beyond her own use of digital tools, Samantha has to be concerned about her children's online activities and expressions. Yet she finds that new ways of relating to them and their friends are possible, while the cross-cultural reach of the technology also gave her valuable resources that contributed to shaping her perspectives as a parent. Sasha found capabilities to explore her artistic skills that allowed for new modes of expression with her friends and family. James and Ryan are both highly skilled in the use of digital tools but struggle to not let them pervade other ways of being in the world. Importantly, all four people show something of the range and identities that are more variable through the use of digital tools.

Identity Rejections

Some interviewees and members of their social networks consciously rejected or expressed ambivalence about identification of themselves by race, or gender, or sexual orientation. Samantha's interactions with her children and their friends revealed a number of instances where expected ways of identifying were rejected. In the case of her son, for example, rather than encouraging a typical masculine identity of what society considers hardness and strength, she instead supported his need to cry over something that was sad or to passionately express himself. Another example is in how her daughter's best friend, who Samantha said "has blonder hair and whiter skin than I do," chooses to reject an identity of being white, in favor, in this case, of identifying as African American. What is important here is the exercise of prerogatives rather than merely accepting an identity that is socially constructed.

In Sasha's case there was a time in her life when she decided that she was not white. The high school she went to was more diverse than her elementary school, with about half the students identified as white and the other half as a mix of Asian, Southeast Asian, Latino, and African American. As noted earlier, her best friends at this school were mainly Filipino/a, but she also had friends from Vietnam and Afghanistan, some of whom she has kept as friends to this day. All her Filipino/a friends were into hip-hop, and she would on occasion proclaim to them, "'I'm not white.' I would say that. And they'd be like, 'Yeah, you're not white.'" Sasha continued, "I think identifying with some perversion of hip-hop culture was, um, I didn't know it at the time, but now looking back, I think it was a way to participate in a culture that was outside of dominant, American culture." Eventually, when she matriculated to one of the top University of California schools and started taking classes on race, class, and gender, she decided to explicitly acknowledge her identification as white. Her act of choosing not to be white, however, is important as an example that people can actively and consciously reject that identity and, ultimately, construct ones that are more ancestrally and scientifically accurate.

On the flip side, Sasha talked about how she and her parents sometimes rejected their Russian-immigrant identities. "There's ways of pretending," she said, "where it's like, you're at the grocery store, and your parents are talking in Russian, and like you distance yourself because you don't want to be associated with them." At times her mother did similar things. "Like, we'll be at the store or on a hike, and we'll hear some Russian people, and she kind of gets like, she doesn't want to be associated with them. And she's not doing anything really active, but it's almost this aversion, which feels like it's an aversion to yourself." James also talked about ways he rejected the identity expected of someone identified as white American. "I kind of see myself as a bit outside of most of the mainstream U.S. system," he said. "And coming back from having experienced a significant amount of my life living in different cultures and kind of understanding my identity that way, I always have found difficulty integrating back into American culture, even among the people that I knew before I left. I feel like there's a lot of difference [because] I don't really subscribe to most of the values that I see in people in the U.S."

The negation of identity with Ryan's German heritage has already been discussed, but there were instances when his mother did things to negate even their Irish identity. Her proclivity to define her family members in terms of whomever it was cool in the moment to be connected to included identifying them as "people of color" when it suited her socio-cultural purposes. Ryan described how when his older sisters were going to a public school in Los Angeles during the time of busing, to get them into a certain school his mother argued that they had a considerable amount of non-white ethnicity. As the story goes, his mom created a whole lineage back to Mongolia and convinced the school that her daughters had a significant percentage of Mongolian and, therefore, were people of color who would add to the school's diversity. The rejection of socially constructed identities as white or specific notions of being male in the lives and families of Ryan, James, Sasha, and Samantha are indications that alternative identities can be agentively constructed.

Challenging Binaries

As partially evidenced by Sasha's "I'm not white" comment, some interviewees actively worked to disrupt conceptions of themselves as being defined within a framework of reductive binaries. Sasha's hope for the future is a continuation of this challenge. "My hybrid nationality or identity became something I really, really value and I constantly try to learn more about," she said. When she and her husband have children her hope is that "they understand, oh, I'm Russian, and I'm American, and I'm Spanish, and I'm Jewish, yeah, and bilingual or maybe trilingual. And they would have this really cool identity where they can be like whoever he or she wants to be, and live where they want to live, and engage in all these different communities and cultures, and see this as a strength." Her hope for the future fleshes out what Baldwin (Mead & Baldwin, 1971), cited in Chapter 2, meant by being witnesses to a possibility for what human beings can become that we might not live to see, but have to work now to bring about.

The cold reality of how far we have to go is partially captured in one of the acts by Samantha to challenge reductive, racial binaries. During the time of the killings of Trayvon Martin, Michael Brown, and other lives that matter, she wrote an editorial that presented what we know from research about how strong teachers can make a significant difference in the lives and learning of students of color in underresourced urban schools. She was viciously attacked in the comments section below her article by people who claimed that low achievement had nothing to do with teaching and was solely the parents' fault. Samantha critiqued how some American ideologies inherently promote racial binaries, with a powerful one being the false notion that we live in a meritocracy. She called it the "Ameritocracy," the idea that people are made to believe that some groups simply "work harder than others without acknowledging the advantage that whites have over many people of color." She does other things to challenge behaviors and beliefs that support reductive binaries in her work as a professor, as a parent in her children's schools, and as a board member of a nonprofit community organization that's kind of a watchdog group on issues of equity in her city and it's schools. "I've seen how policy changes *can* increase equity," she said.

Within this group of interviewees, Ryan was the most active in challenging binaries. Although his focus is disrupting the male/female binary, I believe he models a stance that also must be taken against the white-versus-others binary that undergirds the forces of white supremacy. In addition to his other expressions of identity, his challenging of binaries is vital to his being queer. He indicated that *queer* is a reclaimed term that used to be derogatory for gay folks but has since become more of a self-identifying term. It's now more closely related to liberation from boundaries of identity, particularly within the context of gender and sexuality. He feels terms like *bisexual* continue to reinforce boundaries. "You're saying there's two pieces and you happen to be into both of them, but you're still reaffirming that binary. Whereas the idea of queerness is that there is not a binary. There's not only one spectrum. There's a whole bunch of spectrums . . . [and] I exist somewhere in all of this."

Ryan teaches at a continuation high school with a population of mainly African American males, and it is marked by and in many ways condones expressions of hypermasculinity. "Since I haven't broken the rules in all these other ways" (by being a cisgender male), he feels, "I'm able to push back a lot on the normative notions of gender, gender roles, and gender relations." He's not pushing identities on other people or saying they need to identify in a certain way. Yet he sees himself "bringing these walls down a little bit so they can feel like there's more space to explore different ways of being and of understanding oneself without feeling the pressures of potential exclusion or ridicule or degradation that come along with breaking social expectations."

In his school, Ryan would do things like wear a small, gold belt that looked like a "lady's belt," that he knew would provoke questions from his students. But because he doesn't feel that his masculinity is jeopardized, he would respond by saying, "Oh, yeah, that's my lady belt. I love wearing it." Or, as he describes another occasion, "I got this new shirt that has polka dots on it, not a particular[ly] masculine shirt. And now I'm in this place where, you know, there are young men who in other spaces have to be really puffed up and tough. But this young lady was like, 'Hey, I really like that shirt.' And I'm like, 'Thanks, I just got it. I love the polka dots.' And, you know, this tough young boy sitting there was like, 'Yeah, man, that shirt is saucy. That shirt is dope. Whatever. That shirt is wet.'"

Ryan feels he's established a place where when he gets pushed back, and he handles it, then there are moments in which some of the students feel like they're able to push back too on being reductively defined. "They don't have to always subscribe to those rigid notions of masculinity and femininity, and what it means to be a man, and what it means to be woman, and what it means to be straight, and what it means to not be straight," Ryan said. But he believes that when these young people get to see someone they feel is a strong man, someone who does tough things, and also has this other side that they hadn't associated with masculinity, they begin to see multiple ways to enact masculinity and femininity. Importantly, Ryan said, "I personally find masculinity and the way that boys are socialized to become men to be one of the most destructive pieces of society. I'm not saying that sexes or patriarchy is more destructive than, say, racism or xenophobia or anything like that. But what resonates for me is I see how this power of normative, masculine socialization is a destructive force . . . particularly for young boys."

LIFTING THE WHITE VEIL

Ryan's stance and commitment can also be linked to ways to countcract the destructive forces of racism and white supremacy as well as gender biases. People can perform and model actions to challenge the binary identifications of white versus others in order to create space and safety for ways of being along multiple spectrums of personal-cultural identities. An article by the Santa Cruz Feminist of Color Collective's (2014) also provided similar insights regarding the significance of developing and using a multidimensional conceptual lens to critique the Western, male-centered, heteronormative structures that define the institutional, intellectual, and cultural spaces that constrain our identities. Practices and perspectives of all four interviewees in this chapter contribute to lifting the veil and making the workings of whiteness more visible in terms of the power and privilege it bestows. Their stories lift the veil to show how porous, variable, inaccurate, and politically motivated the identifications ascribed by white supremacy are. Across this chapter, the description and discussion of the interviewees' personal-cultural identities and affinities complicated and even obviated the white racial category.

Samantha indicated how the emerging perspectives of her children's diverse friendship groups indicated that some of them were less concerned with or resistant to being identified as white. She sees them developing understanding and responding to socially constructed racial categories in much more nuanced and complex ways than her generation has. As adults, James and Ryan in separate ways have worked to reject or challenge reductive constructions of their identities as white males. At a point in her life, Sasha acted as a race trader by proclaiming that she was not white. Although later in college, she learned to make her privilege visible, she was actually correct in her prior claim. Key scholars discussed in Chapter 3 argue that Sasha, Samantha, James, and Ryan are *not* white, and I further suggest that everyone behind that veil is essentially pretending to be white. The interviewees reveal and affirm multiple ancestries, ethnicities, nationalities, and affinities reflected in their personal-cultural practices, choices, and perspectives with respect to their interactions with other individuals and in institutional frameworks. As shown in Chapter 3, the census is one of the key institutional frameworks where the abolition of whiteness can begin to take place.

The next four chapters argue for abolition of the other color-coded racial categories in favor of ancestral, ethnic, and national origin identifications. Their organizational schemes differ from that of this chapter, but they continue to illuminate themes of hyperdiversity, stereotyping, and identity constructions along with all the other associated categories surfaced in the data, although not necessarily in that order. The design of the rest of the book is to present the stories and perspectives of the interviewees in compelling ways and often in their own words, then bring these portrayals together in a discussion of "Micro-Cultures" in Chapter 9. Chapter 10, "Challenges of Multicultural Education," explores the education challenges, along with three pedagogical examples that offer considerations for addressing these challenges.

CHAPTER 5

Passing for Black

There were these distinctions in the community of well, you're not really black; you're West Indian; you're an immigrant. . . . And I experienced a lot of tension and cultural shame. . . . It became easier to pass for black. I lost my accent, dressed more urban, changed my hairstyle and clothes, started to read the bodies, and adopt African American language. It was an active project . . . to make socialization easier, to make relationships across cultural differences easier, and, maybe, to not be a target.

—Relene (May 11, 2014)

Culture has been defined in hundreds of ways by anthropologists and other scholars. People have different kinds of cultural knowledge that, like language, is both acquired and learned. Culture is made visible and, thereby, observable and recognizable through practices. It is also associated in overly simplified ways with people's physical characteristics. In Chapter 2, I discussed how acquisition and learning of cultural practices can be related to Gee's (1991) definition of discourse communities with respect to the notion of "identity kits" that specify appropriate ways of acting (talking, dressing, gesturing, eating, dancing, etc.) that allow people to be recognized as members. In the quote that begins this chapter, Relene, who is one of the interviewees in this study, describes particular practices that are learned and her motivations for performing them that allowed her to "pass for black."

In an article titled "Passin' for Black," Fordham (2010) challenged the idea that the United States is becoming a postracial society simply because of the rising number of interracial relationships and marriages and the increasing expression of biracial and multiracial identities. Her argument is that people whose ancestors were enslaved in this country are compelled to embrace a black identity even when they have white as well as African ancestors. On the basis of an ethnographic study of female competition and aggression in a racially mixed suburban high school, Fordham contended that historical memory and inclusive kinship grouping combine to make it necessary for virtually every person who is connected to enslavement and socially defined as black to "perform" blackness regardless of their skin color and other physical features. Fordham's analysis of why people positioned as such are compelled to embrace a black identity is insightful in indicating the defining power of white supremacy and reactions to it by others. But how do we go further in disrupting this power? I suggest that being forced to perform a black identity and being forced into enslavement are certainly different, but only by degree. Also, the blackness being performed is essentially the same as how blacks are racially constructed within the hierarchy of white supremacy. A more agentive approach would be to embrace the full range of one's identity constituents rather than only those allowed and reinforced by the inclusive kinship groups within assigned racial categories. And how should we understand the case of Relene, who would not initially have been included in the kinship group of the black girls in Fordham's study until she learned how to act in ways that allowed her to pass for black?

The controversy surrounding Rachel Dolezal brings up additional complications with respect to how cultural practices can be learned and performed such that identification with an ascribed racial group is accepted and sustained. This controversy blew up in the media about a year after Relene talked in her interview about passing for black. The different sides and shades of Ms. Dolezal's actions, and the reactions to them, directly connect to discussions in this chapter of the lives of interviewees who are identified as black.

Ms. Dolezal is a civil rights activist and former Africana studies instructor at Eastern Washington University. From 2008 to 2010 she was education director at the Human Rights Education Institute in Coeur d'Alene, Idaho. She resigned that position because of alleged discrimination. She was president of the NAACP chapter in Spokane, Washington, for about 5 months until June 2015, and she was chair of Spokane's police ombudsman commission for about a year before being dismissed for misconduct, also in June 2015. After she reported to the police and news media that she had been the victim of hate crimes, her Caucasian parents made a public statement on June 15, 2015, that she was a white woman passing for black. She subsequently resigned from the NAACP after allegations that she lied about her racial identity. The organization later issued a statement saying that a person's identity is not a qualifying or disqualifying criteria for leadership. In a television interview in November 2015, Ms. Dolezal admitted that her parents were white but that she still identified as black, and since July 2015 she has been working as a hairdresser.

Whether Ms. Dolezal's racial identity was a fraudulent appropriation of black culture or an authentic connection to it has been heatedly debated. In *Vanity Fair*, Samuels (2015) wrote a sensitive, but conflicted, portrayal. He remarked, "It's safe to say that Rachel Dolezal never thought much about the endgame. You can see it on her face. . . . It is precisely the look of a white woman who tanned for a darker hue, who showcased a constant rotation of elaborately designed African American hairstyles, and who otherwise lived her life as a black woman, being asked if she is indeed African American. It is the look of a cover blown." Ms. Dolezal did put pictures on her Facebook page of a man she identified as her father, Albert Wilkerson Jr., an African

American she met in Idaho. Yet she continues to defend her identity construction. Samuels's article quotes her saying, "It's not a costume. I don't know spiritually and metaphysically how this goes, but I do know that from my earliest memories I have awareness and connection with the black experience, and that's never left me. It's not something that I can put on and take off anymore." However, Samuels called attention to how Naima Quarles-Burnleys, who took over as NAACP president, characterized things in a statement in Spokane's *Spokesman-Review*: "I feel that people of all races can be allies and advocates, but you can't portray that you have lived the experience of a particular race that you aren't part of."

In her resignation statement, Ms. Dolezal referred to challenging the construct of race, but as Cobb (2015) wrote in *The New Yorker*, "Many people have challenged the construct of race without lying about their lives." Cobb noted, however, that rather than lying about who she is, Ms. Dolezal was actually lying about a lie. Instead of claiming that her outing made it apparent that the emperor has no clothes, Cobb offered an argument similar to that of Fields and Fields (2012) in *Racecraft* that "in truth, Dolezal has been dressed precisely as we all are, in a fictive garb of race whose determinations are as arbitrary as they are damaging." For Cobb this was personal. He acknowledged how Ms. Dolezal, like himself, is a graduate of Howard University and described it as "a place where the constellation of black identities and appearances is so staggeringly vast as to ridicule the idea that blackness could be, or ever has been, any one thing." Extending this point and echoing Du Bois, quoted in Chapter 2, Cobb wrote, "The spectrum of shades and colorings that constitute 'black' identity in the United States, and the equal claim to black identity that someone who looks like White or Wright [major, early leaders of the NAACP who were indistinguishable from white men] (or, for that matter, Dolezal) can have, is a direct product of bloodlines that attest to institutionalized rape during and after slavery."

Rachel Dolezal and Relene's passing for black are alternate sides of a single coin of U.S. racial currency. Ultimately, it's counterfeit, but it gets some value from the pretense that it's real. Relene, Ingrid, Joshua, and Ethan, the four interviewees focused on in this chapter, may not entirely agree with this point. However, I think their combined stories and perspectives confirm it. Relene, an associate professor at a university in the South, was 40 years old when interviewed. She is 5'5" and has a brown complexion, dark-brown eyes, and black hair. She identifies herself as a black woman, as a mother, as an immigrant of African-Caribbean heritage, and as an academic. She is married to a man from Jamaica, and their son was born in the United States. Ingrid was a recent college graduate from a university in the Northwest and 31 years old when interviewed. She is 5'6" and has a light brown complexion and dark-brown eyes and hair. Her father, whose career was in the military, is African American and her mother is German. Ingrid doesn't claim to be black or African American. She is married to a man who is Russian and was pregnant during the interview, and soon afterward they had a son. Joshua was a graduate student at a university on the West Coast and 39 years old when interviewed. He is 5'11", has a light complexion and black hair, and identifies as African American and as a black man. He is married to a woman whose mother is Danish and British and whose father is a Chinese immigrant. Like Ingrid, Joshua's wife doesn't claim a specific racial identity. Joshua and his wife have four boys all under the age of 9. Ethan, an assistant professor at a West Coast university, is 6' and has a brown complexion, dark-brown eyes, and black hair. He identifies as an "African American, cisgender, queer male."

This chapter discusses each interviewee in succession and illustrates how the themes and categories that surfaced in this research are in play in their lives. Rather than specifically evidencing each theme and category for each interviewee, as was done in the previous chapter, this chapter lets these considerations come through as they are embedded in the interviewee stories. Backlash to passing for black is morphed into the title of the section on Relene as "Blacklash." The section on Ingrid and her experiences of constantly being misread racially is titled "Illegible Skin." The title for the section on Joshua, who is usually responded to as a hypermasculine male, is "Man Up." The title of the section on Ethan comes from his saying that society identifies him as "a 'good' black man." This is followed by a section on the interviewees' digital identities, affinities, and practices in a section titled "Cyber-Lives," then by a section on their influences from hip-hop culture titled "Hip-Hop Life." Then key considerations that emerged in this chapter are brought together in the concluding section, "Clap Back!"

BLACKLASH

In the case of Relene (as well as Ms. Dolezal), identities are lost, but irony is not. Ms. Dolezal elected to trade her white identity and privileges by performing a black identity with its perils of exclusion and victimization. Relene elected to lose her Dominican identity and perform a black one to prevent being excluded and victimized by Bostonian blacks. The blacklash Relene sublimated her Dominican identity to avoid and that Ms. Dolezal eventually received is a stinging reminder of some of the contradictions incurred when subjugated people accept the racial identities they are assigned. Acting as suboppressors (Freire, 1970), they draw artificial boundaries for group inclusion that mimic the fictive boundaries drawn around whiteness to exclude others, even though, as seen in Chapter 3, whiteness can expand to accept others when deemed necessary. As meaning making in verbal language depends on deciphering the slightest differences between audible sounds, racism has also made meaning making about racial identities dependent on deciphering the slightest physical and cultural differences. When said out loud, "Rachel" (Ms. Dolezal's first name), is barely distinguishable from "racial." She may choose to identify as black, or not, but U.S. society still constructs her as racial rather than Rachel, a stereotyped perception of who she is. And the same was true for Relene.

When Relene described her identity as a "black woman of African-Caribbean heritage who immigrated to the U.S. as an adolescent," she wanted to signal that she has lived in the United States for most of her life, is a naturalized citizen, and claims an American identity as part of how she constructs her sociopolitical identity.

She sees that U.S. society identifies her as black, "meaning U.S.-born black," and she is comfortable being thought of as African American. When asked where she is from by her southern neighbors and colleagues, she says Boston because it's the city she lived in for more than 2 decades. After naming Boston, however, she always adds that it was the city she emigrated to from the Caribbean island of Dominica, to emphasize her Caribbean identity.

The hyperdiversity, stereotyping, and identity constructions and other subthemes that were revealed in Relene's experiences as an immigrant who became a U.S. citizen provide another view of how reductive and inaccurate the racial category of black is. First, significant "within-group distinctions" of national origin, ancestry and ethnicity, and variable island languages and cultures are collapsed under the term *West Indian*. But Relene and others whose identities are stereotyped and oversimplified in this way are keenly aware of their differences. Dominica, where she was born, is one of the smaller islands in the Caribbean, in contrast to Jamaica, Barbados, Trinidad and Tobago, and other islands sought out as tourist destinations. She feels that people living in the Caribbean have a collective sense of West Indian identity, but noted, "There's also this sense of West Indian identity . . . that's imposed on them by the larger dominant U.S. society." Consequently, the uniqueness of the different islands and cultures become invisible. Importantly, she said, "Even when we ourselves claim that identity, we still account for the cultural differences that exist among us."

Island Cultures

To exemplify within-group distinctions, Relene described how the people of Trinidad and Tobago have a very different background and culture from those on islands like Antigua, Saint Lucia, Saint Kitts, Nevis, Jamaica, Barbados, and Dominica. "There's more of an Indian [from India] influence often for people from Trinidad and Tobago just because there was historically an Asian, East Asian immigrant stream . . . that has kind of worked out in terms of these people having a different sense of cultural identity." She also talked about how phenotype differences are apparent because the East Asian influence can be seen physically in Trinidadians in contrast to the African influences on people in other Caribbean islands.

Other examples of the complexity of difference under the umbrella of West Indian identity resulted from the varied histories of colonization. Relene said that Haitian immigrants in the United States had the most difficult time staking claim on a West Indian identity because their first language was Haitian Creole instead of English. Hierarchies were created in the broader West Indian community, in which Haitian kids were looked down on because of their language difference. On the other hand, kids from Jamaica or Barbados, who were from islands that were more established or economically advanced, relatively speaking, were higher up in the hierarchy. For instance, the popularity of reggae music and all the new artists coming up in the 1990s made Jamaican culture more respected by other West Indians as well as African Americans. Relene mused, "So as a girl from Dominica, I felt much lower down on the chain of cultural coolness or acceptance because I was not from Jamaica. But still I understood that in a sense I was to be grateful that English was my first language because, sadly, I felt, well at least I'm not Haitian. I'm not that far down on the chain. And it was a reflection of how West Indians and different groups within that collective identity were positioned in the larger community."

Relene drew attention to the island of Saint Martin/Sint Maarten as another example of the complexity of people's identities that were homogenized and made invisible under the West Indian label. From its colonial history, this island has a French half (Saint Martin) and a Dutch half (Sint Maarten). She noted that there also is a large Haitian and Dominican population living on both sides of this island, and that it is a "hub of immigration for many West Indian countries." She captured a bit of the complexity of these collateral cultures by describing the life and family of a good friend she went to school with in Dominica for 5 years before coming to Boston. This Dominican friend also emigrated to the United States, but to live in Tampa, Florida, with her mother and siblings. However, their family kept close ties with both the French and Dutch sides of Saint Martin, often going back and forth between there, the United States, and Dominica. Relene's friend eventually married a Saint Martin native from the French side of the island whose first language is French and moved back to live there permanently.

Relene thought it was interesting to see how these diverse cultural and geographic connections contributed to identity constructions, and she used the 16-year-old daughter of her good friend as an example. This young woman is formally educated in French in Saint Martin schools, but speaks English at home with her mother. Her dialect in English is not like her mother's Dominican one, but rather that of people in Saint Martin, despite the fact that she spends summers in Florida with her grandmother. Unlike her mother, this teenager is a French national because of her country's colonial history. However, she also has developed a deep interest in Japanese culture and language. Relene felt that she might be motivated to explore the Dutch resources available to people on that island, such as options to go to Holland for college if she took advantage of opportunities to become fluent in Dutch. Instead, assisted by Facebook and the Internet, she's teaching herself Japanese and making other personal connections to Japanese culture, including taking on a Japanese name.

Relene feels that "this is indicative of how young people take on these identity projects that we would never imagine if we just think of cultures that they're connected to in terms of where they live or who their parents are or what have you." She was fascinated by how this young woman and others in her generation are choosing identities leveraged by different countries they are able to visit and live in, multiple cultural and family lineages, and what's available through digital technologies that they are able to adapt to modify who they want to be. "Where I'm going with this," Relene said, "is this kind of teasing out of identity or wanting to kind of claim distinctiveness within this monolithic group identity."

Black in Boston

Against the distinctiveness of the identities and histories of these island nations and the discrete individual identities and trajectories within the nations, Relene's experiences with African Americans in Boston was of being stereotyped and homogenized as West Indian. Her family settled in Boston because a network of relatives was already established there. Being 15 at the time, she already had a strong sense of her Dominican identity, but she soon realized that she was not prepared for the blacklash to that identity from the larger community and society she came to live in. As she started high school in the United States, it quickly became apparent that African Americans made distinctions between themselves and youth from the islands. She saw their position as "Well, you're not really black; you're West Indian. You're an immigrant, as opposed to well we're all black. We have different cultural backgrounds, but we're all from the African diaspora." She thinks this may be changing now, but then the African Americans perceived immigrants from the islands negatively as people who were willing to work for less money, willing to work as just nurses' aides, willing to work as hotel maids, willing to work at Dunkin' Donuts. "Just broad perceptions and stereotypes, right? And it's a difficult thing to talk about," she said, "especially now in retrospect, understanding the complexity of the social and political conditions that contributed to how we viewed each other and how we're positioned in society, right? . . . And how the larger society, white society, viewed us."

At the same time, Relene indicated that there were some advantages to being seen as West Indian. Employers would often express a preference for them. In urban schools, West Indian kids would disproportionately be the ones on the dean's list or be selected for the scholarships to exclusive private colleges with whom the Boston public school system had partnerships for accepting high-achieving students. Because of all the dynamics noted, Relene remembered her "teenage years being just incredibly fraught with cultural conflict, and all of these questions, and this sense of jockeying for acceptance. . . . For me as a West Indian girl it was a project of becoming an African American girl. Much later on, I started recognizing and accepting that I wanted to claim my West Indian background. It didn't have to be one or the other. It continues to be a complex project . . . to live with being a West Indian immigrant in the United States who also in many ways is an African American person as well."

Relene's and Rachel's stories demonstrate that rather than race being a stable category, recognition of race is attained and sustained through performance and perceptions. This means that practices and choices that contribute to identity constructions could also be enacted in ways to disrupt hierarchies and enable fuller expression and acceptance of diverse cultural positions and perspectives. Relene's description of her friend's 16-year-old daughter is interesting in this regard. Relene was impressed that this girl and others in her generation could take on identities "that we would never imagine if we just think of cultures that they're connected to in terms of where they live or who their parents are." Perhaps Relene's appreciation of the variegated cultural practices and choices of this young woman help redress her own desires to escape the cultural shame she experienced at a similar age that caused her to pass for black.

ILLEGIBLE SKIN

Excepting some recent immigrants, Cobb's (2015) article on Ms. Dolezal noted that nearly everyone who identifies as African American in the United States has some white ancestry. Cobb mentioned his own white great-grandparent and how his grandparents' four children ranged from two males who are "almond-brown, with black hair and dark eyes," to two females who have "reddish hair, fair skin, freckles, and gray eyes." Cobb claimed that his father, uncle, and aunts were all equally black, despite the quirks of chance that can make ancestry from Africa or Europe (or anywhere else) more apparent. He wrote in conclusion that "for black people, that past remains at the surface—close at hand, indelible, a narrative as legible as skin." I appreciate how Cobb elucidated key issues in the controversy; however, I believe the lives of my interviewees, and Ms. Dolezal's as well, attest that skin is essentially *illegible* for reading race.

"Society, I believe, gets a bit confused on identifying who I am, and where I come from, and what my background is," Ingrid told me. People have read her as Brazilian, Puerto Rican, Cuban, or generally of Hispanic descent, as well as African American and multiple races. She was born on a mid-western air force base, the child of an African American father and German mother. "They got married in Mexico because I guess they weren't allowing interracial couples to get married in the United States yet," she said. "They have stories too." When she was young, the family was stationed in

Athens, Greece, for several years, but she remembers only bits and pieces of that experience. Her mother wanted to move back to Germany, so that's where Ingrid lived from about 8 years old until she was 22. During this time she had only brief glimpses of the United States on short trips with her dad to visit his family in Florida.

Military Brat

Born after World War II, Ingrid's mother had serious problems with her German roots. She was proud to have English-speaking children and did not teach them German. This might have been facilitated by the fact that they lived on a U.S. air base outside a major German city. So Ingrid did not learn German until she went to high school, and she is the only one of seven children by her mother who speaks German to her. Interestingly, no one in Ingrid's family expected or encouraged her to go to college. "If you were a military brat," she said, "you are automatically bred into going into the military. I was the one, and there were a few other siblings, that didn't go into the military, and my parents never talked about college to me." She feels she had a missed opportunity because in Germany one can go to college almost for free. But for her parents, everything was about going into the military. In 2007 as an adult, she moved to Colorado, where one of her brothers lived. She met and married her husband there, and in 2010 they moved to a major city in the Northwest, where she enrolled in college and completed an undergraduate degree.

The hyperdiversity of Ingrid's blended family is reminiscent of the lives of the other interviewees discussed earlier. She began describing her family with a laugh and asked, "Are you ready to be confused?" Her mother was married two times before she married her father. Her first husband was from Spain, and Ingrid believes he was a darker-skinned Spaniard because the two girls and a boy they had together look "sort of mixed." After they divorced, her mom married again and had two more boys. She married Ingrid's father after her second divorce, and Ingrid and another brother were born to that union. But there's more. Her father had a son before he married her mother. He also adopted two children and now has had two more children with a German woman who is not Ingrid's mother. Across all the different skin tones, hair colors and textures, and body types, every one of the children has brown eyes. Ingrid's family might be even more diverse than those discussed in Chapter 4, but echoing them, she said, "We all love each other."

Growing up in Europe gave Ingrid "a different kind of mindset" on race. She sees European and American societies as very different entities. According to her, they both struggle with similar issues but don't approach these in the same way, particularly with regard to race and ethnicity. In the United States, "it's as if they have to put you in a box so they can release expectations about you, or feel comfortable about you in society and know how to adjust or act around you," she said. In Europe, she felt she didn't have a racial or ethnic identity. She talked about always having a mixture of friends from different ethnicities and backgrounds and how it never really occurred to her that she should just be in one group or another. Also, her parents never spoke to her about who she should identify as. Instead, they accepted her for who she decided to be, and she noted, "I always identified myself as just 'Ingrid.' No confusion there."

For many people in the United States, however, Ingrid's racial indeterminacy is both confusing and problematic. "I let people play the guessing game of 'What are you'? And, they start labeling things, and I'm like, 'Nope. Nope. Nope.' And it's really funny that they pretty much get really upset because I won't tell them what my ethnicity is." People here still attempt to box her into a category, usually as African American or Hispanic, and she experiences stereotyping and discrimination as a result. "Oh she must be of African descent, so she must be angry or have an attitude," she said. "It's more of a brainwash that America has put on its citizens for generations. They label you a certain way, and make you feel a certain way, and have the people treat you a certain way in order to sustain privilege, but, of course, there are other implications as well."

Checking the Box

Ingrid described a number of instances of stereotyping, relational identities, homogenization, invisibility, and discrimination that she and her husband have experienced. She met him at a rock-climbing gym in Colorado. When they would go rock climbing, which she loves, people would see her and "they'd be like, 'What are you doing here'"? Also, she would meet a lot of Germans while rock climbing, and being fluent in German, she would start conversations with them. "They just get really shocked," she said. "I tell them I used to live there. . . . My mom's German. Again, they get kind of confused." Ingrid mused about how these same Germans are aware of their own history as colonizers. One result of this was that there are now a significant number of people from Africa living in a number of cities and towns in Germany.

Although her husband is identified as white in the United States, he considers himself mixed race. His mother is Polish and Latvian and his father is Russian and also from one of the native groups in Siberia that total about 10% of the 40 million people there. Ingrid said that her husband doesn't see himself as white as it is understood in this country because of these multiple lineage constituencies, but in the United States most of these aspects of his identity remain invisible. He does get pushback in some situations though, such as in applying for jobs, because of his accented English or because of what's happening politically in Russia with regard to the United States.

Before Ingrid and her husband started dating and eventually married, her husband was not confronted with overt discrimination. He was with a lot of Russian friends in Colorado and was somewhat insulated within that group. But American racism became more apparent when he saw how Ingrid was sometimes treated when shopping in stores or how people otherwise responded to her. As a couple, they often got "looks" while walking around holding hands. "It was kind of weird because in Colorado we faced discrimination from the Caucasian, Euro-American side for being together, but when we moved to [the Northwest] we faced discrimination from some African Americans staring at us and being like, 'Oh, my gosh, you guys are together'? We were shocked." Interestingly, she felt more accepted when she traveled to Russia with her husband to visit his family. "I met his family in Siberia where there's no people of color whatsoever. They were very friendly. They were welcoming, and, you know, they treated me just like their own," she said. These experiences are a testament to how their identities were relational and responded to differently in different contexts like Colorado, the Northwest, and Russia.

Ingrid experienced discrimination by being homogenized in institutional structures that intentionally propagate ascribed categories of race. While filling out medical paperwork in connection with her pregnancy, she remembered being excited because she was aware that since the 2010 census, as noted in Chapter 3, people were allowed to indicate their identities as more than one race. "I was like, 'Yay!' They have two or more races. I was very happy about that." She filled out the paperwork accordingly, and the aides put all her choices in. Later, however, when her husband checked the paperwork, he found the aides had changed their selection of "two or more races" to "African American." "I guess they just want to label me in a certain way and put me in a category," she said. She wasn't angry, but the next time she went to the medical office, she requested that they change her identity, and thus the identity of her coming child to "two or more races" instead of "African American," and they said, "Oh, that's not a problem."

But it is a problem. Social constructions of race are encoded and enacted within the spectrum of institutional structures in U.S. society. It's not a small problem to permanently alter or reinscribe a person's identity; it's a racist act. If it's unconsciously motivated, it's still just as problematic. Ingrid, like Sasha at different points in her life, rejected the socially assigned identity and actively negotiated one suited to her personal-cultural positioning, practices, choices, and perspectives. Like Sasha and Samantha, she hoped her children would represent and help bring about a society that was more equitable, less hierarchical, and without rigidly imposed racial constructions and constraints.

Little Pushkin

Regarding her son (who has since been born), Ingrid said, "I'm really excited. I kind of resemble this child. I know it's a boy, and so I kind of resemble him as a little Alexander Pushkin." I asked her to expound on the Pushkin reference and she said, "Alexander Pushkin identified with both sides. He was very proud of his African descent . . . but he also had, of course, Russian nobility. He was very proud of that too. He combined two of them together and wrote marvelous books and fairy tales. I hope my son has this similar life. Of course, I hope he doesn't get shot in a duel, but I hope he's going to inspire the world, and that he's definitely going to change perceptions. . . . If he has my mindset and determination, he's going to be just fine." Ingrid felt her son might have thick hair and a broad nose, or he might have very light skin and blue eyes. Either way, his skin will not be legible as a reading for race. She fears, however, that she might be out with her son "and someone may think of me as a nanny or something instead of the mother." But she added, "It's going to be quite an adventure, and I'm looking forward to it."

MAN-UP

When his first son was born, Joshua started listing all the ethnicities he was going to put on the birth certificate. His wife finally said, "I'm just going to put American." He reminded her how important it was to capture the newborn's range of ethnicities, but being the person having just given birth, his wife said she couldn't handle it. "I couldn't fight that battle at that point," Joshua said, "so I had to let it go."

Birth certificates, as was also seen with Ingrid, as well as things like the census, reflect ways that U.S. institutional structures subtly and overtly work to define individuals and groups in society even though these definitions can be continually and even radically changed in different historical or political contexts. One example is a person I know who has a much older brother and a much younger brother. He recounted how his older brother was identified as "colored," while he was identified as "Negro," and his younger brother was identified as "black" on their individual birth certificates.

The birth certificate incident with Joshua was with the first of his four sons, whose skins, like Ingrid's, are also unreadable with respect to race. Identifying himself as African American and Portuguese/Irish (from his father) with a splash of Native American and his wife as Danish/British and Chinese, he said affectionately, "Our kids are all mixed up." Joshua couldn't tell me how his wife identifies herself. "It's hard to get her to pin anything down," he said. She grew up middle class and Asian and white, and her Chinese-immigrant father is a dedicated believer in the idea of an American meritocracy. His daughter, however, rejects specific identities as European, or Asian, or mixed, and prefers to think of herself simply as American. Joshua said that for a long time she considered herself to be "a-cultural." Her perspective has changed somewhat as a result of being married to him, but he feels it's still difficult to pin down. When asked how society identifies her, Joshua could say only, "It's hard to say." Absolutely no clue can be gained from how she looks either. I've seen her and she could be the poster image of racial indeterminacy.

Their family now lives in a suburban area that is primarily European and Asian American, without a lot of African American kids around. When their oldest son got to be 5½, the son started to identify himself as African American, although Joshua is not sure if his son really knows what this means. His second son "is really interested in his Chinese-ness. . . . If you ask him what he is, he'll first answer by saying his name, but if you dig deeper, he identifies his Chinese-ness for whatever reason." Joshua thought his connection to being Chinese was particularly interesting because this son has blonde hair and blue eyes. Although Joshua's primary personal iden-tification is African American, his choice of a life partner and the racial indeterminacy of their four boys controvert the traditional notion of black family. He talked about how his children have cousins who are European, African, and Asian Americans, and reminiscent of how Samantha's hyper-diverse family is discussed in Chapter 4, he noted, "At our family reunion they're all in the picture, and [my children] see all these different ethnicities as a normal family."

Mixed Messages

Joshua identifies as African American although some people think he is mixed race because of his light skin. He has a younger brother who has a different father, who is African American. His mother, who identifies as African American and was a community activist, pretty much raised them. Privileging light skin, people would tell his mother in reference to Joshua, "You have a really handsome son." She would always respond by saying, "Yes, I have two really handsome sons," to not let them play the pigmentoc-racy game. Still, from an early age, Joshua remembered that people treated his brother very differently, more quickly perceiving him as a threat, "and it had to do with his complexion."

Joshua's biological father was not really in the picture, and his brother's father was his first real association with a man on a daily basis. Joshua came to hate this man. "He beat my mom, and he also abused me," Joshua said. "There was one point in my life ['dealing with the anguish of him trying to kick a hole in my mom's throat'] when I concocted a plan to get rid of him." Joshua and his brother grew up in a tough neighborhood of a city that has sometimes been described as the murder capital of the United States. He was the first in his extended family to go to college, but his route to undergrad-uate and graduate degrees had many dangerous detours along the way. He recounted, "When I was in high school, there was no shortage of drugs. . . . I had this moment in my life, I was 17 years old; I looked in my backpack for a pencil . . . and all I had was a Glock [a semiautomatic pistol], and I was going to school."

When asked how society identifies him, Joshua noted as an aside that there have been times when people assumed he is Middle Eastern. But, he definitely stated, "I'm perceived as an African American male irrespective of my complexion. . . . The police for sure identify me as an African American male because I've been stopped several times. Once when I was younger, I asked why I was stopped. They said there was a report of an African American male just by the store, so they stopped me." He described how when he first started dating his wife-to-be, she was in awe and fear of how he had to act and how he was treated when they were pulled over by the police. "We would be driving somewhere and the police would pass by. We wouldn't necessarily be pulled over, but I would sit up straighter in my seat, take off my hat, and when I did get pulled over, I put my hands out the window." His future wife was incredulous, and he had to explain that this is what he has to do to not be seen as a threat, to assure the police that he was unarmed. These behaviors continue even though he is approaching 40. "For her, it was mind boggling," he said. "She actually said the other day that her biggest fear in life is that something is going to happen to me out in public with the police."

Many people who identify as white or Asian also respond to Joshua as a hypermasculine black male, which is a bit ironic in that his father is Irish and Portuguese and his wife is Chinese and Danish. He reflected on how he has to be hyperaware of the way that people view him. "It's not as though I can just get up and leave the house and not have some type of consideration of the ways that my being, my maleness, my African American maleness, is going to make people feel," he said. "So in elevators I always assume the furthest corner away from people. . . . Even though I'm in elevators with people or I'm walking close to people with [my] Gucci shoes on, women still clutch their purses. . . . If I start moving my hands, people are paying attention to what I'm going to do. . . . I have to be aware whether or not I'm perceived as some kind of looming threat, and I gotta tell you, it's tiring."

Although going to college was collateral with turning his back on the vicissitudes of urban street life, Joshua recounted many instances when he was stereotyped, discriminated against, or had to enact relational identities there, including dressing quite differently for the different contexts of his home, school, and work lives. He said his closet was divided into a side with clothes he wore in the community and a side for college and work. "I always felt as though I had to be really, really measured in the way that I answered questions . . . because I didn't want to be dismissed as an angry black man, and I always felt like just based on my tone, irrespective of whether or not what I was saying was cogent or pressing or any of those things, I had to be hyperaware of my tone and my comportment. It was like a performance. And, you know, performers get tired, and it wasn't just physical—it was psychosomatic. I was drained cognitively and emotionally, and it manifested itself physically." He concluded by saying, "I feel like all those instances are indicative of the way that we are viewed in this country—the conflation between black male and threat."

It's sadly ironic that the person who was a real threat to society was Joshua's white-identified father. He said his father's notorious criminal activities actually deterred Joshua from committing crimes, despite the stereotypes that link him to such behavior. His father has a nickname, Fast Eddy, and was attracted to African American women. Joshua has an older sister who looks a lot like his dad, and her mom looks a lot like his mom. "On his best days," Joshua said, his father was "George Clooneyesque—he was like a zoot suitor, a real character." He sold drugs, and he robbed 16 banks, 15 successfully, and was caught on the 16th. That final robbery attempt was featured on Jay Leno's *Tonight Show* in a segment called "America's Dumbest Criminals." Apparently, his getaway driver went across the street to get the car washed, and so the headlines read, "Two Bank Robbers Failed to Make a Clean Getaway." Fast Eddy went to prison, and for a long time, Joshua thought his father had died there, until years later he received a letter out of the blue from his dad wanting to connect with him. An intravenous drug user, his father was eventually let out of jail because he had AIDS, and Joshua regrets that his father died without ever getting to know the four boys who would have been his grandsons had he lived.

In the Body of a Black Man

While in graduate school, Joshua created or directed several different after-school programs that were very effective in helping youth of color develop interests and competencies in science, technology, engineering, and math (STEM). One that was for African American males in middle school met for 3 hours every other Saturday morning over 3 successive academic years. Of this program Joshua said, "I work with 70-something African American males on a regular basis, and I don't want them to be paranoid, but at the same time I have to have honest conversations about ways that they are perceived in this world. It's not positive in my experience . . . and I need to prepare these young men to, you know, be able to navigate these spaces." So these academic programs are designed to be a safe space for developing STEM identities and skills for youth of color, but also for developing critical perspectives regarding uses and values of STEM disciplines and careers in society. This is both political and personal for Joshua, who talked at length about the numerous young black boys and men, some the age of middle schoolers, who have been killed by the police. "I have nephews that age," he said. "I have sons who will be that age. I work with young men who are right at that age, and they need to be able to have a childhood and make childhood mistakes, right?" In this regard, Joshua quoted a good friend of his who said, "The most dangerous place for a black boy to be is in the body of a black man."

This danger is one of the compelling reasons for deconstructing race. Stevenson (2015) and Alexander (2012) have painstakingly analyzed the inequities of our racialized society in terms of the onerous consequences of unjust deaths and castelike systems of incarceration for those at the bottom of the hierarchy of white supremacy. Of course, this will not change by simply proclaiming that race doesn't exist, but the lives of people discussed thus far in this book illuminate the contradictions and constraints of race as a social fact. Joshua's diverse personal-cultural positioning is made even more so through his marriage and their resulting hyperdiverse family in which his wife and four children are racially indeterminate. Their lives and her identity rejections subtly work to challenge binaries. And though there were within-group distinctions that led to varying life trajectories and differing relational identities such as between Joshua and his brother, as one of the examples, societal perceptions and forces homogenized both of them as hypermasculine blacks with all the attending acts of stereotyping and discrimination.

Clearly, continued political actions to expose the institutional mechanisms that perpetuate detrimental impacts of race are needed. It's also clear that people's perceptions of racial inequalities and constraints can be changed through authentic relationships with others from different backgrounds. This is partially seen in the examples of Ingrid's husband and Joshua's wife. More deliberately, multicultural education is crucial to increasing productive relationships and socio-cultural activities across racial lines to help people question, reject, and even trade social constructions of race for more ameliorative and agentive ethno-cultural identities and ways of acting and being.

A GOOD BLACK MAN

Joshua and his brother are objects of the fear and threat that society sees in men it has constructed as black with slight additions or subtractions of preference for varying shades. Conversely, when asked how he felt he was identified, Ethan said, "I would say that society would describe me as a good black man, with *good* in quotations." He explained that his background has followed a normal trajectory from high school through higher education: "Someone who is, um, a little overly theoretical, a little overly temperamental about societal issues. . . . [But] I think it would kind of be this nice person who can kind of be particular about how society functions in the United States, right?" Being an academic is central to how he constructs his identity. Prior to being hired as an assistant professor of math and education, he completed undergraduate degrees in math and sociology, masters degrees in math and education, a PhD in mathematical education, and a postdoctoral position. Russian and German were the languages he passed proficiency exams in as part of his doctoral program. He also studied for an extended period at the National University in Singapore and used that time to travel all around Asia and Southeast Asia. He scheduled his classes for Monday and Tuesday and was on a plane every week going somewhere like backpacking in Vietnam from Wednesday through Sunday, or longer when he decided to skip classes. He was kind of a tall, black Gulliver, and the various people he met during these travels were constantly in awe, asking him where he was from or what sport he played. These experiences outside the United States, in conjunction with those in undergraduate and graduate school, contributed to his sorting out his identity as an African American and, eventually, as a queer, cisgender male.

Ethan's parents were not college educated, and he grew up in a family of five children in a city in the southeastern part of the United States. His family lived in the projects, and although he hung out with kids in his neighborhood after school, his family never really talked about race while he was growing up. He felt he grew up in a family-friendly neighborhood, but he also noted, "All of my male cousins, there are nine of us, are dead or in jail. All of my female cousins—they're still at home, right?" This background motivated him to succeed academically, and he consciously created the kind of "public identity" he needed to get through college. He also grew up as a Jehovah's Witness and felt this significantly contributed to his identities. He would go to the Kingdom Hall, and they taught that there was "no such thing as race, or class, or gender or all these other things." At one point during high school, however, his father asked him directly, "Are you gay or not?" His answer was, "Maybe I am. I don't know. You know, I'm kind of attracted to everyone." He had a girlfriend at the time whom he had been dating for 4 years, and the expectation was that they would get married after high school. The church leaders had had several meetings on the issue, and although he was still trying to figure out who he was, they actively tried to make him identify as a heterosexual male. College was where he began to explore and ultimately affirm two core aspects of his identity—sexual and racial—being black and queer.

Orientations

While indeterminacy for other interviewees was associated with race, for Ethan it was associated with sexual orientation. In line with his focus on succeeding in his college majors, he described how he was willing to assimilate into whatever culture he needed to get through. He joined a fraternity and as part of that process created a public identity that was acceptable to its members while privately working through his identity as a cisgender male. He was also working out the racial component, which was getting problematized in ways that he had not been prepared for in his experiences growing up, where "it was just black folks and not black folks, [like] white folks and Asian folks." In college, two frat brothers that he became good friends with were from Nigeria, and until then he had not really thought about the differences between Africans and African Americans. "So I began to understand, like, how they felt about black people in the United States, right?" This sensitized him to within-group distinctions that had not been visible to him during his upbringing.

Ethan carried these sharpening perceptions into his graduate studies, where "it just kind of all blew up in my face, right?" His math department was composed of mostly international students, mainly from China and Korea. "There were two African guys, [but] I'm the only black man sitting in all these classrooms . . . that's from the United States." Race became more of an issue for him than it ever had before. At the same time, he was still working out the other key aspect of his identity, which graduate school provided opportunities for him to also explore. Realizing that his math program allowed him to take electives in other departments, he took a number of classes in the sociology department and learned more about *cisgender, transgender,* and other designations that he had not heard of. In concert with Ryan's definition in Chapter 4, Ethan noted that "when we say 'cisgender' it's basically you are following these designations that have been given to you, right? So you were born male, and you identify as a male, and your behaviors, for lack of better words, follow traditionally what we would call, like, masculinity as opposed to femininity. When we think of transgender, it's when your original designation as a male based on your sex is transitioned over to your sexual identity as more what we call femininity, etcetera."

In Deep

Identifying Ethan as a good black man requires us to interrogate along with him what should be considered "good," "black," and a "man." Thirty years in the making, Ethan's life is a window into the dimensionality resident in each of these terms. "I'm in deep," he said. "I'm trying to do more in terms of my identity." He left the world of his upbringing to explore beyond that horizon. In addition to Asia, he traveled through Russia by himself for a few weeks "to understand what it was like to just be in that space, to understand, like, the racial dynamics, the international dynamics." Along the way, he noted, "I created these identities . . . nice, little cookie cutter identity markers to help me think through things" that he enacted in transit through learning experiences in college, graduate school, and far reaches of the globe. "I see these shifts," he said, "and it's this constant evolving question of, 'who am I'? So I'm having to rethink those three particular buckets, right? The gender, the race, and the sexuality, but in the larger frame of how they work together and intersect, and as I tug on one, something else shifts, right?" He wondered if instead of there being some kind of authentic self, that identity should be conceived of as many selves.

Ethan journeyed deep within himself to places where thoughts and feelings can reside without words to express them. Enduring the innuendo of certain friends and family members that silently said, "You can save your-self," he dated both men and women—"I had this thing about women in heels"—and he has considered dating a transgender person. If someone came out and directly asked, "Are you gay"? he would "clap back" with something like "Well, what does that mean? . . . I started to try to remove myself from these boxes." Yet he struggles with how some gays may have homophobic tendencies and that he may be one of them. He also struggles with what it means to be black and queer. And he struggles with how he sometimes feels like an impostor in being a college professor. He indicated he was seeing a therapist to help him work through these struggles. I immediately told him he did not have to discuss this (and checked again when writing this section), but he said, "Therapy has been something in my family that's been kind of public. So I've always been comfortable. It's kind of like going to the gym. You work out your body. You work out your mind. Keep it all healthy." So he told me about hanging out with a good friend who was a gay man along with some of the man's other friends. "I just generally don't enjoy myself," he said, "and I started to keep myself away [from them]. And I think that looks—I would say mildly homophobic in the sense that I consider homophobia not only actions, but also a fear of this idea that a particular group of people, particularly gay men or lesbian women, are going to, like, interfere with who you are. Like they're going to hit on you. And I think some of those times I feel that way. And so I intentionally stay away from certain places or certain types of people, and I've been trying to work through that." He has also tried to work through whether he would date a transgender person, as well as the fact that he wants to have biolog-ical children and how to make that happen. He said that all this "difficult stuff has a lot to do with the racial pieces."

For example, when Ethan joined the black fraternity in college, it was partially about asserting a black identity. "It was African based, right? And I feel bad to say this as I still work through it, but I think it was the first time I felt I could actually be publicly proud of being black." But black fra-ternities can also be extremely homophobic. "And so here I am joining this fraternity, and I have all these, I wouldn't call them issues, but I'm trying to figure stuff out." He remembered when he was 21 and how gay black males like him needed to openly perform their gayness. "I wanted to be as far away from it as possible," he said, "and I'm not sure if I joined my fra-ternity for that reason." Despite the clash with his emerging gender identity, he said it felt good to publicly claim a black identity, particularly in contrast to growing up as a Jehovah's Witness, "where being too black was a bad thing. Being too anything was a bad thing. Retrospectively, Ethan came to see "all these full-circle moments" that required him to go back to his early upbringing and hit some kind of "restart button" to more fully understand. "I'm able to look at these moments and see some distance between different aspects of who I think I am. What I see is there are many, many versions of me, right? And they are always engaging with society, always performing."

These deep dives with the help of therapy are "giving me more answers than I thought was there before." He doesn't believe that there is some kind of authentic self to be found. Instead, he said, "life is a constant process of finding out who you are."

Through it all, Ethan felt he was broadening his perspective on essential questions he has been struggling with all along, such as "What does it mean to be African American? What does it mean to be male? What does it mean to be queer?" And what does it mean to be a "good" black man? We learn from Ethan—and Joshua, Ingrid, and Relene—that answers to these questions are intricate and changeable in ways that cannot be apprehended within simple binaries of race, gender, and sexual orientation.

CYBER-LIVES

All interviewees in this book were born after the early 1970s and the emergence of two global forces that inevitably contributed to their identity constructions—the rise of the Internet and the rise of hip-hop culture. In this section and the next, we see how the identities of these four people were shaped and expressed through digital and popular cultural texts and tools in ways that also challenge any essentialized way of identifying them racially. All four connect their identities to hip-hop culture, but they have widely varying opinions about and uses of digital and particularly social media. Relene and Ingrid try to minimize their use of social media, although things like email are entirely necessary for Relene's work as a professor. Joshua and Ethan are much more involved with social media, and both try to leverage it for purposes that are political as well as personal.

Relene describes her participation in digital culture as moderate. She emails and texts colleagues and friends, and she joined Facebook, partially because her colleagues have a strong presence there. She also uses it for personal reasons occasionally so that family members in Boston can see her young son, since she only gets to visit her family there about once a year. She accepts friend requests but rarely friends anyone else. She also signed up for LinkedIn in 2013 but never bothered with it after a few months and ignores any requests to connect. She doesn't have a Twitter account, and outside her presence on and use of the web for her job, she pretty much avoids cyber-life.

Ingrid is 9 years younger than Relene and has an even smaller digital presence. "I don't have Facebook. I don't have Instagram. I don't do any social media. I steer clear of it. I think it's kind of a waste of time," she said. She does use WhatsApp to stay in contact with family members in Germany, and she has telephone conversations with her dad from time to time and every day with her mom. Beyond that, she said, "we mostly just text or call, or send postcards or gifts during the holidays, or something like that. But yeah, I don't really go online or anything like that." Her husband *is* an active Facebook user who posts many pictures online, including some of their son, I later learned. She doesn't contribute to it and says she rarely looks at it. She considers herself more of an artsy person who likes painting and doing drawings and cartoons and illustrating her own stories. She prefers to express herself in material rather than virtual modes.

But she has other reasons for not getting involved with social media that she has thought a lot about. In part, she is influenced by her father, who works for the government and warns her about all the ways that digital records are kept on everyone. More fundamentally, she doesn't like how this "new norm" in social media is so egocentrically oriented. "I don't want to just focus on me," she said. "I don't really want to post pictures and boast about, 'Oh I did this. I did that.' I don't want people to be jealous. I treat people as if we're all equal. We all have the same kind of feelings, and we strive for one thing, and that's happiness. So I don't want to make anybody feel envious of me."

Joshua is an active user of digital media, particularly Facebook and LinkedIn. In both mediums, he is sensitive to "curating a persona because you don't have control over who is able to view it." He keeps his guard up even in personal conversations in social media spaces. Because he is socially constructed as an African American male in these spaces, he feels restrictions that don't exist for other people because of an oversimplification of the archetype of the angry black man. Yet he works to use digital media to disrupt these very kinds of racialized stereotypes. He makes efforts to stay abreast of what's going on in these arenas with specific regard to depictions of African American males, and he uses his various forums with young people of color to question and critique narratives of violence and criminality that get associated with them. In the after-school programs he worked in, for example, he would guide young people to type words like "thug" and "engineer" in to Google's search engine and see the first 15 images that come up. For "engineer" the images that come up are all white and all male. For "thug" the images are all of African American males. In addition to demonstrating for young people that digital media is not neutral regarding how it can reference and contribute to constructions of identity, he feels he is also using it to counter the very stereotypes it helps to perpetuate.

In conjunction with his personal use of digital media, Ethan has a similar political object to Joshua's, although he approaches it in a completely different way. "I became a professor," he said, "and that professional identity affected how I read stuff online." He said he looked at the sociology on Facebook. "Why do they say that? What does this mean? What type of people are these? And I'm also looking at myself as a participant. So as I identify these groups, where do I sit?" His profile says "justice seeker"; despite this stance, he said that using Facebook was still difficult for him. However, he does use Twitter and Tumblr a lot as vehicles for identity creation. "Tumblr is very interesting," he said. "It's like the angry version of the things that I'm not willing or I don't want to say on Twitter." He also talked about using these digital affordances to extend Afro-pessimism and Afro-futurism conversations. The former is focused on acknowledging the plight and pain of the African American experience across society and using that to generate conversations, and the latter is about reimagining opportunities for society with regard to race, class, and gender.

HIP-HOP LIFE

With respect to hip-hop music and culture, Relene was a very active participant through her teens and mid-20s, constantly listening to black radio stations, watching Black Entertainment Television (BET) endlessly, buying tapes and CDs of favorite artists, going to concerts, and dressing and styling her hair in hip-hop fashions. As she got older, she realized hip-hop music was changing, with less R&B influence, among other things, and it resonated less with her. It wasn't just the music that was changing; there was a new generation of hip-hop artists coming in and replacing some of the originators of the music and culture. She was also getting older, and although she kept abreast of some of the music through her students, her participation was only peripheral. She still listens to African American radio stations, but when she does she's looking for older hip-hop and R&B and often doesn't know who the artists are for contemporary popular songs that she hears.

Ingrid doesn't believe that hip-hop exists anymore. Although she loved early hip-hop, those artists are no longer at the center of what's happening now, and she feels it has just become commercialized and colorized. "I just feel as if that music industry is, kind of, fading away; or am I just getting older?" she pondered. She affirms how hip-hop is global and vibrant and has met many people from different places in Europe who were into it. Her husband has a lot of Russian hip-hop albums. "They speak so fast. I have to really, like, slow it down and break it down, but they sound wonderful. French hip-hop is amazing. German hip-hop, hmm; it's kind of strange. Spanish hip-hop is really good. I love everything as long as it has passion, and it aspires to move the world, or change the world, or make people happy. But now we just have rap. I don't believe there's hip-hop anymore." Despite her contention of its demise, hip-hop has clearly had a considerable influence on her identity, and she sees how it offers cultural connections for people all over the world.

Hip-hop culture is more than music, and I think Ingrid's drawings and cartooning (or graphic novels) represent another vector of it. She talked about a story she had written and was illustrating at the time of her interview called "Space University." The main character is a woman of color who wants to be an anthropologist or archeologist, and her classes are with not just typical human beings but a variety of different kinds of creatures from around the universe. The story line of "Space University" is to illuminate the boundaries and possibilities of how we interact with other beings—the same story line as this book.

Joshua wanted to make it clear that there are many different kinds of hip-hop. He listened to gangster rap, and his high school years were filled with images and events that were rapped about. "There was no shortage of drugs when I was young," he said. As mentioned earlier in this chapter, there were times when he carried a gun. But now he uses his understanding of the influences of hip-hop on young people to help him reach them. For example, he will wear Air Jordans and True Religion jeans when interacting in some neighborhood contexts. He's not deluded that there is some kind of cultural authenticity gained in dressing this way, but he said that in certain situations with young men, it's a conversation starter. "Every hip-hop song mentions True Religion jeans or a certain type of shoe, and so I still listen to hip-hop to see what contemporary kids are up to." Interestingly, he doesn't let his own kids listen to rap music. "I don't feel like it's age appropriate," he said. And, like Ingrid, he doesn't identify a lot of rap music as hip-hop. "It's radio stuff. It's misogyny. Everything is about strip clubs, and that's not even music to me anymore." But, as with his use of digital media, he uses hip-hop to talk with young people and to get them to raise questions. "Why does this gangster have no shirt, lots of tattoos, guns, all of these hypermasculinity symbols merged with some type of criminality"? For Joshua, hip-hop is a vehicle for getting young people to question the ways that they are socially constructed and positioned in society.

"What's interesting about hip-hop culture and me," Ethan said, "is it has allowed me to get closer to my understanding of racial identity." He used his love of the music of Kendrick Lamar and his album titled *To Pimp a Butterfly* to illustrate his point. On the front cover of the album Lamar and several other men are standing in front of the White House with the flag in the background, and they have blunts and 40-ounce beers in their mouths. "I identify with that more than I have ever in my life. . . . It's a means to an end that's allowing me to realize, like, where I kind of got some things wrong." He talked about how albums like this allow him to explicitly attach to his racial identity. He said he reads the lyrics as he would read an academic article, that it is similar to what he is doing when he writes a paper or does other academic work. "It's performing, and our performances are literary," Ethan said. "We use words, whereas artists use vocals, sounds, and music. I'm seeing this for the first time, and it's helping my professional identity as well. I want to think of my career trajectory like an album. What's the first song going to be? What's the interlude? What's going to be the end? And this has actually helped me to figure out that I'm talking about the same issues [as Lamar], but to a different audience.

CLAP BACK!

Relene, Joshua, and Ethan see blackness as core to their identities, while Ingrid does not see it as core to hers. Curating their stories lifts the veil on blackness and exhibits that, as with whiteness or any of the other color codes for people, there is no essentially definable or uniformly recognizable core. As Ellison's preacher in the prologue to *Invisible Man* exhorted, Black is . . . an' black ain't. . . . Ain't it the truth" (1947, p. 9). The irony of Relene and Rachel Dolezal working to be seen as "good blacks" by approaching a fictive core of blackness from opposite directions shows how arbitrary and contradictory the sting of blacklash is on skin that ultimately is illegible. One woman was rebuffed after her performance of blackness had been initially accepted, while the other was rebuffed until she learned to acceptably perform. As Joshua said of feeling forced to perform, "I gotta tell you, it's tiring." Performance threads the stories woven from all 20 interviews presented in this book. They learned to perform their identities, yet their stories reveal how these performances necessarily change as they elected to or were influenced to play different roles in contexts that vary across time and place. This raises two crucial questions: Will we merely perform racial identities that are scripted for us by white supremacy? Or will we enact practices and choices that disrupt oppressive hierarchies and enable fuller expression and acceptance of our diverse cultural positions and perspectives?

In this chapter we saw a wide range of positionalities, practices, choices, and perspectives that were further complicated and multiplied with digital texts and tools. Relene's Dominican roots and culture should not have to be lost so she can avoid being targeted and shamed. More hopeful stories are needed like that of her friend's 16-year-old daughter and others in her generation who take on identities that cannot be imagined within the restrictions of current racial/cultural categories. Ingrid's complex, blended, international family and the spectrum of physical features of its members is not an anomaly but a new norm. Her multicountry, multilingual, and multicultural experiences allowed her to inhabit an interstitial space that did not need race to affirm it despite institutional forces that attempted to define her and her child within its racial taxonomy. Society's response to Joshua as a hypermasculine black male veils the kaleidoscope of cultures that intersect in his family as well as the family he and his wife brought into existence, with four boys who, like their mother, are racially indeterminate. Ethan's quest to make sense of the racial/sexual/intellectual constituents of his identity took him on journeys around the world and deep into his own being. He came full circle to the realization that rather than his finding some kind of authentic self, his identity was composed of many selves that are always trying to integrate with each other while also constantly changing, performing, and engaging with society.

The stories of these interviewees provided glimpses of hyperdiversity that's invisible behind the veil. They also revealed instances of the tragic stereotyping and discrimination predicated on blackness as a social fact that can exist only in a post-truth society. To paraphrase Cobb's (2015) point about Ms. Dolezal as a question, how can someone lie about his or her race when race itself is a lie? When lines of exclusion are drawn, some people, even in oppressed groups, feel a responsibility to judge who has the right to perform certain identities as well as to decide on the "authenticity" of the performances. The standards for judging can be as capricious as styles of hair, dress, music, and dance or approximations of skin to brown paper bags. A couple of months before completing this book, for example, my "blackness" was questioned by an African American woman I've known for more than 40 years because I told her I liked sushi in one situation, and the evidence from another situation was that I didn't play my car stereo with enough bass. I responded with a chuckle, but she clearly was not making a joke.

In addition to rights of performance, blackness entails rites of performance. Witness the rites of suboppressive hierarchies created by Boston blacks with regard to West Indians, and by West Indians internally with regard to different island groups. As noted earlier in this chapter, when Ethan began to consciously remove himself from boxes placed on his identity, he did what I feel we all must do to challenge and change the constraints of race—clap back!

CHAPTER 6

No Body's Yellow

I've never heard "yellow" in Chinese identified with Asian people. It seems like the term is a manifestation of the binary of black and white needing spaces for now red, now brown, now yellow in American discourse. I think it's weird for Asian people to think of themselves as yellow. I feel similarly about the term "Asian American." It just glosses over a literal world of differences.

—Phil (July 18, 2016)

Under the newspaper headline "Korean American Rapper Knocks Down Racial Walls," Mendoza (2017) described Jonathan Park's rip-rap titled "Safe," a track that responded to #OscarsSoWhite. In the music video, which shows Park's face superimposed on white male movie characters, among them Indiana Jones and Jack Sparrow, he rapped, "The other night I watched the Oscars / And the roster of the only yellow men were all statues." This refrain offers a point of entry into the complex issues surrounding people in the United States who have been homogenized as Asian Americans and colored a derogatory yellow tinge. Although the Oscar statue may have a yellow tint, as Phil, one of the interviewees in this chapter, emphatically indicated in the quote at the beginning, nobody's skin is yellow. Park's video also addresses another crucial issue. Instead of being portrayed as invincible heroes, people identified as Asian are expected to make heroic efforts to be invisible within America's cultural scene and psyche. Park's superimposed face on those of select movie characters flips the superimposition of whiteness on the character of everyone else that glosses over, as Phil noted, "a literal world of differences."

Chloe, Halle, and Felix join Phil in taking us into this world of differences. Age 22 and single when interviewed, Chloe was the youngest of the 20 informants. She was born in the United States to parents who were immigrants from Southern China. Chinese are the largest group of Asian immigrants in the United States. An English teacher in an urban high school, she is 5'2", has a very light complexion, black hair, and dark-brown eyes, and she has one brother, who is a year younger. She identifies as Asian American, and the title of her section in this chapter is "Sassy." Halle's father is Japanese and Hawaiian, and her mother is Native American and white. The director of special education in an urban public charter school, she is 5'8", has a light complexion, black hair, and brown eyes, and, like Chloe, has one brother. She was 34 years old and single at the time she was interviewed and identifies as "Hapa," which is the title for her section. Phil's parents were immigrants from Taiwan. He was born there and came to the United States at 2½. He is about 5'8" and has a light complexion and black hair. His wife is Chinese American and they have one young daughter. He has one older and one younger brother and was 34 at the time he was interviewed. He identifies as Taiwanese and Chinese American, and "Hyphen-Nation" is the title of his section. Felix's parents emigrated from the Philippines, and he and his identical twin brother were born in the United States. People from the Philippines constitute the second largest Asian immigrant group in the U.S. behind the Chinese. When interviewed, he was 43, single, and the associate director of a student learning center at a university in California. He is 5'6" and has a light-brown complexion, black hair, and dark-brown eyes. He identifies himself as Filipino American and also as a gay male, and his section is titled "Pigmentocracy." The interviewees' engagements with digital media are addressed in the section entitled "Media Portrayals" and with hip-hop culture in a section entitled "Mediums of Hip-hop." The concluding section is entitled "Enter the Dragon."

SASSY

Chloe feels that U.S. society identifies her as a Chinese American female. She accepts this and adds that she is multilingual and can speak Cantonese, Mandarin, Spanish, and English, and also that she is a Christian. Her mother has been a strong influence on her and felt it was important to maintain traditional Chinese values that included Chloe eventually getting married to a Chinese man with the same values. Within this cultural framework, Chinese women in particular are supposed to be quiet and submissive. In her family she was told to never speak out: "you need to respect your elders. Respect your parents. Don't talk back to them." Initially she was shy, but when she went to middle school she hung out with a lot of Latino/a and African American students as well as Asians. "We all wanted to be cool, and a lot of the guys stared acting out, so-called 'acting hard.' We listened to hip-hop music. We sang along, and we rapped and all that stuff. And I think that's when I started learning from all these different people like, I want to speak my mind." Clearly, interactions and relationships with students from other backgrounds changed how Chloe thought about them, as well as how she thought about herself. Also, her mother was the one who ran their household. "My mom is like the boss. My dad listens to her so well. She handles all the finances. She's the one that makes the rules in the house, and that's what I grew up seeing, and I'm like, you know, I can be a strong woman." So, she began to speak up for herself. But when she left middle school and went to the most academically competitive high school in the city, other

9th-graders started asking her, "Why are you so ghetto? Why do you talk like you're African American? Why do you listen to 'their' music? Why are you so sassy?" These mainly European and Asian American students would frame these questions with statements like, "Obviously, you're Asian." Reflecting on the memory that "They keep telling me I'm too sassy," she said, "Does that mean it's just because of me as a person, or because they think I'm an Asian woman, and I should not be that way?"

Soon after she started 9th grade, Chloe felt she needed to reject a part of her identity. "I was like, I need to fit in. There's no way I'm going to have someone be calling me 'ghetto.'" Beyond the irony in how she used the "state of being" verb in the previous sentence, we see the pressure on her to conform and perform a different relational identity. "I felt like they were looking down on me," she said. This high school had mostly white and Asian students, and they were not that into hip-hop music and culture. "I needed to listen to more pop or more classical music, and I didn't even realize at the time that, you know, what I'm learning, it's like, that's totally 'white' culture. That's just, like, what 'American' students listen to." She concluded, "I feel like people were imposing views on me, and I wasn't able to use that language before. But now that I'm able to say that, 'I need to find out who I am for myself, not because people are telling me.' Am I this, you know, super outgoing person who's outspoken? Can I still be patient and gentle while being outspoken? I'm in this, like, twenties stage, and I just need to figure myself out."

"Obviously, You're Asian"

Chloe's friends sometimes felt that they had to remind her that she's Asian, but this cover term hides tremendous within-group distinctions. She talked about the range of differences among those who identify as Chinese, as one example. Many defining distinctions exist based on where a person or family emigrated from. Chinese from Hong Kong, Taiwan, Vietnam, and even from different parts of mainland China have very different histories and experiences in coming to the United States. Chloe's mother took pride in being able to speak both Cantonese and Mandarin so that she could communicate with more Chinese people, and she helped Chloe learn both. Mandarin is the main language in China, but there are over 50 other dialects spoken across that country.

Whatever their first language, the level of English proficiency results in other distinctions among Chinese, as well as among other groups that come to the United States. For example, Chloe has cousins who live here that have difficulty defining themselves as she does because of language and other cultural considerations. "They don't call themselves Chinese American," she said. "My cousin doesn't feel American because she knows that her English will never catch up to the, she calls them 'ABC's', American-Born Chinese, like me. She calls me an ABC. She's like, 'I will never catch up to you because you were born here.' And so, I mean she just told me it's frustrating. . . . All she can do is pick up bits and pieces here and there, but she can never call herself 'American' because she doesn't feel like she is." Chloe disagrees with her cousin and feels that in addition to the language issue, she can learn to be American by understanding more about the culture, and popular culture specifically, including ways to dress. But she also understands her cousin's frustration. "She's been embarrassed and humiliated for not being able to speak English well," Chloe said, "and it's really interesting that that's her marker for what it means to be American."

Chloe encountered other within-group distinctions while in college. During part of her time there, she worked at the Office of Graduate Studies as a clerical assistant. Chinese immigrant students would come in who had trouble expressing themselves in English, and she would talk to them in Chinese. "Like, hey. You can talk to me in your language, and I can help you out." But she still felt there were significant differences. "That was mainly the only time I was able to communicate with them," she said. Despite the importance of language to identity, other cultural factors and practices are also determinative in ways that can create within-group distinctions, even when there is no language difference. Language might be the tool of tools, but other cultural tools are needed. Chloe's experiences growing up in the United States and attending urban schools resulted in cultural practices and perspectives that were obviously different from the foreign-born Chinese graduate students with whom she was able to communicate in Mandarin or Cantonese in the academic setting, but not in social settings.

Cultural Dissonance

On the other side of the coin, Chloe talked about within-group distinctions and cultural dissonance regarding American-born Chinese who mainly or only speak English and not the first languages of their parents or other family members. She encountered this with the person she was dating during the time when she was interviewed. He was Chinese and Korean but only spoke English, and yet he still reflected a particular masculine model and place of privilege attributed to men specifically in Chinese culture. Tension developed in their relationship because Chloe was outspoken and would not play the quiet, submissive female role that he and the cultural model he was enacting demanded.

Before she even started dating, her parents continually told her they wanted her to marry a man who speaks Chinese. And, though they would be polite and accepting when she dated Asian men who did not speak Chinese, she always knew their hope was for her to connect with one who was fluent in their language(s). This also meant that men from other ethnicities should not be considered. Chloe noted that her parents had considered the possibility of her marrying someone who was not Chinese, but it was always very superficial talk, like, "If you marry a white guy, you might have cute babies." What they really cared about was being able to communicate with her future husband. They want someone who understands their culture, but it's also practical. She noted, "My parents are like, 'Once we get older we'll need you and your spouse to be able to help take care of us. If we can't talk to him, let's say you're busy, we want to be able to contact him. But if he can't speak the language it makes it really difficult to communicate what we want, or even just to have a conversation with him.'"

Being obviously Asian is also linked to specific academic disciplines and professional careers. Here too, Chloe did not fit societal stereotypes. "I knew from, like, elementary school that I wanted to be a teacher. I knew since then because I had a really great 3rd-grade teacher and a really great 4th- and 5th-grade teacher." One of the teachers was African American and the other was Asian American. One was male and the other was female. "They were just role models for me, and I really wanted to be like them," Chloe said. "So I knew from the start that I wanted to be a teacher, and I wanted to teach English." Her mom has always been against this, and, interestingly, she had been an English as a second language teacher before coming to the United States. "I did not leave China for you to be a teacher again," she told her. She was upset that Chloe would not change her mind, and then she would ask, "Why not teach math? Why not teach science"? When Chloe was a girl, her mother wanted her to be a doctor or a pharmacist. "She was like, 'That's a very stable job for a nice, young woman. You'll be fine.'" But Chloe felt science and math were boring, and because she didn't like them, she didn't do especially well in these subjects. "It was like I just love reading and, you know, that's what I want to do." Her parents knew how "stubborn" and determined Chloe was, and she said with a laugh, "Yeah, I'm not a 'good' Chinese daughter. Yeah, exactly, I'm so rebellious."

Despite cultural dissonance with graduate students from China, Chloe has many Chinese friends, as well as African American and Hispanic ones. She admits that there are "certain linguistic codes or experiences that I do not share with other ethnic groups," but some of her Chinese friends go back to her childhood, while her friends from other groups are mainly from the college where she recently graduated. In her story, we see more of the diversity and within-group distinctions that are homogenized, stereotyped, and rendered invisible under the labels of Asian and Chinese. We also see some of the relational identities she performed and how her own identity constructions worked to reject constraints and challenge cultural binaries. In juxtaposition to hypermasculine stereotypes associated with men like Joshua and James, for example, Chloe resisted conforming to hyperfeminine ones. "People have this idea that Asian women are supposed to be submissive, quiet, and gentle," she said. "They rely on their husbands, and they don't speak up for themselves." Chloe is too sassy for that.

HAPA

While growing up in Honolulu, Halle's family took her on summer trips to visit relatives in Washington State. After high school she went to college in Boston. These locations differentially index an assortment of ways people have tried to construct or define her identity. Based on how she looks, it's impossible to link her to a racial category. Her father is Japanese and Hawaiian, and having grown up in Hawaii she feels this state is her strongest cultural reference point. This is why I joined her story with others in this chapter on Asian Americans. Her mother is Native American and white, and people in her family descended from a tribe in Washington. In Hawaii, Halle never gave much thought to her identity "because everyone is so mixed, and that's kind of the norm there." But in Boston her identity came into constant question. "I was asked on a daily basis what I was," she said. "I primarily identify as Hapa, which I define as just being of mixed heritage. . . . I don't want to identify myself necessarily by one cultural background."

Although her mother is Native American and white, Halle feels she identified as white when growing up. She embraced living in Hawaii and felt its welcoming spirit. According to Halle, "there is kind of a freedom for her too in being there and being in a place where nobody ever asks you what you are . . . everyone is really mixed. Parents are mixed and their parents, and it's so generational at this point that I think it is more kind of a cultural norm there. . . . She went there and never moved back because it was a more comfortable place for her as well, I think." Halle's identity was never questioned in Hawaii, but she recognizes that her background causes confusion for people in other parts of the United States. She has been asked if she is white, Polynesian, Asian, Hawaiian, or even Latina. Her identity is most often constructed in relation to the context she is in. Halle: "Since I'm kind of ambiguous in appearance," she said, "I float in and out of different areas, and . . . I found that if I'm with friends who are white, then there's an assumption that I'm white. And if I'm with friends who aren't white, then there's an assumption that I'm not white. It's a very interesting experience, and I tend to be defined by whoever I'm around in that moment." But always, people attempt to put her into a single box. "I'm defined in many different ways," she said, "and I don't think there's a consistent theme other than it's usually one category. . . . But it was usually just, 'What are you?' There was no, like, answer."

The State of Washington

For different reasons, there was a tendency on both sides of her family to pass for white, but it is much stronger on her mother's side in Washington State. Particularly, her mother's father was adamant that he *was* white right up to the point when he was close to dying. Halle remembers finding photos of his grandparents that made it clear he actually had relatives who lived on a reservation. She asked her granddad about the pictures, but he wouldn't talk about them, "said they were visiting friends of friends or something like that." However, her grandmother confirmed, "No, that's his grandparents." Finally, just before he died, he was willing to talk about why he rejected his Native American identity. Halle said, "He very much associated that lineage with being poor and being impoverished. He was very proud of the fact that he had come out of poverty and that he was able to make a good living for himself, buy a house. He was a plumber, but he very much associated that success with being white and being able to pass."

Like Ethan in the previous chapter, Halle's identity quest took her "in deep." Her grandmother is German and Irish, and Halle's mom and all of her mom's brothers look pretty white. "They all married blonde-haired, blue-eyed people, and that was something he [her granddad] took a lot of pride in—how white they were." My dad, when he was in college, actually went to Japan for a while, and he went to college in Michigan. And he really felt like he didn't fit in anywhere. He said that he felt uncomfortable in a lot of places, that in Japan he wasn't Japanese enough and on the mainland he didn't felt like he could find a peer group, so he ended up moving back to Hawaii. And then I think there was a little bit of a question among my parents about where they would raise us, but given my mom's family context I think Hawaii clearly being the winner for where they wanted us to grow up. And so that's where we were raised."

Living in Hawaii, Halle and her brother would mainly visit their granddad's side of the family about once a year. "I remember when we were little," she said, "and my brother and I would run around and get very tan, and they hated it. They called us the ethnic grandkids." Her granddad would blatantly tell her and her brother, "Get in the house. You guys are getting too dark." Halle also associated these kinds of statements with being Japanese and Hawaiian. Her dad also made casual references to how her mom's side of the family made him feel and that he was always uncomfortable visiting that part of the family.

Statements privileging whiteness were directed at Halle as a girl and later as a woman, even more so than at her brother. When she got old enough to decide for herself if she would go on the trips to Washington, she chose not to. She continues to maintain connections with some of her cousins, but noted, "I think in a very powerful way that I, kind of, limit[ed] my relationship with that side of the family because he was so adamant about those things, and it was such a different frame from how I grew up in Hawaii." She remembered visiting her Washington family after coming back from college and being much paler than she had ever been in her life, and her granddad told her, "Oh you look so pretty. You look so nice. You've been out of the sun in Boston." Although her brother had similar experiences, she didn't feel that he had to deal with the overlay of standards of beauty. "When we were little," she said by way of example, "I was the one told to go in the house. It wasn't cute or pretty to be dark. And he was allowed to

run around, but we look pretty similar." In Hawaii her brother was usual-
ly read "on the Japanese side," but when he ended up going to college in
Washington State, for the first time in his life, people thought he was Native
American, the very identity part of his family was so eager to hide.

Yet, some family members embrace the Native American part of themselves. One of Halle's cousins actively identifies herself in this way and
strongly feels that it's the best way to define herself. She's upset that the
rest of the family doesn't disclose this part of their identity. Halle also feels
something integral is lost by not acknowledging and embracing all of the
ancestral lines that contribute to a person's identity. Regarding her Native
American connections, she noted, "I think a lot of the things that I see as
overlaps are just, kind of, seeing yourself as part of a larger picture. Um,
and a lot of the connections of respect for nature in the world and, kind
of, where your place in it is and not disrupting things, and just having that
frame of how tiny we are and being really thankful for those things that we
do have and our role in, kind of, a greater scheme. You know, terminology
is different, but a lot of those frames are very similar in native Hawaiian
as well." So, there was always tension in the family around these issues of
identity, tension in raising questions, tension in providing answers, tension
both from knowing and not wanting to know.

Boston Commons

Halle landed in Boston and went straight to the new student orientation
for her college. The first question her R.A. asked her was, "What are you?"
She remembers being taken aback and not really knowing how to answer
the question. When she finally was able to give him a run-down, he had a
bunch of follow-up questions: "How much Japanese? How much Native
American? How much Hawaiian?" It wasn't something she had thought
about and she struggled with answers. And the same thing continued to
come up throughout the day. At the end of her "orientation," she called
one of her best friends and told her, "Seventeen people asked me, 'What are
you?' today. Did this happen to you at your orientation?" Her friend, who
is also Japanese and Hawaiian, went to a college in the South. On her first
day, she was read as African American. Later, they found it surprising that
she was actually from Hawaii.

Ongoing attempts to construct Halle's identity became the norm in
Boston. Although she perceived these questions as a bit forward and strange,
she initially just thought that they were funny. "Over time," she noted, "I
started to be offended by it because it became the primary focus of conversation, and it was always, "What's your name? What are you?" She formed
friendships with other students from places like Tonga and Samoa as well as
Hawaii, and these were common questions for them in Boston too. "What
became interesting to me," Halle concluded, "was that my read of myself
didn't necessarily match how people were reading me, and there were a lot

of assumptions about where I was from and what my perspective on things was." This was a rude awakening for her because her upbringing did not prepare her for what she encountered in Boston, and she felt a little naïve. "I didn't realize the little bubble that we were in," she reflected. "We were literally on an island, and I didn't really have any awareness of that until I was out of it."

Tipping Point

"In my ideal world," Halle told me, "[people] would just be able to define themselves. I think what's been problematic for me is feeling defined by other people or feeling a need to counter the definition other people have given me. I also think moving away from, kind of, this like, 'I'm one quarter this, and one eighth this, and another one eighth this,' and thinking those things somehow add up to a person. That definition is problematic because that's not the way it actually plays out. It's not a neat, you know, mathematical division, and how each of those contributes to who you are as a person. So, I think some understanding that there are those lineages, and there's that history, but then how they come together is going to be different. Those things don't necessarily add up into one clean, little picture."

This part of Halle's interview captures an essential aspect of the argument I am making in this book. I also asked her what her hopes are for a child if she decides to have one. She began by saying, "I doubt there's someone else out there that has the exact background that I do," and she felt her child would "irrevocably" be even more mixed than she is. Consequently, she doesn't see the definitions or reference points of ascribed racial groups being helpful. She gave the example of if she had grown up in the Washington side of her family instead of the Hawaiian side, she might have a different definition of herself. So, she feels that background and positionality have strong influences, but stated, "it's not in the neat, categorical way people want it to be." She further believes that "at some point there's going to be a tipping point of just how people identify themselves. There's going to be, you know, a large enough number of people that it's not going to be so easy to ascribe categories for anymore. . . . I've seen a lot of pushback about those things that I find really interesting, and I think is helpful. Every time I fill out an application . . . and I get to the check box of what your background is . . . I pause [because] there's a lot of us that don't have an appropriate box to check, and don't want to check a box."

HYPHEN-NATION

"I identify myself as a Chinese American, transnational, ethnically cosmopolitan mix," Phil said. "A Hyphen. I live in a Hyphen." Negotiating different identities, languages, and practices was the norm in his upbringing

rather than feeling settled in any one place both geographically and culturally. "Whether I was one of those FOBs (Fresh off the Boats), or I was somebody who was trying to create distance from them, I was both within a day,
you know? I was the kid who brought the food that's wrong, you know, and
also the kid who wanted to just show how much I liked, I loved, American
culture, you know? How much I knew about it." Phil was born in Taiwan,
came to the United States when he was 2½, moved back to Taiwan at 5,
and returned again when he was 7. From 9 to the present, Phil has lived in
California. His mother and father both graduated from college in Taiwan.
Both of them received bachelor degrees in Taiwan, but as immigrants in
their mid-thirties, they went from being white collar workers to having to
do some blue collar jobs in the United States.

Immigration also affected the birth patterns in Phil's family. One of his
brothers is 4 years older, and he sees specific differences between himself and
his brother that he called "micro-generational." "Being older, he feels his
brother had to make hard choices in the back-and-forth between countries.
"It's a more jarring thing when he comes back home with my parents and
has to switch into this Chinese mind frame." Phil said his brother actually
had fewer memories of his early childhood than he himself does "because I
think he just sort of forgot and erased a whole lot of us being in Taiwan and
being Chinese." Although no body *is* yellow, Phil talked about how Asian
peoples' varying skin tones were other manifestations of hyphenated spaces
between them. "There's a lot of stuff about, you know, dark skinned, light
skinned in Asian cultures, but it's all very fraught," he said. "It actually has
a lot to do with indigenous cultures versus, you know, colonizers from within Asia. And my own skin color and my own being Chinese among other
kinds of Asians and other kinds of Asian Americans is an unusual thing."

Here, Phil is echoing what we saw in the stories of Chloe and Halle and
what we also will see in Felix's story—that intricately woven into within-
group differences are micro-cultural distinctions for each individual that are
revealed through their specific positionality, practices, and choices. For example, although each interviewee has a brother or two (Chloe's and Halle's
brothers are about a year younger; in addition to the brother who is 4 years
older, Phil has one 9 years younger, and Felix's brother is the same age), their
micro-cultural identities and practices are dramatically different from their
siblings despite their growing up with them in the same family contexts. For
example, Phil and his two brothers attended the same high school. When his
older brother was there, the school was 30% Asian. When Phil attended it
was 45% Asian, and when his younger brother attended, it was 75% Asian.
So was it the same high school? When his older brother attended, he got
into heavy metal music and had mostly white friends. He became comfortable identifying with European American culture and eventually married a
woman who identifies as white. Their children, interestingly, do not fit into a
neat definition of being white. When Phil was in school, he was embarrassed
to be caught reading Asian comic books (manhua or manga comics); by the

time his younger brother went to the same school, kids from different groups were reading various kinds of Asian graphic novels, playing Pokémon, and engaging Asian and Asian American culture more generally. As will be seen later in this chapter, these personal-cultural differences and unique trajectories are just as interesting in the case of Felix, whose brother is an identical twin.

Erasure

Noting that U.S. society sees him as Asian American, Phil thinks that it sees neither the broader cultural distinctions nor the micro-cultural, personal distinctions of people it lumps into this category. "Aspects of the distinctive Chinese identity tend to be sort of smoothed over, you could say, or you might say, erased," Phil said. "But Asian Americans come with different kinds of packages, different expectations, different kinds of privileges, opportunities, and constraints. And I've sort of been bouncing back and forth along those lines, you know, for my whole life." He gave several examples of erasure based on stereotypes and homogenization-like experiences of having his identity mistaken for another Asian group that he said every Asian who looks like him has had. "I remember times that we were talking about World War II and Hiroshima, and somebody asked me what it was like for my family to be in the internment camps," he said. "I explained that I wasn't Japanese or Japanese American. Or times when people assumed things about what I knew about food or culture, language. I grew up speaking Mandarin, and people just kind of go, you look Chinese so there's some people speaking Cantonese over there. . . . I have a lot of memories and experiences of just bringing food to school, and someone saying, 'Why does it stink around here? Oh it's your lunch.'"

Before returning to graduate school, Phil was a high school English teacher and chair of the English department. He led and coached 20 other English teachers at his school. At school meetings, however, he would regularly get asked what level of math he taught. Outside school, people often assume he is a tech worker in Silicon Valley. Like Chloe, he talked about how Asian American kids of his generation sometimes distanced themselves from the most recent Asian immigrants, which was conflicting for him because of his own immigrant background. "There was kind of intergroup distinctions trying to be made, and how you aligned yourself culturally and language and dress with being somehow assimilated, or somehow being Chinese or at least Chinese American as opposed to Chinese immigrant. Those kids would frustrate you because they never knew what was going on, and they were just not culturally with it, you know? They were into the wrong music; they would be cloistered and speak Chinese with each other at school, and you wanted to separate yourself from them."

Added to these within-group pressures was what Phil termed "a certain kind of white gaze that you felt. Kids called me chink, kids made fun of me and, you know, ridiculed me. Non-Asian kids but especially white kids."

Like Chloe, Phil had a lot of childhood friends who were Latino/a and African American as well as a few white kids and lots of Central Asian and Middle Eastern kids. The high school he attended in Northern California was about 45% Asian and 40% white. In this context it was assumed that if you were Asian American you were going to either assimilate white or you were going to assimilate "urban," meaning the ways of talking and dressing and the kind of music listened to. For Phil, in middle and high school, to be Chinese American meant to be in the FOB category, or to fit into a good Asian American kid category of pleasing your parents and doing well in school, or to adopt various kinds of cultural identifying markers to align with other groups. "And all of that was in the mix in my taking on different identities as an adolescent," he said.

Writing Identity

Pop culture and unguided reading were other influences that affected Phil's identity as an adolescent and later as an adult. He loved comic books, and he got to read them, as well as many other books, in the library, where his mom would leave him for hours at a time. "Kind of free babysitting," he laughed. "But it was also a gift, right"? As a kid, comic books were, in his words, "metonymic for culture." Reading them not only helped him to learn English, it also gave him a sense of textual narrative and critique that really helped him in school. Early on, he wrote an essay that his teacher read to all her classes as a model of originality. Soon, people began to see his writing talent as something that needed to be further cultivated. "So fast-forward through high school. I loved history. I did okay in science and math. But English class is where I thrived. I got to college and just followed that interest." He was also into social justice activism, but he became an English teacher as a choice of career.

Phil also talked about influences he felt from a diaspora Chinese identity connected to what's going on geopolitically and culturally with Chinese people around the world. By identifying as Taiwanese his family is relating back to Chinese who left mainland China around 300 years ago and the complications stemming from the fact that there have been a series of colonizers throughout the history of Taiwan. Whereas some Chinese people feel their families have 5,000 years of history in China, Phil noted that his family can't claim that. "We were generationally somewhat itinerate," he said. "So I think the term *Asian American* obscures the distinctiveness of who I am, and that's something we're struggling against.

PIGMENTOCRACY

Felix's parents are immigrants from the Philippines who he said had a very strong Filipino cultural identity. He and his twin brother were born in the

United States. Yet he lived in the Philippines twice for extended periods, when he was in 2nd and 3rd grades and his parents decided they wanted to return to their home country and again after he finished college. Therefore, he has strong connections to Filipino culture, but he's also very American in his ways of thinking. However, he also feels somewhat disconnected from, or positioned between, both cultures.

One way Felix connects with his parents is by hanging out at their house and watching Filipino television with them. This is also a way that Filipinos connect globally as well as keep abreast of what's going on in the Philippines, he said. Soap operas in the Philippines are called *telesaria*; and their equivalent in Hispanic culture is the *telenovela*. They can blend in what Ocampo (2016) termed Mexipino culture. At one point while watching with his mom, he had to ask whether it was Spanish or Filipino TV because all the actors looked European. Brown people in the telesaria are always cast as servants or the masses, and there is clearly a color-line between light-skinned characters and everyone else. This colorism hierarchy also reflects the standards of beauty, with light-skinned characters cast as desirable, rich, and intelligent and darker-skinned characters cast as possessing the opposites of these characteristics at the opposite end of the "pigmentocracy." Felix was the one who first mentioned this word as standing for a concept that underlies stereotypical associations with marginalized groups based on a hierarchy of skin tones. He noted how it is as intense in Filipino culture as it is in African American, Hispanic, and Asian cultures. He also feels that for Filipinos, pigmentocracy is part of the history of colonization and the colonial mentality. "If you're light skinned, or if you have a heritage within the Filipino ethnic group that you're mixed with Chinese or mixed with Spanish heritage, like you're a little bit higher in the social hierarchy," he said.

Personally, Felix sees himself as one of the most Filipino-looking people there is. "I'm definitely not light skinned, definitely kind of have a mix of features, but I think for Filipinos they're all over the map—light, dark, and everything in between." In addition to the spectrum of skin tones, the hyperdiversity of Filipinos is reflected in the fact that they are a global people with a diasporic culture who speak multiple languages and participate in many national and ethnic cultures as they move around various places in the world. As noted in Chapter 3, the Republic of the Philippines is composed of more than 7,000 islands and has almost 200 distinct living languages. "It's complex," Felix said, "and as I get older, I'm kind of being more resigned to this complexity."

Ambiguous

When he has to fill out a form that requires him to identify himself by a racial or ethnic category, he usually checks the "Asian American" box. Sometimes he gravitates toward the "Pacific Islander" category and feels a bit more comfortable with that. But he ultimately identifies himself as a U.S.-born Filipino American. He described how relational that identity can be depending on the context he's in. For example, in a mostly white municipality in the San Francisco Bay Area as the gulf war broke out, a woman who lived in the same building told him, "Oh, it must be horrible what's going on in your country." Of course, she did not mean the United States or the Philippines, but Kuwait, because it was being invaded by Iraq. Similar things happen often, such as when he was in Chicago a couple of weeks before being interviewed for this book. A group of school kids at the greenhouse of the arboretum in Garfield Park ran up to him and started asking him questions in Spanish, thinking he was Latino and must be fluent in that language. His looks confuse people because they see him as having an affinity with many different groups. "I'll get Hawaiian. I'll get African Japanese. I'll get Middle Eastern. Many times I'll get Latino. I went to Puerto Rico, and they were upset that I wasn't communicating with them in Spanish. I have also been identified as 'Chino'—so Chinese is in there too." Amid the fray of these misperceptions, Felix came out in his late 20s and identifies as a gay male. He's appreciative that his family is very accepting of who he is and doesn't compare him with his identical-twin brother, who is heterosexual, married, and has a child. He also noted that in Filipino culture there's a kind of acceptance of the gay element, particularly in the media, although it reflects a sort of feminine representation of male gayness. So he identifies more with gay American ideas of gay Filipinos, while still feeling "very invisibilized as well," even living in the San Francisco Bay Area.

At times Felix had hopes of finding a life partner who is a gay Filipino male. But he said it's rare that he runs into gay Filipino males who are interested in dating other gay Filipino males. "I find it prevalent that gay Asian men or gay Filipino men are more into interracial dating," he said. And he too has dated men from different groups, from white, to African American, to Caribbean. He thinks the resistance he sees in Filipino men's dating each other might also be linked to a colonial mentality, particularly regarding pairing with whites. "Well, if you're Filipino, then you should strive for like a higher social status," he said. But he also indicated how considerations of preference are more complicated than this basic stereotype. He talked about numerous elements at play in romantic pairings. "Are they the dominant one or the submissive one, top or bottom, sero-positive or sero-negative? You need to parse out all of the possible identity connections that someone may be attempting to make. . . . It's so complex that even ethnic pairings become a small sliver of what's really meaningful to a person."

Belonging

A high point of Felix's life was meeting Paulo Freire. Like Ethan in the previous chapter, Felix felt a tripartite intersectionality of his ethnic, sexual, and scholarly identities. Freire spoke to a packed audience, and Felix was moved to tears. It wasn't just being starstruck; Freire's lecture touched Felix personally. Freire talked about political choices and how they had consequences. He talked about his experiences as an exile. He talked about in-between-ness, and about feelings of belonging and not belonging. He also talked about our human connections to nature, to water, to feeling the air and ocean. There were almost no other Filipinos in the audience, and Felix felt a wave of nostalgia for the Philippines, where he had spent the previous summer, at times wading in the ocean and feeling the calm. Air and ocean connect the 7,641 islands of the Philippines, but Felix was an island of his own. He felt alone; there was no place where he really belonged. "It was weird," Felix said. "[Freire] was talking about theories and about liberation and education, but he also was signaling these feelings of belonging and not belonging. And it was one of those profound moments . . . that's unexpected but very real, and not just about ideas, but kind of affirming humanity and affirming you as a human being."

MEDIA PORTRAYALS

"When I think of digital culture, I think of the culture that we in our generation participate in through social media," Chloe said. "These are the ways I interact with people, and it's very popular nowadays to stay connected 24/7." All four of the interviewees in this chapter were active users of a wide range of digital tools—Facebook, Twitter, Snapchat, Instagram, blogs, emails, and so on. Felix said he was on social media way too much, but Phil was the most avid user of digital media. Feeling he was on the crest of the Internet explosion, he said, "I got Facebook in 2006, and if I'm not mistaken they started in 2004. I was a little later on Twitter, but I use it. . . . I have an iPhone, an iPad. I currently use my Surface Pro. I have my MacBook. I have a desktop, many different devices." There also was considerable distance between digital activities of these four and their parents. Yet digital connections also brought them together across generations and geographies.

Although her mother eventually got a smartphone and followed Chloe on Facebook, Chloe's connection with her family through digital media was more old school. She and her mother bonded watching TV dramas in Mandarin; in addition to being a vehicle through which Chloe learned to speak that language, it connected both of them back to China. "Hey, daughter," her mom would say, "this is what I watch, and this is what people usually think of when they think of Chinese dramas." This is similar to how Felix connected with his family. A point of interest is that Filipino TV is geared to the global Filipino market, with news hours for Filipino Canadians that are separated from the news shows for Filipino Americans. They actually show the Filipino Canadian news during one hour and the Filipino American news during another. Another development in the past few years is that all the soap operas, the telesaria, have subtitles in English.

Although the telesaria was seen as lowbrow, for the masses, it was also a space for familial, language, and cultural experiences. They call this media *bakya*, a term that means "a wooden slipper worn by servants or lower-class people and women usually." Pejoratively, people would say, "Oh that's for the bakya crowd, or that's so bakya," Felix said. Halle was also sensitive to negative ways that her culture was portrayed in the media. She described a movie that came out recently that was based in Hawaii. The lead character was supposed to be Hapa, and the narrative was of both Native Hawaiians and Asian culture that was grossly inaccurate. Further, the Hapa character was played by a white woman.

Like Chloe and Felix, Halle used digital media to become closer to her family. In her case it was posting photographs and other materials that authenticated her granddad's Native American ancestry, despite his claims to being white. Her cousins started finding things out, such as their family's connection to the Klallam tribe in Washington State. Postings of these things on Facebook started a lot of conversation among the cousins that Halle feels would not have otherwise happened, because they were hardly ever in the same geographical place. Something similar happened on her dad's side of the family, where one of her cousins started doing research and posting what the family had done when they were in the internment camps during World War II. Halle's grandmother on her father's side was Japanese, and this grandmother's father was a doctor who enlisted in the U.S. Army and fought in the war. "Everyone else got sent to internment camps," she said. Halle also talked about the problems of depictions that can be found on social media, particularly Native American and native Hawaiian portrayals. "There is this romanticizing of these portrayals, or stereotyping that reduces people to a picture or one definition."

Phil also thought the portrayals of Asians in mass media were negative, at least at first. As a young kid, it was jarring to feel that he was being connected to Chinese movies, language, and culture. "My early childhood was a process of disassociating from that," he said. But in late adolescence he became attached to "a lot of digital culture, digital communication," and he also saw other groups starting to take interest in Asian culture as it was portrayed in the media. Bruce Lee was a big contributor to this, but also characters like Jackie Chan. More and more of his Asian peers were also reconnecting, appropriating, and taking pride in Asian and Asian American culture, and he began to take pride in it too. Additionally, he observed a good friend get more fluent than he was in Chinese in just a year and a half by using Chinese movies to develop her language proficiency.

MEDIUMS OF HIP-HOP

All four interviewees were influenced by hip-hop culture growing up and into adulthood. We saw this with Chloe earlier in the chapter, while Halle did not go into much detail about how it influenced her identity. Phil and Felix, on the other hand, talked at length about their connections to hip-hop. As a teenager Phil realized that there were choices about the cultures he would identify with. He described the crassness of teenage social life at his high school, which was 40% white, in terms of a kind of cool he had no access to and a kind that was potentially within reach. Hip-hop was the latter; the former was "white cool." His brother crossed the line into white cool, but Phil noted, "He was always a marked case." Alternatively, Phil listened to the hip-hop stars of his day and particularly loved the Wu Tang Clan, with its explicit nods to Asian culture in the group's name and in the titles of some of its albums and songs. The title *Enter the Wu Tang (36 Chambers)*, regarded as one of the greatest hip-hop albums of all time, alludes to Bruce Lee's classic film *Enter the Dragon*. Phil saw what everyone did, that "these guys were very cerebral."

Phil was insightful regarding how hip-hop culture influenced the identities of Asian youth. "A lot of my friends became some combination of who we were as Asian Americans—rice rockets (you know, the cars), the emphasis on computers and technology, and certain kinds of fashion—with a lot of that derived from black culture, hip-hop culture, urban culture generally." He noted that Chinese immigrants did not necessarily think to identify themselves as people of color, and to begin doing so was to recognize affinities with other people of color while acknowledging that there are still very different experiences between them and African American people and Latino/a people. As he grew into adulthood, Phil saw hip-hop as a bridge for exploratory crossings of cultural divides. He arrived at a point where he could say that the songs they sang also resonated with his own experiences of life in America.

Felix said, "Yeah, it's interesting because my parents haven't lived in the Philippines for decades now, you know, and we have family and friends in the Philippines, but when they do get together, when they visit the United States, they get all into what's currently happening in soap acts or what's happening with whatever celebrities are on blast at that moment in Philippine media. So that's really interesting. So does that mean that we're losing Tagalog, or are there more people who are going to be able to learn the language more with this kind of subtitling? But, yeah, those are very emerging and new things that are happening within that medium. I think it's more popular with Filipino immigrants than it is for American-born Filipinos, but then . . ."

Hip-hop was born during Felix's generation, and in the urban area in which he lives it's just "in the air." He feels there are ways that hip-hop culture is almost like Filipino culture. "Looking at the ethnic, political fabric of hip-hop across generations and nations, there are connections that are inter-ethnic and across genders," he said.

Although there is denigration of women and people who are gay in hip-hop, Felix noted, "There's always remnants of bigotry or prejudice or stratifications that we know are present in our everyday life, but there also is potential for change, for growth. The hip-hop I knew is very different from hip-hop now, and there is the complexity of evolution that will continue to make it different over time."

ENTER THE DRAGON

Not only is no body yellow, nobody is obviously Asian. As noted earlier, the term "Asian American" did not exist before the late 1960s (Ocampo, 2016). As Phil indicated in the quote that began this chapter, the term itself has problems similar to those of *yellow* as a designation for people. Without language clues it's not possible to reliably guess what Asian nationality or ethnic group an individual is in, whether the person making the guess is from within or outside the groups identified as Asian. As Halle said, "It's not a neat, you know, mathematical division, and how each of those contributes to how you are as a person." In coming to terms with personal and societal constructions of identity, Chloe, Halle, Phil, and Felix each revealed how distinctly complex every person is. Chloe's sassiness did not fit the stereotype of a quiet, submissive Asian female. It conflicted with her family's sense of how she should behave as well as with the hypermasculine male orientation of her boyfriend at the time. Growing up in the United States also created cultural dissonance in college between her and Chinese immigrant students despite her fluency in both major languages of China. Halle's indeterminacy was read quite differently in the various contexts from Hawaii to Washington State to Boston. Her Native American background was rendered invisible by her family in Washington, while people she encountered in Boston continually sought to box her in to some category they could understand within the simple typography of race. On the other hand, her Hapa identity was never in question in Hawaii. Phil, an immigrant himself, at times felt cultural distance from other immigrant students in high school who had different trajectories based on contexts surrounding how they came to the United States. Like Chloe, he did not fit one of the pervasive Asian stereotypes, by being an English teacher. However, he felt himself to be in a hyphenated space at the intersection of elements of Asian American, immigrant, academic, and urban cultures. Felix described similar feelings of in-between-ness and lack of belonging, accented by his intellectual quests; his identity as a gay man; and society's pigmentocracy, which could understand him only as racially ambiguous. All four are also quite different with respect to their positionality and practices from their closest sibling, who in each case is a brother. Even being an identical twin, like Felix, is no indication that core aspects of identity will be influenced and manifested similarly by growing up in the same familial and ethnic/national context. As Felix said at one point in his interview, "Man, I kind of need to shut it down and embrace complexity rather than kind of box define my thinking."

This is the challenge for us all. We all exist in interstitial, hyphenated spaces between and beyond the markers of race, and our need to belong must not cast others into exile.

The lives of these interviewees demonstrate that the hyperdiverse positioning and practices of individuals and the myriad distinctions between people in families and ethnic/national groups defy the homogenized boxes that institutional forces in U.S. society try to contain them in. Their stories expose the stereotyping, discrimination, and attempts to render them invisible. When people's appearances are more ambiguous, as in the cases of Halle, Phil, and Felix, these forces may seem more overt. Yet every one of us is just as indeterminate with regard to fitting into the essentialized categories and binaries of race, gender, and sexual orientation. In their own identity constructions over time, all the interviewees challenged or rejected these limited identity constructions, partially by extending their identities and cultural connections across generations and geographies with digital texts and tools.

Although most media portrayals of the vast array of positionalities lumped into the category of Asian are negative, there also were instances during the adolescent development of these interviewees when the media provided glimpses of ways of being beyond stereotypes. Some martial arts films during this period provided those instances. Of particular note was *Enter the Dragon*, starring Bruce Lee, which has been hailed as the greatest martial arts film of all time. Whether youth like Phil were aware of it or not, these films often had anticolonial themes that made allegorical links with mass movements for decolonization. We also saw how each interviewee was influenced by hip-hop, which was an emerging global cultural force as they were developing into adulthood. Although there are numerous critical considerations of hip-hop culture, as a powerful discourse (one that is able to critique dominant discourses) it also indicates that fundamental identity connections are possible across the different positionalities in the United States and globally. Of course, there was also cross-fertilization between liberation themes embedded in some of the martial arts movements and the self-determination themes in the music and hip-hop culture of groups like Wu Tang Clan and others.

Can we enter the dragon of white supremacy and defeat its hierarchy of racial identities? Halle believes we are reaching a tipping point where "it's not going to be so easy to ascribe categories." She's "seen a lot of pushback about those things" and claims that "there's a lot of us that don't have an appropriate box to check, and don't want to check a box."

CHAPTER 7

The Brown Box

> The brown box is the box that was given to us. Where I grew up there was
> no brown box. It's like we're all either Mexicano or Chicano . . . and that
> terminology of Chicano is not uniform. . . . You fill a room full of Chicanos, and
> there are so many different layers.
>
> —Javier (July 21, 2016)

As indicated in Chapter 3, more than 50 million people in the United States
identified as Hispanic or Latino/a in the 2010 census. This is up from 35
million people in 2000, and Mexicans accounted for three-fourths of this
increase, which reflected more than half the growth of the total U.S. population during that period. Interestingly, until 1930 Mexicans were classified as
white in the census. Also of interest is that at the time of the last census more
than half the Hispanic population lived in three states: California, Texas,
and Florida. Importantly, the definition for Hispanic or Latino/a in the 2010
census provides language that with a few revisions can be used to identify
every person in the United States without defaulting to racial categories.
The first revision is to widen the scope of identification beyond "Cuban,
Mexican, Puerto Rican, South or Central American, or other Spanish culture" (Ennis et al., 2011, p. 2) to *all* individuals being identified. Next is
to change how this most recent census defines "Hispanic origin" by sub-
stituting "a person's identity" for those two words so that *all* individuals
are identified by their origin. Changing those two words would create the
following definition: "A person's identity can be viewed as the heritage,
nationality group, lineage, or country of birth of the person or the person's
parents or ancestors." An additional revision is needed to drop the two
prepositional phrases originally included at the end of this statement, "before their arrival in the United States." Finally, there is a need to better account for complexity by making the defining categories plural. Thus, a more
accurate and viable way of defining ourselves in this country would read: *"A
person's identity can be viewed as the heritages, lineages, nationality groups,
or country of birth of the person or the countries of birth of the person's
parents or ancestors."* This definition does not account for ways that selected activities and affinities also connect to identity, but here, the attempt is
to first redefine identity for census purposes. Also, sexual orientation is not

in this definition, and, of course, there are contexts in which it should be accounted for. But I don't think that should be the government's business with regard to identifying people as residents in this country.

Carmen, Suzana, Anton, and Javier reveal many different layers of personal-cultural positioning and practices that are outside the brown box. Carmen's parents are Puerto Rican. Like Ingrid's, Carmen's father was in the military. Carmen was born in upstate New York but raised in Puerto Rico, then lived a good portion of her life in California. She is 5'7" and has a light complexion, black hair, and brown eyes. Married with two sons, she was 39 and in graduate school when interviewed. She identifies herself as Puerto Rican but also identifies with African Americans. Suzana was born and grew up in California as well as in Colombia. Forty-one at the time of her interview, she is 5'4" and has a light complexion, light brown hair, and brown eyes. She is an assistant professor at a university in Southern California, is married, and has a young daughter. Suzana identifies as a Latina, as Colombian, as a woman of color, as a person born in California, and also as queer. Like Susana, Anton was 41 when interviewed. He's 6'1" and has a light complexion, black hair, and brown eyes. He is married and has two children and was the dean of students at an urban high school in the San Francisco Bay Area. He identifies as Chicano but says he is seen by society as Latino. Javier's parents are from Mexico, and he was born and grew up in California and was 47 when interviewed. He is married, has children, and is the principal of an urban high school in the San Francisco Bay Area. He is 5'8" and has a light brown complexion, black hair, and brown eyes and identifies himself as Chicano to connect both his Mexican and American backgrounds. "Blacxican," "Colombian," "Cholo," and "Chicano" are the section titles for these four interviewees. Their activities with digital media are discussed in a section entitled "Digital Acts" and with hip-hop culture in a section entitled "Hip-Hop Action." The concluding section is entitled "Breaking the Piñata." The positioning, practices, choices, and perspectives revealed in the following stories of these four interviewees indicate the hyperdiversity they and their families reflect, the stereotyping they experienced, and the ways they actively constructed complex identities as also specified through all the subcategories associated with each of these themes.

BLACXICAN

Both of Carmen's parents are Puerto Rican, but her mother's family is very light skinned from Spanish influences while her father's family has much darker skin tones from African influences. "You would definitely think they were black," she said of her father's side of the family. Carmen, however, is in multiple ways invested in both Puerto Rican and black culture. She is often asked, "What are you"? and feels her identity is relational in terms of how she is perceived in different contexts. Mainland U.S. society generally sees her as biracial or more specifically as a mix of Mexican or Puerto Rican and black, or what she termed "Blacxican." When she was younger she was also perceived as African American. But when she was living in Puerto Rico and attending school there, people called her "La Americana" although she was completely fluent in Spanish. Painfully she remembered, "So I wasn't even Puerto Rican. It was very much like, 'You're American. You don't count as being Puerto Rican.'" Her experiences convinced her that Puerto Ricans "could be as racist as any white person" toward people with darker skin . . . favoring the spectrum around being more valued if you're lighter skinned." Despite the rejections she experienced, she identifies herself as Puerto Rican. She understands, however, that "black is in me. It's part of the whole historical process of colonialism, you know. In many ways, I'm a black person."

Like the father of Ingrid in Chapter 5, Carmen's father was a military man, which influenced how Carmen grew up, but in very different ways from the military influences on Ingrid's life. His being stationed at an army base in California is how the family ended up there. He eventually moved back to Puerto Rico, and that's how Carmen ended up going to elementary school there. When Carmen's mom and dad divorced, they both started new families. So she has two much younger brothers by her father, and two sisters more than 15 years younger than she is by her mother. After the divorce, her mother never married again, and she had relationships only with white men. There was a period in Carmen's home life when her mom had a white domestic partner. "The way she experienced growing up, she sort of identified Puerto Rican as being related to poverty, or like cultures of poverty, and she just didn't want to identify that way. To this day she's still very much like, 'I'm a human being. I have no desire to identify with being Puerto Rican.'" With a twist, this is reminiscent of Halle's grandfather, as discussed in Chapter 6, except that the alternative identity was human rather than white.

One consequence of her mother's positionality was that when Carmen returned from Puerto Rico to live with her mother in California at around age 12, her mom would not speak to her in Spanish and also put her in all-white schools. "The teachers were very discriminatory, and I would have wishes to be blonde haired and blue eyed," Carmen said. "I could see that the fact that I was a person of color, or that I looked different, was a problem for these people I was around, and I would just, you know, get teased mercilessly by kids." They said things like, "Oh, your shackles are loose," and they called her the N-word. In one incident at school when everyone was washing up after playing outside, kids teased, "Oh, look! Maybe the brown is coming off. Maybe she has something underneath." In another incident while doing a coloring activity, a student next to her mentioned that his favorite color was black. "I'm black," she told him. "Why don't you like me?" He responded, "You're not black. You're brown." Like Phil and Felix in Chapter 6, Carmen felt exiled in a state of in-between-ness. "It was just very obvious to me that whatever I was, I didn't really belong," she said. It wasn't until high school that she started to get her bearings. While watching a TV show with her mother on the African slave trade, they had a conversation about its impacts on the people of Puerto Rico. "So I'm Puerto Rican and African," she told her mom, who responded, "Yeah. We're mixed with all that."

After that, Carmen embraced her identity as a person with multiple lineages, including African ancestry. She read books like *The Autobiography of Malcolm X* and *Roots*. "This literature really helped me understand why I was seen in particular ways, why I was treated differently." She saw that she had internalized a wish to be white. "It just helped me be more confident in who I was, and I didn't have to feel so alienated. It was like, 'Well, I can see you're racist . . . [and] this is why you have a problem with me, like skin color." She started a Black Student Union in her predominantly white school. When she got to college, and had more exposure to what it means to be black, she began to question if she would be comfortable staking that claim as an identity for herself. "I understood that I couldn't identify as black because I'm not black." But she does feel she can identify with the black experience politically. "When something's happening to black people, I feel like it's happening to me, that it's part of my experience, even though I know I'm not black. I'm Puerto Rican."

Carmen's story demonstrates, however, that U.S. society makes every positionality outside the boundaries of whiteness subject to victimization, discrimination, and stereotyping within the pigmentocracy of race. By her own account, her life was made miserable, and it was particularly difficult while growing up and not being conscious of the pervasive ways that forces of white supremacy worked to divide and distort. "As a child I didn't understand, right? What's everybody's problem with me? And all because I look different. There was, like, serious feelings of, like, people hating me, or had, like, disgust for me. Even teachers, there was no respect or care. . . . And so I would just wish that I could look different so that I wouldn't be treated differently or be teased so incessantly and be treated so, like, inhumanely, right?" Carmen went on to describe how all the microaggressions made her become withdrawn from social interactions, but also from learning activities. She was passed along without having fundamental skills, particularly in math and science. "I was just sitting there," she said. "Nobody engaged me or made sure I was doing what I was supposed to. It didn't matter what I did. As long as I stayed quiet or stayed out of trouble, then I was just passed along." Fortunately, she was internally strong. Instead of letting these experiences beat her down, she redoubled her determination to prove her self-worth to others, but mainly to herself. "It was a hard thing," she said, "but my spirit was never killed." Initially, she blamed close family members for not doing more to protect her when she was a child; however, she came to see that circumstances of powerlessness and poverty had harmed them too. She decided as a teenager that she would no longer be under the authority of adults in her family. Yet she found that developing her own resilient identity also required that she be able to forgive them, understanding that they too were victims of the racial perspectives and practices that hurt her. "Have I found a place?" she asked rhetorically. "You have, like, choices around who you want to be and what you want to be" was her answer. "These can actually be experiences that you can turn around and use to bring other people up and make differences in their lives. That's where I think I became comfortable, maybe."

At 17, Carmen was working and taking care of herself. She became closer to her mom once she was out of the house and on her own. She was rebellious, precocious, and athletic. She said she was sent back and forth between the United States and Puerto Rico, in part because her family did not know what to do with her. Her mom couldn't control her, and her dad expected her to be a polite girl and into dresses and things, but that was not who she was. She went to a Division 1 university on a full track scholarship, but dropped out before graduating because she decided she wanted to act. She was selected as an extra in one of the best-known films of this century, and afterward just left school and moved to live in Los Angeles for 5 years. She did a variety of jobs and also had a child while in Los Angeles. Then she went to a community college to get her grades up while being a single mom working up to 14 hours a day. Eventually, she returned to the prestigious university she had left and finished her undergraduate degree, 10 years after she had first started college. "Yeah, I lived a number of lives," she said.

One way she challenged her family's color politics was to date only black men. Her husband is African American, and the father of her first son has an African American dad. "Why do you always want to be with the Morenos?" her family constantly asked. Her answer is, "Well, I consider myself black. We're black people! What are you talking about?" The father of Carmen's first son was a professional basketball player. His mother says she is Blackfoot Indian, Creole, and Jewish, but Carmen thinks she's not claiming all aspects of her identity. "I'm like, 'Lady, you got blonde hair and blue eyes. You look white to me, but okay.'" . . . If she doesn't want to identify as white, she still has the privileges of a white identity. Her son with the professional athlete has bright-red hair, hazel eyes, and very light skin, and he's really tall. Talking about her son opened a conversation about the hyperdiversity in her family. Since her son's hair is red, the recessive gene that determined it had to come from both sides of the family, and she talked about aunts on her side that have auburn hair in one case and reddish-tone hair in another. "I even have some red undertones if you hit me in the right kind of sunlight," she said. "It's a reflection of heritage, of colonization. We're a bunch of highly mixed people."

COLOMBIAN

Like every interviewee, Suzana indicated that society's identities for her are relational. In general she is identified as Latina, and in California she is seen mainly as Mexican. She is a U.S. citizen who was born and grew up in California and also lived in Colombia. She identifies herself as Latina, Colombian, a woman of color, "and queer, of course." I asked why she emphasized being queer by saying, "of course," because it's not obvious from anything that can be externally observed about her. She responded that rather than as emphasis for me, it was more an emphasis for her as affirmation of this specific way of self-identifying. She'd had relationships with men before she married a woman, and they have a young daughter. She also knows that some people might identify her as bisexual or lesbian and that people who use those terms are older or white. "I said 'of course, queer,'" she added, "because I was only thinking culturally, and I was like, oh, there's other aspects of my identity, right, like I'm queer. I said 'of course' because . . . it wasn't that you can't necessarily tell by looking at me that I'm queer—I don't look butch, you know—[but] . . . I prefer the term *queer* because it's a much more open-ended category. It's not fixed the way that a lesbian identity or something like that would be. . . . Things aren't binaries; they're much more open than that."

Suzana emphasized that in addition to sexual orientation, identifying as queer and also as a woman of color is political. People have varying associations with both terms, but for her they are expressions of political identity. "It's a coalitional identity. And the organizing that I've done through that category of 'woman of color,' it's been mostly queer women of color that have led a lot of that organizing, you know? Even from academic to community spaces. So thinking about people like Cherríe Moraga, Audre Lorde, Gloria Anzaldúa. You know Angela Davis is also queer." She's been a big influence on Suzana's development as a scholar. "Queer politics signals to other people that the categories aren't white and black, that we can change, that our identities are fluid," she said. "It's not always a clear-cut question. . . . So that's why I identify as queer."

Suzana thinks representations of fluid identities are extremely important at this historical moment in the United States and across the globe. They work to disrupt fixed identities not only in the realm of sexual orientations. They inherently challenge notions of fixed categories with regard to peoples' positionality and practices, including ascribed, hierarchical categories of race. She believes that queer people of color, and particularly queer women of color and queer trans people, have led the way to coalition identities and coalition politics, which are bringing a lot of communities together. "They're the ones that are able to kind of span . . . and show multiple intersecting identities to allow people who identify in different ways to kind of come into the circle, as opposed to just sticking to one aspect of someone's identity."

In addition to sexual orientation, Suzana addressed how relational identities are in other arenas by talking about her growing connections to Mexican and Chicana cultures. Interestingly, her travels to Spain accentuated these connections as they etched against the surrounding cultural context of that country. Almost every interviewee indicated the importance of travel in sharpening and broadening their cultural awareness of others as well as themselves. As with the other interviewees, Suzana's travels revealed both affinities and dissonance with others as their personal-cultural positioning, practices, choices, and perspectives intersected. Her time in Spain revealed things she had not been consciously aware of regarding how some of her own perspectives and practices were influenced by Mexican and Chicana cultures. In Northern California she grew up living in an area between San Francisco and Sacramento that had a lot of Mexican residents. She noted that she did not have a real problem with the term *brown* being generally applied to Latinx* people, particularly in the context of its use by community activists applying it with regard to organizing and coalitions across communities. She talked in detail about the histories of Asian Latinos, white Latinos, and black Latinos. But growing up in Northern California, she held to a more specific identity as Colombian to make it clear that she wasn't "something else," because people were always making erroneous assumptions about her. When she went to Spain, she further realized "how relational identity is," although she did not have this terminology to describe it at the time.

Suzana went to Spain in a study-abroad program sponsored by the university she attended. She had always heard that Colombian Spanish was similar to Spanish from Spain, and in conjunction with other things she had heard about Spain, she felt she would be very comfortable there. Instead she said, "I found people very dry and just very different from me." The first real friend that she had was a Chicana from another school in the university system she was in who was also studying abroad at the same university in Spain. Her friend took her to a party that the Mexican students at the university hosted, and Suzana said, "I knew all the music, and all the food, and I finally felt at home. I was like, wow, I must be part Chicana, part Mexican too because I'd grown up around it, you know?" Of course, what Suzana was expressing was not limited to food and music. Instead, it was a beginning discovery of how she related to other kinds of Latino identities. For her whole life, she had thought of herself as Colombian, but in Spain she became aware of how connected she also was to Mexican culture. "I didn't realize how much I had just grown up without seeing it," she said. "It wasn't until I left my context."

It was disconcerting in Spain when she told people that she was born in the United States because they would then tell her that she was not Colombian. "I was like, what? I started having to tell a whole story that I

"Latinx" has been used to circumvent the gender specificity of the term "Latino."

was born in the States, but both of my parents are Colombian. Ironically, when she went to Colombia, people there rejected her identifying herself as Colombian despite her expressing that identity for her entire life. "Oh, the gringa's here," they would say, "and I was like, gringa, me?" Suzana is fluent in Spanish, but in Colombia they could tell she had an accent. "They could hear the Mexican influence on my Spanish," she said. In Spain, however, they attributed her accent to South America. "I don't think they could hear the English side of the accent, but they could hear the Colombian side." The way Suzana looks also came into play when others constructed her identity. She said she's never been seen as white, but in Spain people thought she might be Moroccan, or Middle Eastern, or North African, depending on where she was or who she was with. In college she had a lot of Iranian friends, and people there thought she was Iranian too. In one very uncomfortable situation, her Iranian roommate's African American boyfriend was checking Suzana out and made inappropriate comments about her body (which he thought were compliments) before asking, "Are you black? Are you part black?" In other contexts people would ask if she was Egyptian; Israeli; Indian, as in South Asia Indian; Italian; or Portuguese. While she was waiting on the street to meet a friend in Spain, somebody stopped and asked, "Do you need a job? Are you Portuguese?" Also in Spain she was asked to show identification papers because they thought she was Moroccan.

Suzana's identity is further complicated by her family life while growing up. She has one brother 2 years older who became a surgeon, while she became a professor. Her dad came to the United States from Colombia in 1961 and became a citizen after being drafted into the army. He was able to get a GED and a little bit of college through the GI Bill. Her family is Catholic, and Suzana went to Catholic schools. She got teased in school because of physical characteristics like her full lips and thick, curly hair. She played on the boys' soccer team in high school because they didn't have a team for girls; she was made fun of and called "fluffy" and "Diana Ross" because of her hair. When she got to college, these same features became attractive and "exotic." One of her uncles is a priest, so family relationships have been challenging since she became a queer woman, although they have become a bit more open as a result of the stance of the new pope. After college, Suzana began doing activist work for human rights and on issues surrounding Colombia.

When she goes to Colombia, however, Suzana feels she has to be aware that expressing an overtly queer identity could have problematic consequences. Yet her sense of herself does not require her to dress or look a certain way to signal queerness. She didn't start dating women until after college, and unlike some people who have an earlier sense of the range of their sexual orientations, her attraction to women didn't happen until after college for her. "I've never chosen to not look a certain look; I just look the way I want to," she said. "I just like to dress a certain way, and I don't think, 'Does this look queer?'" You don't have to look a certain way to be queer.

I come out to my students in my classes, but I don't have to. A lot of times people separate sexual orientation from gender presentation. I'm more close to femme, you know, or sporty femme, as some people like to say."

CHOLO

Anton grew up in Los Angeles. Like Javier in the coming section, he identifies as Chicano. However, he adds a number of relational identities. "It kind of depends on what setting I'm in," he said. "But I guess I would be seen as Latino. However, if you look at me, you would think I was white. . . . But if you heard me talk on the phone, you would think I'm black. . . . What am I? I'm Yaki; I'm Mexican; I'm Chicano; I'm Cholo. If you want to go back scientifically, we're African. So you gotta throw that in there. In terms of society, I guess I'm identified as Hispanic—and I'm not one to panic—but I'm not accepting that! It's my way of resisting being colonized and being told who we are." Anton has a master's degree in social work and was the dean of students at a majority Hispanic, urban high school in the San Francisco Bay Area at the time of his interview. The following slice of his story indicates the hyperdiversity of Anton and his family, the stereotyping he and they experienced, and the ways he and they constructed identities while reflecting the subcategories associated with each of these themes. Most of the subcategories are in three intersecting parts: "Street Life," "School Life," and "Home Life."

Street Life

As a young man, Anton enacted hypermasculine behaviors in street life and Latino gang culture. "Hood life is like dog years," he said. "You live with a lot of stress, and you deal with a tremendous amount of worrying and watching your back. You develop physical ailments from fighting in the streets, getting shot, getting stabbed, being on alert, and just kind of wrecking yourself. So, I'm 41, but maybe it's more like 70s." Literally everybody in his neighborhood, including all his family members, was connected to street life and gang culture. He came from a family that he described as "generationally deep in the street life, in the gang culture." His grandfather was a Pachuca gangster early on, his dad was a Cholo, and his uncles and aunties along with his siblings were deeply involved in gang life as well. "Pachuco," he explained, "is just like the old school. It started with the riots back in the days with the naval men and the Mexican Americans. They formed, in ways, to protect themselves from racist clans of white people. A Pachuco was also a well-dressed zoot suitor, if you will. A Cholo is just a more modern-day version of that, what it evolved into. It got a little bit more lax on the dress code, maybe not quite so fancy, but a Cholo is like a descendant of a Pachuco gangster." Now, "it goes down to my nieces and nephews who begin lining up in elementary school with gang initiations where you are jumped and beat to a pulp."

Anton described how there were always lots of beatings. "Giving 'em and receiving 'em." He took pride in never being defeated in one-on-one fights, but has gotten jumped by six or seven rival gang members. He has been shot three different times and once stabbed with a screwdriver. "I got shot through my shin, shot in my tibia. I still have a metal rod in my leg. I was shot in my arm and the bullet is still inside. I was shot in the chest, and it punctured both my lungs and just missed my aorta by two centimeters." That final shooting, from which he almost died, was the beginning of an awakening. He lamented how this was something he didn't necessarily want to do, but that he and his family were born into it, that it has spanned generations, and that as a youth, he didn't see any options until he almost died from being shot.

A number of Latino and African American gangs operated in the same neighborhoods, and some of his best friends, "road dogs who would 'ride' and die for each other," were African Americans. "We just grew up right next to each other, you know, black and Latino, black and Mexican." He uses *Latino* and *Mexican* interchangeably. Different areas were claimed by specific gangs, such as Sureños, the Southside gang. African American gangs like Crips and Bloods also controlled large areas. A big part of being in gangs was the culture, and initially some events were shared by both Latino and African American gangs. There would be big cookouts with African American and Latino gang members sharing food and music: "oldies, soul music, and funk." Eventually, however, the Mexican mafia moved in and with prison connections to some of the Latino gangs, they essentially said, "Okay, you can no longer affiliate and you have to, kind of, cleanse your neighborhood of black gang members, of black people." So the connections between the two groups were broken, while up to that point, some of the African Americans talked, dressed, and acted like Cholos themselves; some had taken Cholo names; some learned Spanish, sometimes becoming fluent. Anton said the Mexican mafia/Latino gangs consolidation "really was about money, power, and drugs, and it just had huge, huge effects on the community, and just created these divides that were just sad and tragic and, you know, still continue."

Anton had a larger critique of these conditions, however. He talked about how Latino gangs were used as scapegoats and projected as having "values at the margins of society." He saw these things, instead, as being core American values in terms of violence, control, and power—things he said this country was founded on and that were glorified in the media. He explained how this was also an expression of hypermasculinity, noting, "The greatest gangster on the planet is the U.S. military, the American government." Anton brought this perspective to Latino and African American youth he worked with as a high school dean of students with conscious aims to contextualize and disrupt the stereotypes that U.S. society holds for them.

School Life

Anton never went to prison, although he always thought he would. "I'll be dead, or in the pen," he said. "I couldn't even imagine being alive in my mid-20s. In my neighborhood, you hit your mid-20s, and you're considered an 'Old G'" (an old gangster). Almost dying from being shot at 17 changed him, and echoing the experience of Joshua, in Chapter 5, Anton's going to community colleges was collateral with his turning his back on the vicissitudes of street life. He tried manual labor for a while, and although it taught him the value of hard work, he also realized that he wanted something different with his life. He knew he wanted to work in some capacity to help develop and heal the community he grew up in. It took him 6 years to complete community college, which he began attending despite never having received a high school diploma. After being shot he never returned to the continuation high school he had been attending. They would not allow him to go back. "It took me 2 years to finish my first two courses in community college," he said. "My mom would say, 'Go to school, fool; go to class.' Just to get me out of the neighborhood. And little by little, baby steps, I finally transferred to a 4-year university." In his last year of undergrad he began to see, "Oh yeah, I can do this. I got this." He eventually went on to complete a master's degree in social work.

Interestingly, while he was in community college, they put him in English as a second language (ESL) classes despite his being born in the United States and having English as his first language. He is the only one of his siblings who is fluent in Spanish. One ironic consequence of being grossly stereotyped in this way was that his academic confidence was actually boosted because he was easily the best student in the ESL classes. He also enjoyed the relationships he was building with some people he met in the community college context. There was an African American woman who was a secretary who continually encouraged and inspired him. After he completed undergraduate school and eventually got into graduate school, he and his wife had their first child, a girl. To make ends meet, he said, "I did multiple things, even going back a little bit; I still would make trips home to supplement my income. But when my daughter was born, I was really able to sever myself with the neighborhood. It was kind of like, 'All right.'"

Home Life

"I'm mixed," Anton said. "I clearly have European blood." He and his wife have two children. His wife's family members are from the Yaki Indians in Mexico. "They have a cultural heritage that was never conquered," he noted, and the names he and his wife gave their two children come from one of her family's Indian languages. His hyperdiversity is reflected by his racial indeterminacy; his cultural connections as Mexican, Chicano, Pachuco, and Cholo, as well as with "road dogs" who were African American; and his marriage to a Mexican Indian woman who works to sustain cultural practices extending from her family's Mexican Indian traditions.

Anton explained that Mexican Indians are stereotyped, discriminated against, and marginalized in their society in similar ways to the experiences of American Indians in the United States. "It was better to be Mexican than it was to be Indian, so Indian people learned Spanish and attempted to look Mexican so that they weren't immediately deemed and treated as if they were outlaws. And so, there was a lot of that." Instead of dividing North, Central, and South America, this Indian culture sees it all as "the land between two seas." He supports his wife's efforts to reconnect the family to their Yaki Indian roots through reclaiming aspects of that culture and its language. Anton said this also is a way he and his family resist vestiges of colonization by exploring their ties to this indigenous Indian culture that has never been colonized—"not by the Aztecs, not by the Mayans, and not by Europeans."

CHICANO

Javier grew up in a small town about 10 miles from Los Angeles that was 95% Mexicano/Chicano. As with Anton, there was lots of gang activity in this area, but Javier questioned the use of the word *gang*. He said, "I understand gangs and gang culture. But where I was growing up it wasn't a negative. To me it was family. To me it was friends. . . . Now some choose to go into the negative and start causing mayhem. But at the end of the day, you still live next door to each other, you hang out together, you have common interests, you take care of each other. You have squabbles. But it's still family."

Javier's parents are from Michoacán, Mexico, and growing up and straddling both Mexican and American cultures, he identifies as Chicano. He prefers the term *Chicano* (sometimes spelled Xicano) over *Mexicano* or *Mexican American* because it signals more of a political consciousness with respect to societal forces that are threatening yet position them as a threat. "It'd just be easier if we just didn't exist," he said. For him, however, "*Chicano* is a term embedded in pride and understanding, in that I'm brown and I'm proud. To me, the beauty is I am multiple. I can access multiple worlds, multiple experiences. I'm educated. I have a sense of history. But to me, the Chicano part also goes to the indigenous part that most of us who are Mexican American, American, Latino, and Hispanic people don't realize. We're a combination of everything. But instead of seeing it as a negative, I see it as a positive. Think about the beauty of the fact that we are a combination of so many different cultures, you know? And it's to me the celebration of the acknowledgment that we are indigenous; we are black; we are white; we are everything. And so to me the Chicano part is the consciousness, the understanding that it's about embracing the beauty of the diversity that's within us. But it's also an understanding that this country, from the get-go, from the founding, tried to confine us into boxes."

People in society identify Javier differently depending on who *they* are. He feels that white society generalizes him as Mexican or Hispanic "because they assume we're all Mexican or Hispanic." He said that other Mexicanos and Chicanos see him as Mexicano or Chicano because that's the dominant group in California. Sometimes people find it easier to just say "brown." He said this is bothersome because he doesn't like how it lumps people into a general category, but at times he identifies himself as "brown" because it seems to put some people at ease. Asserting himself as Chicano makes some people nervous. He feels they fear having a conversation with an educated Chicano, and he asks, "Isn't our business as educators to have those conversations so we can model for our kids how to have conversations about race and racism as they enter the real world . . . and give them the language so they don't have to identify in a brown box or black box or white box?" He continued, "We don't have enough conversations in schools, let alone outside of schools, to really accept you for however you may identify. I think in this country we want to put people in boxes because it makes us feel safe. If you start identifying in a way that I'm not comfortable with, it sort of questions my identity, my worth, and I can't have that. So I need to control you. And the easiest way to control you is to put you in these broad categories that kind of affirm, 'Okay, I'm good.'" Javier's question to educators is "when can we talk about racism and sexism and homophobia and all these other 'isms' that separate and make our kids and our families and our communities feel less than, that makes them feel they're not normal." For him, part of the challenge of educators is to present curriculum content and learning activities that enable students to question and critique difficult issues, including how identities are socially constructed and controlled, understanding who benefits from this control, and what needs to be done personally and collectively to bring about more human and sustainable relationships among people in our society.

Javier is concerned that adults and youth learn how to explore and embrace their commonalities across groups as well as their distinctions within them. Rather than leaving stereotypes unquestioned (and, thereby, perpetuating them) being willing to drill down to specifics with students and colleagues, as in "You know, that individual, that family, that group, they're from Nicaragua. They're not Mexican. They speak Spanish, but they have different histories and varying cultural practices." He feels it's important for Spanish speakers to sustain that language as one way to keep connected to their cultures, but he admits that it's a struggle. He has to seek out others to talk to, to maintain his Spanish "literacy" even when he is surrounded by Spanish speakers. This invitation and activity alone creates a higher level of familiarity. Yet he still has a lot of work to do to improve his academic Spanish as well as to make sure that his two young children become fluent in that language. He made an interesting point that was consistent with

Anton's development of fluency in Spanish also. "I have three siblings and . . . it's like a common trend. The older children or the first child tends to hold on to the language and values of the culture more than the younger ones. . . . My sister and I, we're much more fluent in Spanish than my two younger siblings. My younger brother has two daughters, and I don't think I've ever heard him speak Spanish to them. It's difficult because his wife does not speak Spanish, whereas my wife does. It's also sad when it comes to my mother, his daughters' grandmother. It's just lack of communication with her because language is the bridge. I think about everything that the grandparents have to offer, the sharing of stories, the sharing of our culture, where we grew up, how we were when we were little. The grandchildren are losing a generation of information. And, 'knock on wood,' the clock is ticking. You realize that as much as you may love your grandchildren, or they may love their grandmother, much is lost. All of that is lost."

In a larger sense, Javier talked about how losing one's culture leaves a person with no sense of history and, therefore, nothing to stand on. "For my children, the value is 'no mijo. Tienes una cultura,' you know?" Every individual needs to be aware of the richness of his or her history because this is what enables resistance to social forces that work to minimize certain people's sense of personal value and self-worth through stereotypes and the homogenization of identities. Using his son as an example, Javier noted that without a nuanced understanding of his cultural positioning and background, he will be more subject to the forces in white America that work to reject him because of the shade of his skin or the way that he speaks. "This way," Javier said, "he's like, you know what, I can enter any world I want to because I'm grounded. I know who I am." He will be able to counter what Javier called "the master checklist" of what is projected to be American from the dominant paradigm. "The master checklist is you're white, you're Christian, you're this, and you go down the line. And then you start asking, Well, if that's normal, if that's American, then what am I? And you realize, wait a minute, we were here way before any white people or anybody else was here and we have a rich history here in what they call the Americas, so then I must be American. There's so many layers to that, and people don't understand or have the context or the background to engage in that conversation or accept you for who you are."

Javier feels that when Chicanos understand more about who they are, they see that they are not victims, but fighters, and they have been fighting for centuries. Yet he also noted that there are so many layers to that identity that "there is no common definition of what is a Chicano. There's some general understanding, maybe a consciousness, a language, an appreciation for history, or the struggle that we continue to fight, but that terminology of Chicano is not uniform. It's not common within everybody that may identify or operate within that brown box that people put us in." He used himself as an example of this last point. "If someone were to ask me who are you or what are you, it's like Chicano's not the first thing that comes to mind. It's more like my name, who I am, or what I am as a profession, as an educator. . . . In a room of Chicanos . . . you don't have to frame it. But as soon as non-Chicanos enter the conversation, and by 'non-Chicanos,' it doesn't only mean white. It can be people from Central or South America or the Caribbean, where we may have the language in common, but the cultural experience is different. So then that changes the dynamics as well. And for someone that grew up Chicano, you quickly pick up the nuances of differences."

DIGITAL ACTS

Each interviewee's use of digital media and participation in hip-hop culture further revealed his or her micro-cultural positioning, choices, and perspectives. Carmen was initially reluctant to use social media because of privacy concerns. "Putting yourself out there so publicly bothered me," she said. "It felt strange." She finally joined Facebook in 2009 and started really getting into it because of how it allowed her to extend her interests in influencing and organizing people around important societal issues. In her words, she became a "social media activist." She still worries about privacy, but since she believes that digital tools are now so pervasive that no one has privacy anymore, she's decided to use them for her own activist purposes. Now she considers people who don't use them being like hermits. "It means, like, isolating yourself from a lot of the world." She talked about some of her social media activist projects and noted how new critical perspectives must emerge to fully understand the potential of digital activities for both harm and good. She used the example of the recent Supreme Court ruling on gay marriage. When it passed, she said, "I was like, 'Yay! Love wins!'" However, she soon saw the need to use social media to raise questions of equity regarding differential treatment and for various groups within the gay community such as trans people or people of color who are gay but may not benefit from this ruling in the same way based on their social positions and conditions. Carmen also learns a lot from activists and scholars "who bring really unique points of view to the table" through the affordances of digital media.

Suzana also appreciated how social media allowed her to enact her affinities with a number of communities from "Colombians in the Bay Area to Colombian human rights defenders and networks, to women of color in academia." She feels that a lot of digital spaces for women of color are driven by queer women. She also participates in a group of queer mothers from all over the United States. Like Carmen, she sees the viability of social media for social action and talked about the Orlando massacre as an example, particularly in how it also indexed racial tensions in addition to the viciousness of attacks on gays generally. "I saw a lot of the queer mothers, and especially the queer mothers of color, kind of reaching out to this community, to other mothers to say, you know, we need to teach our kids about race, and we need to teach them young, you know? We can't hide it. And especially calling out to white queer mothers to pay attention to this question, you know?"

Anton expressed his practices with and perspectives on digital media primarily though his observations of the young people he works with. Although he uses Facebook to stay in contact with some of his "homeboys" and family members back in Southern California, for the most part what was posted by them was very toxic. "I would see something inspiring on Facebook, and it would be great. But the majority was just drama. Seeing how toxic what was going on with my family was, I decided not to use it." He also doesn't like the impact that social media has on youth. In the school where he was dean of students, he noted, "I feel like it desensitizes, contributes to lack of empathy, to instant gratification from notices popping up, to anticipating new messages. . . . It's just really sad, and I feel like it really inhibits their thought processes." He used the example of notifications from Snapchat popping up that encourage immediate responses because they disappear so quickly. It did the same thing to him when he would be in a meeting and get a text message. It would trigger his thoughts into a completely different realm. "I just really feel like it hampers the learning process. . . . [Although] there are some wonderful things in terms of being able to access information."

Javier is the oldest of the interviewees, and though he recognized the potential of digital tools for accessing information, he made it clear that he is very traditional and just likes reading things on paper, such as newspapers and paperwork for his job. "I prefer to hold a hard copy," he said. "But I know that our students use digital culture much more than I do. I mean, they grew up with iPhones, you know? I was an adult before those even came around. So, I'm familiar, but even to this day I don't embrace it as much." He of course uses email in connection with his work, but when I asked if he had a Facebook page or ever used Twitter or Snapchat, his answers were "No, no, and no." Television and radio were the primary mediums he experienced growing up, and "Trust me," he said, "there was nothing positive, only negative images of brown men on TV."

HIP-HOP ACTION

Looking back on her teenage years as an adult, Carmen felt she appropriated hip-hop music and culture in order to identify as black. "I was specifically getting into it as a way to affirm an identity of being black, right?" Hip-hop was what blackness meant to her as a teen. So media projections of hip-hop culture influenced how she wore her hair, how she dressed, how she talked, and the kind of music she listened to in order to "perform, in order to demonstrate" (her words) what it meant to claim blackness and to identify as a black person. She argued that her appropriation and her performance of black identity and culture were different from the actions of Rachel Dolezal because as a teen Carmen was "anchoring" her identity in a culture to which she had an authentic claim. Interestingly, although U.S. society defined her as a black girl, members of her family both in the United States and in Puerto Rico vociferously challenged her taking ownership of that identity. The key difference I saw between her and Ms. Dolezal was mainly the specific youth cultural material within hip-hop used to identify with blackness rather than other, older adult ways of performing it. She eventually married an African American man, who was, in her words, a "connoisseur" of hip-hop. Carmen keenly pointed out that societal institutions such as music production companies and the media highlighted certain representations of hip-hop music and culture over others, essentially all others over conscious rap. She talked about two major production companies that controlled the rights to most hip-hop music and how one of them was also one of the largest owners of private prisons. She also talked about the extensive appropriation of hip-hop music and culture by young white males. So her hip-hop action has always been tinged with personal and political conflicts.

Suzana said hip-hop music was "part of the soundtrack of my life." Yet she was also really into salsa music and all the fusions between Latin music and hip-hop. She also made note from her travels of how hip-hop is being used in other countries as a form of resistance and as a way for oppressed people to tell their stories. She told her own story of taking a group of people deep into Colombia to visit an Afro-Colombian community. The trip was long and arduous, involving taking a tiny plane from the major city, changing to a car and driving through banana plantations to the coast, taking several small boats across the gulf and three different rivers, and then walking for 10 kilometers to get to this community in the rain forest. The cultural presentation they received on the first night showcased some Colombian music from that region, but the teenagers from that community performed rap. "And in this community they did a culture presentation for us that night, and so some of it was Colombian from their region but there was two high school–aged kids that sang rap." She's aware of how hip-hop had been perverted for money, but she is also impressed by how she has seen in her travels hip-hop being used as a powerful voice of resistance.

In Anton's experience, hip-hop was also a bridge between Mexicano/Chicano and African American gangs. His first gang was a breakdancing crew called the Chain Breakers. His African American friends influenced how he danced, and even now when he sees his son dancing stiffly, he tells him, "Come on, man, you gotta put some flavor to it. Put some soul in it." He feels rooted in African music coming through black and Puerto Rican sources, he constantly listened to the African American radio stations, and he was greatly influenced by singers like Bob Marley—all important strands in the emergence of hip-hop. "We shared bonds over songs and what they meant, and just the nostalgia, still, that it brings back when I hear that type of music," he said. "I enjoyed it so much; I didn't care what anybody had to say because I really felt that spirit. Later on, spending time doing ceremony and getting more in touch with my roots, I understand why and where that comes from, but that's still sacred to me, and I share it with my children." For Anton, hip-hop and other cultural connections between African Americans and Chicanos in his neighborhood were vital to how he defined himself as a person. "We not only shared the same area; we also shared the same culture. . . . Soul music, funk, hip-hop—these were a big part of Latino culture."

April 29, 1992, the day of the LA riots, resonates strongly with Javier, and it was influences from hip-hop culture that really articulated the anger and frustration he felt while simultaneously reaffirming why he identifies as Chicano. "This bullshit is still going on, and here we are decades later, and let's not talk about the recent incidents that have been popping up" (all the police shootings of men of color). He talked about how Ice Cube's documentary and music about what happened really spoke to how a lot of Chicanos also feel. "It really hits home," he said. "It kind of like captures the anger that we feel. When I hear certain songs come on, it's sort of like I can't believe that here we are in 2016 heading into 2017, and we're still dealing with the same stuff." He explained how 1992 connected to 1965 and ultimately connected to 1492. "No matter how far back you go in this country," he said, "it continues to repeat itself."

Javier also talked about hip-hop culture in terms of his role as principal of an urban high school. He keeps abreast of it because of the students he works with. "I have to listen or pay attention to the nuances of what my students are listening to so I can understand the influences or narratives that are shaping their identities. . . . When they use the N-word or the B-word or any other words to dehumanize themselves, to belittle themselves, or hate each other, part of my responsibility is really to present that *other* narrative. I need to give them the tools to understand their context, but for me to meet them where they are, I need to know where they're coming from. I talk about the ideas of certain people, that's there's a history behind this. So I just use hip-hop as a tool to really work with my young people."

BREAKING THE PIÑATA

A piñata has many colorful toys and goodies inside, but it has to be broken to get to them. To free its contents requires taking aim and forcefully striking successive blows. No matter how well it's constructed, it will succumb, and the good stuff inside makes all the efforts worthwhile. The stories of Carmen, Suzana, Anton, and Javier provide more evidence of the hyperdiversity of individuals and their families and communities. They also evidence the destructive impacts of stereotyping and discrimination as each one worked to construct and embrace personal-cultural identities and explore affinities that others denigrated or felt threatened by.

People tried to confine Carmen within the limits of what they had learned to see her as, and their continual rejections of her emerging identities were traumatic. She was not allowed to be comfortable affirming parts of herself that connected to her African American father in some circumstances, yet her Spanish and Puerto Rican identities were made problematic for her in other circumstances. Instead of blossoming in public schools as she later would in college, she withdrew, and her teachers did not shield her from harm or nourish her. She was called names at home and school. "In Puerto Rico it was like, 'You're not Puerto Rican. You're American,'" she said. And when she was in the United States people would say things like, "I'm gonna call you the N-word. I'm gonna call you Shaka Zulu because you have those big lips." People also tried to confine Suzana because of the limited ways they had learned to perceive others. Again, pejoratively calling her names like "fluffy" and "Diana Ross" make it imperative that we work to deconstruct race. Their stories, like the stories of Anton and Javier, illustrate the within-group differences, the racial/ethnic indeterminacy, the learned and selected proclivities and practices that don't fit within the reductive construct of a "brown" race. As Suzana said, "It erases a lot of people. You know, and it simplifies. Brown is essentializing, and you know sometimes people mobilize those essential identities strategically, but it can be exclusive, right? There's not a lot of awareness of the spectrum of people within the Latino community."

This chapter began with a quote from Javier about "boxes" and ends with another quote from him. Here he directs us to a critical place for striking blows to free our appreciation of the full spectrum of people in all communities. "I thought more about your question about how I identify," he said. "That conversation begins with structures that the government has put in place—all the documents, all the forms where you are asked to identify by race. We know that race has no biological foundations. Yet the government continues to put out surveys and forms that force us to limit and confine our conversation to those boxes. So it becomes a fight to explain to people why I'm not a race, you know? Part of the movement, and this applies to education as well, is, like, not to have that box. Don't force us to identify within a box and limit us. Just keep it open ended, and let people write in what they want."

CHAPTER 8

Red Rum

The term *red* . . . is really hurtful when I hear it. It makes me angry that it's still something we see, like the stereotypical cartoon Indian with the red face and big nose saying, "How." Or white people dressed up as Native people with their skins painted red. The Washington Redskins, like right there. . . . Why are we the last group where this is okay to be publicly racist?

—Lily (June 14, 2016)

At the end of February 2017 as I finished writing this book, President Donald Trump signed the documents needed for Energy Transfer Partners to complete the review and approval process for building a section of the Dakota Access Pipeline (DAPL). Building this section of the oil pipeline, this "black snake," has been fiercely but peacefully contested by the Standing Rock Sioux Tribe and many thousands of other protesters. If this oil pipeline were ever to break, it could contaminate the water sources for millions of people. On February 22, 2017, the Standing Rock camps were raided and evacuated, and any remaining campers were arrested. For the Standing Rock Sioux Tribe and the 10,000 other protesters who joined them as water protectors and water warriors, after spiritedly withstanding attacks with rubber bullets, tear gas, high-powered water hoses, and sound cannons, this evacuation raid was devastating.

The Standing Rock Sioux Tribe is part of what was known as the Great Sioux Nation, which included tribes that fought the U.S. government in the Great Sioux War of 1876. Led by Sitting Bull, these Indian warriors fought to prevent illegal U.S. incursions into the Black Hills, which are sacred lands for these tribes. The Black Hills are in the center of lands ceded to the Great Sioux Nation in 1868 through treaties with the U.S. government. In 1874, however, General George Armstrong Custer led the U.S. Army into the Black Hills to secure them for exploitation of their gold. This brazen treaty violation led to the war that included the Battle of the Little Bighorn, also known as Custer's Last Stand, which was a resounding Indian victory. The standoff at Standing Rock is a continuation of centuries of war between American Indians and the U.S. government. At the center of this current struggle is the need for clean water, the gold of the 21st century. The Standing Rock protest is a harbinger of the most important struggles we face as a global community. The lines are drawn between those invested in power, profit, and violence and those invested in people, sustainable progress, and peace. These are crucial issues on which we all must act and take a stand. They also are integrally connected to deconstructing race. The color-line is another divide used to increase power, privilege, and profits for a few against larger human interests and needs.

The stories of Lily, Darien, Mila, and Alexandra again accentuate the hypocrisy of race. As in the previous three chapters, priority is given to the fluid telling of their stories, understanding that they could also have been told as was done in Chapter 4 through the 13 themes and subthemes identified in the research. Instead, the hyperdiversity, stereotyping, identity constructions, and all other associated themes are seen as they emerge in the stories, and the titles for each person's section are taken from his or her own words. Interestingly, although none of these interviewees identified as LGBTQ, two of them discussed considerations of multiple "energies" and "spirits" that are in direct dialogue with issues addressed by those in previous chapters who identified as queer.

Lily is enrolled in the Citizen Potawatomi Nation, a federally recognized government of the Potawatomi people. Her mother "looks" Indian, while her father's Indian and Caucasian mix is indeterminate. Lily identifies as a biracial woman, but U.S. society sees her as white. She is 5'5" and has green eyes, dark-brown hair, and a very light complexion. "I'm definitely a sunscreen person," she said. She has a PhD, works as a school psychologist, is married, but did not have children and was 35 when interviewed. Darien identifies as Lakota because his mother identifies as Lakota. Both of his parents are Indian and Caucasian, and he has one younger brother. He feels that U.S. society identifies him as a white man. He is 6', has very light complexion, gray-green eyes, and dark hair and was 38 when interviewed. He is married to a Polish woman and has one child. He works as a scientist for the Environmental Protection Agency, providing technical and financial assistance to tribes developing environmental programs. Mila was born in Mexico and became a U.S. citizen after coming here with her family when she was young. She is 5'2", has a light-brown complexion, brown eyes, and black hair, and was 23 years old and single when interviewed. She had recently graduated from college and worked in an administrative position in an urban school. Although she identifies as Mexican American, she also said, "I feel comfortable identifying myself as Native American because my family, my culture comes from there a long time ago. She has ancestors who were indigenous Indians in Mexico. She feels that U.S. society identifies her as a Mexican immigrant or as Mexican American. Alexandra was born on the Navajo reservation in Arizona and identifies by the name of her mother's clan, Tótsohnii, which translates into "Big Water Clan," as well as by her Navajo tribe's name, Diné. She said that people in U.S. society identify her as Latina and think she is from Mexico or Central America. She has a light-brown complexion, brown eyes, and black hair, is 5'5", and was 32 years old and single when interviewed. She is self-employed.

Lily's section is titled "Citizen Potawatomi" and Darien's is "Urban Indians." These two had intricate connections to American Indian life on reservations and in cities through Lily's mother, on the one hand, and through Darien's job, on the other. Like Anton's in the previous chapter, Mila's family was connected to indigenous Indians in Mexico; the title of her section is "Mexica." "Res-Girl" captures the fact that Alexandra is the only person in this chapter who was born on a reservation, although her family left to live in California when she was around 5 years old. I discuss their practices in digital and hip-hop cultures in sections titled "Virtual Presence," and "Presence of Hip-Hop" before concluding this chapter with a section titled "Listening to Spirits." Following the uses of terms by the interviewees, in this chapter "Native Americans" and "Natives" are used interchangeably with "American Indians." As I noted, the voices of these four have been used substantially in telling their stories. Clearly, the stories of American Indians are essential to understanding the kaleidoscopic story of the United States with all of its cataclysmic episodes and intrigues.

CITIZEN POTAWATOMI

Lily is enrolled in the Citizen Band Potawatomi Nation, her father's tribe. This tribe is in Shawnee, Oklahoma, but was formerly in the Great Lakes area. Enrollment rights vary from tribe to tribe, and in her tribe benefits included things like receiving a tribal ID, being able to vote in tribal elections, and other things such as mortgage loans and academic scholarships. Enrollment in her tribe required having a relative with a certain amount of ancestral blood, but some people are not able to be identified with the tribe because their ancestors may not have been included on the government lists of tribal members.

Lily has always been a bit secretive about her tribal membership. Disclosing it is a bit like "coming out," and she has to develop a lot of trust before she will talk about it. Or she feels it's often not worth the effort to get into all the details. "I'm going to have to go through at least a one-minute explanation. This is who I am. This is where I come from. These are my parents. I look like this; they don't. You know, it becomes this tiring experience." She's also sensitive because people might think she has been given favorable treatment in competitions, such as getting into graduate school. "People might think I was only here because of my ethnic background, you know, one of the boxes I checked on my application. So I kept it more private, even though I studied it." She feels she has to define her claim to being Indian American or that she has to prove her legitimacy. She also understands that she benefits from a lot of privilege because the U.S. society sees her as a white woman. "It's definitely shaped who I am," she said. "My day-to-day interactions are filtered through that. I know that there are a lot of fake people out there, and I don't, you know, want to be perceived as someone who is trying to get in on something that I'm not entitled to."

Lily has a close relationship with her mother, who raised her. They didn't have a lot of income coming into their family, and they were on welfare for the first few years of her life. She says her mom decided that education was the way out of poverty, so she continued going to school until she completed a doctorate degree. Her mother is Northern Cheyenne, Crow, and also of Danish ancestry. According to Lily, her mom "is much more phenotypically Native. She's got, you know, dark hair, dark eyes, dark skin, the strong bone structure of a Native person. You look at her and you know that she's got something in her." The visible contrasts between Lily and her mom are striking. "We look alike in that we have similar facial structure, but coloring is, you know, hundred percent different." Even as an adult her mom reminds her how shocked she was by the baby she gave birth to. "She was like, 'Who is this pink baby?'" She would jokingly tell Lily that she was adopted, and when they were out together people always thought her mom was her nanny or babysitter. Her father was born on a reservation and is much more mixed looking. He has a light complexion, brownish hair, and, like Lily, green eyes. However, she has never had a relationship with him and only sees him in photographs he left behind.

In Lily's mom's tribe, the blood-lines are maternally inherited, and because her mom's connection was through her father, she is not technically a tribe member. So Lily, who looks white, is enrolled in a tribe, while her mother, whose Indian identity is never questioned, is not. As a consequence, her mom has not been allowed to apply for certain jobs or to be on certain boards. "It's frustrating. It's maddening," Lily said. Nevertheless, her mom does extensive work with numerous tribes across many states. When Lily was 8 years old, they moved to Colorado for her mom to attend graduate school, and her mom immediately hooked up with American Indian student programs and started building relationships with the surrounding Indian communities. Lily would sometimes sleep on a sofa in her office while she was there studying.

After graduating with a doctorate, Lily's mom worked her entire professional career on different reservation communities in North and South Dakota, Montana, Arizona, and New Mexico. She took Lily with her when she went to work with different tribes, and from childhood on Lily got to see and experience the differing cultures of the various tribal groups. "You'll have what we call different bands of people, subgroups within a larger tribal community. So, there's this Cheyenne group, but then there's a Northern Cheyenne and Southern Cheyenne. In the Lakota tribe there's at least three or four different reservations, and they all consider themselves different bands of Lakotas. Each reservation community has its own set of issues, obviously its own culture. Within the Lakota tribe, for example, you have the Pine Ridge Reservation and the Rosebud Reservation. These are two very different communities. They have similar shared history but, you know, different circumstances now and in more recent history. So they consider themselves separate, but also part of the same larger group." While accompanying her mom while she worked on all of these reservations, Lily also saw lots of people who looked like her: "freckles, and lighter eyes, lighter hair; usually their skin was not quite as light," perhaps because of being outdoors more. All these experiences contributed to her understanding of herself as a Native person.

Lily was constantly aware of the swarm of stereotypes and other societal aggressions experienced by American Indians. Her grandfather was forcibly relocated to California in the 1920s. His youngest sister was identified as Negro on her birth certificate. The family lore is that it was just as bad or worse to be a Native American as to be a Negro. So identification as an Indian was shunned in many ways, and when embraced it was often in the context of blood quantum—how much Native blood one had. These things were directly linked to their oppression by the U.S. government. According to Lily, when Native people were relocated and removed from their lands, they were enrolled or put on a registry as a means of tracking and controlling them. Over time, tribal organizations formed different criteria for how to enroll members. It was all very sloppy and inconsistent across the country. Also, within different tribal groups being enrolled became something of a badge to flash. "You've got your tribal ID, and that proves that you're Native. It gives you that legitimacy," she said, "and it determines who can participate in tribal affairs, tribal government, who can access scholarships, housing benefits, health benefits. The [U.S.] government has the Indian Health Service (HIS) that gives health care to Native people, and my mom can't go to IHS and get health treatment, but I can." Even in university programs and admissions, Lily feels there are instances where an American Indian cannot simply state his or her identity; it has to be proven with a tribal ID. "No other group has to do that," she said.

Her great-grandfather was used as an extra in Hollywood movies and had to dress up as "the Indian," "the redskin." The persistence of these stereotypes is clearly painful for Lily, who said, "I don't think you can talk about using that term *red* without talking about our nation's acceptance for using it for mascots, sports teams, or you know, using Native peoples' names as car names." Picture Washington Redskins, Atlanta Braves, Jeep Cherokees (and the now defunct Comanche), General Motors' Pontiacs (whose hood ornaments were in the visage of Chief Pontiac). In the 1930s General Motors discontinued a model named the Viking that had prompted protests by outraged Scandinavians, but these shameful stereotypes of Native Americans continue in the United States. "It's a really hurtful word when I hear it," Lily continued. "It makes me angry. I think of the stereotypical cartoon Indian with the red face, the big nose, and, you know, saying, "How." Or white people dressed up as Native people and have their skins painted like a reddish brown. Um, where I get the most frustrated and pissed off with is that it's still something we see. . . . Why is this still okay? Are we the last group where it's okay to be so publicly racist? You know, like not even trying to hide it."

Painfully, some Native people make within-group distinctions among themselves, and Lily has experienced microaggressions in this regard, in part because of being seen as white. Between college and graduate school, for example, she interned at an Indian Health Services organization in Washington, DC, that had a mixed group of Native and Caucasian employees. Positioned somewhat between these two groups, she reflected on having a number of really negative experiences with both. Although she noted that some of the negativity might be coming from their being burned out as government workers, some of the things that happened to her were, in her words, "really, really hateful." She has also experienced similar negativity from other "people of color," such as the occasion of going out for dinner with her fiancé, who is a Filipino immigrant, and another mixed couple. Jokingly, she said their children will be "'Whindipinos'—white, Indian, Filipinos." The tone at the dinner changed when her fiancé was verbally criticized by the African American man in the other couple as "an Asian boy dating his white girlfriend." Use of the word "boy," misidentification of Lily as "white," the comment coming from an African American who himself was dating a Caucasian woman—all this is tragically racist on so many levels. Her hope for her future children is that they never have to experience these kinds of racist acts.

Lily expanded these issues beyond the problems of the stereotypes and microaggressions because they open deeper wounds that have been inflicted on American Indians. She talked about how other groups had been brought to this country for labor and profits, and how "a lot of murder happened to these people," but they also needed to be kept alive to be useful. Native people, on the other hand, stood in the way of "manifest destiny," the belief by whites in the United States that they were destined to expand across North America because they felt they and their institutions had special virtues. "Many groups of Natives have been completely eradicated," she said. "There's lost languages, lost cultures, lost tribes. Lots of California tribal groups are completely gone, you know. There's not one person left, and they were wiped out in a matter of, you know, months." She talked about all the relatively recent stories in the United States of mass shootings, mass genocides. The horrific shootings in Orlando had been characterized in the media as the worst in American history. Discussions of this unfortunate event with many Native American friends also surfaced how invisible the plight of American Indians is in this nation's consciousness. "In the Sand Creek massacre in the 1800s, hundreds of women and children were shot in cold blood and their bodies were mutilated," she said.

Additionally, Lily pointed out that not only were many Native peoples wiped out; there also was intentional destruction of the resources needed to sustain themselves—food sources, fur trading, wiping out the buffalo. She talked about the idea of historical trauma from these events being carried on from generation to generation and revealed in things like higher instances of substance abuse, suicide, domestic violence, and alcoholism, particularly in rural Native communities that have larger incidences of issues than any other community. "White people gave Native people alcohol as a way of keeping them more content, subdued, you know, jovial," Lily said, and she felt the title of this chapter was appropriate. "Red Rum" spelled backward is "murder."

URBAN INDIANS

Toward the end of the section above, Lily drew attention to American Indians in rural communities. Darien focuses attention on Indians in urban settings as well. He works with numerous American Indian groups in his role of providing technical and financial support as a scientist for the U.S. Environmental Protection Agency (EPA). His educational background included majoring in environmental policy analysis and planning and minoring in Native studies and geographic information systems. He said that sometimes the terms *urban reservation*, and *urban res* are also used to indicate the current spatial, socio-cultural, and political contexts of some of American Indians.

Darien defined and contrasted urban Indian communities to reservation communities saying that urban Indian communities consist of a collection of individuals from diverse backgrounds who are tied together by place and possibly by common activities and common history. Things that led to these communities were relocation programs of the 1950s that brought a lot of Native Americans from reservations to urban areas. Oakland was one of these relocation centers. Others, like himself, came because of being in the military or having relatives in the military. His father was in the air force. Also Native Americans came to the city for the same reasons as other groups—jobs, education, city life. Because Native American communities in cities come from many different tribal backgrounds and some have lost access or connections to their families and tribes, a kind of urban pan-Indian culture emerged through the adoption and blending of cultural practices and perspectives from the various groups. As a Lakota person, his closest reservation is that of the Rosebud Sioux Tribe in South Dakota. He gave the example of how urban Indians who are not Lakota will end their prayers in the Lakota way with words that mean "all of my relatives, all my relations." In the Lakota tradition, "to pray, we pray for everybody. We don't just pray for ourselves," Darien said. "So when I think of an urban Indian community, I don't think of one tribe; I don't think of one history, or one story collection. And the approach for engaging the urban Indian community is *inclusive,* regardless of tribe, regardless of history, regardless of racial makeup."

In his work with federally recognized tribal governments, a contrast that Darien sees between urban Indians and those on reservations is that because of the politics of the tribal governments, the latter tend to be more *exclusive* than *inclusive*. For example, he is not able to work with some of the Native Americans from the Bay Area because they're apparently un-recognized. He's obligated to work with the elected representatives in each tribe, but it's exclusive in that some people who are descendants of the tribe are not enrolled. Especially in California, there's an epidemic of disenroll-ment of people who have formally belonged to the tribe through a process of having their identity, their political identity, their legal affiliation with the tribe taken away. Although Indian people included and excluded each other before, the system in place now is one imposed by the federal government stemming from the Indian Reorganization Act of 1932, which created tribal governments. "They said we need to set up figureheads to run tribes who *we* can deal with," Darien noted. "So we have now, with the tribal councils; we have the chairmen and we have several elected officials; and that's not a traditional concept. It was given to us. So, yeah, that was the first thing, working with a tribal government that's not representative of who we are, and our ideals, and our culture."

Darien detailed a bit of how these tribal governments actually work. To understand them one has to think of the tribe as a political entity instead of a collection of people of the same ancestry or history. As a political entity, the tribe is able to establish its own membership, and the definition of what constitutes a member can change in an instant. He gave several examples of how variable definitions of membership could be. "So you can say the litmus test is that you need to have one out of your four grandparents to have been a tribal member. Or it may be that you have a fraction of blood, maybe you're an 8th, or you're a 16th. Maybe it's that for your dad's tribe you need to be a matrilineal descendant. So even if your father is [of matri-lineal descent], if your mother is not, then you belong to your mother's tribe. So we have situations where elected officials can say we're going to take the charter or the constitution; there are different ways tribes are made political entities, and just change the definition [of membership]. They take a vote on it, and then that changes. So you can add people or delete people based on that."

The insider/outsider legacies of imposing "foreign" institutional struc-tures on the cultures of American Indians as well as their massive reloca-tions shaped their cultural identities and practices. Darien gave a personal example. "As a Native person, as a Lakota person, I have a way of living, and ideals, a way of being, a way of being generous. It's the way we live," he said. So I'm grateful that I have some connection still to who I am, where I come from, and teachings and people. But one of the ways living in an ur-ban setting has shaped my own identity is you're removed physically; you're removed from the history; you're removed from the people. So you live outside. In a lot of ways I feel included, but also I'm an outsider, right? For example, if I go to a reservation somebody might say, 'Oh, look, Darien's here. He's visiting,' instead of, 'He's come home.'"

Darien talked further about connections to land and consequences of being removed from it. "Part of being Lakota is a connection to the land. It all starts with the land," he said. "We talk about sovereign people, you know, sovereign without the land? There's an issue about how a certain group is polluting our water, right? Or, the U.S. Forest Service has raised the level of our dams, flooding our sacred sites. . . . And people would ask me, 'Hey, why don't you come to this public meeting we're going to? Can you come and march with us'? And I'd have to tell them [to really address these issues] you need a lawyer, you need a political advocate, or you need an engineer." He also talked about another solution, that of getting the education needed to be more effectively involved in these issues. He feels that social justice for Native Americans around land and environmental issues is served by also having the scientific and technical skills to be able to engage and make a difference.

Darien said that people in society identify him as Caucasian, as a white man. Yet if it's summer and he is wearing his hair long, people then think he's mixed race. He was born in California and has never lived on a reservation. He identifies as Lakota because his mother does. Within this tradition, he has also been "gifted" with a Lakota name but said it's a name that you kind of keep to yourself. "You don't share it with everybody. And it's more for identification in the afterlife," he said. Although he embraces a Lakota identity, he made it clear that this inherently means seeing yourself first and foremost as a human being. I return to this point in the conclusion section of this chapter. Darien has a younger brother with a different father, who is Chinese, and his mother would joke, "He looks so much more Indian than you." On both sides of his family, he has a Native grandparent and a Caucasian grandparent. So, in addition to the Lakota tribe, his ancestry goes back to England, Austria, Hungary, and France. His 5-year-old son has this lineage combined with that of his Polish mother.

Because Darien is mixed, he sometimes chooses how to identify. "On the census, some might say I'm Lakota; for work, Native American; my driver's license, I'm white. Yeah, there are layers to my identification depending on how much information I'm allowed to present and what the purpose of the identification is." Within the cosmology of being Native American, of being Lakota, however, Darien understands identity to be more comprehensive. "[If] we were talking about how to change the way we think, and how to keep people from having to choose and put themselves in a box, I think the conversation shouldn't be limited to human beings. How I was raised, we respected animals and plants for the beings that they were. So bears were beings; bears were to be respected; bears were teachers, right? We learned from animals. We lived alongside them. I mean, there's a difference, but in our worldview we all belong and this conversation about races of people and colors of people is very—I wouldn't know the term, but it's 'anthro.' I guess I would say it's human focused."

Darien used the symbol of the medicine wheel to describe more of the Native American cosmology. It has four colors, and some might say these indicate four major races, but he quickly noted, "I'm no more white than you are black; we're all shades." The medicine wheel is actually a symbol used for understanding and connecting people to each other and to all things. "Most things we do are in a circle," he said. "It's a symbol used for understanding. So most things we do are in a circle. When we pray, we pray in a circle. When we set up camp, we set up in a circle. When we gather, we sit in a circle. When we have a dance, we dance in a circle. And so it's a representation of the universe, of everything."

MEXICA

Mila's connection to Indian ancestors is through Mexico rather than the United States. She was born in Mexico and came to the United States with her mother and brother when she was 5 years old, her mom escaping from domestic violence. Mila has not personally returned to Mexico since she came to the United States. At 23 years old, she had just graduated from college. Although she identifies as Mexican American, she also strongly identifies with her indigenous Indian roots. Her grandfather and great-grandfather were indigenous Indians in Mexico. "I have to be very flexible and versatile," she said, "because I'm in a place where I can't be fully indigenous; I can't be fully American; I can't be fully Mexican. I just have to be very flexible." In part, because she doesn't know the exact tribe that her Indian ancestors are from, she uses the word "Mexica" as a term that she feels captures several sides of her identity as indigenous Indian, as being from Mexico, and as Mexican American. The word "Mexico" itself comes from an indigenous language, she said. She also identifies as Native American, but not in the restrictive sense of its applying to only the United States. "It's not necessarily divided by North or South or Central America, or anything like that," she noted. Similar to Anton in the previous chapter, she sees America as the land between the two seas.

Mila and her brother, who is 2 years younger, are both fluent in Spanish. How he identifies himself, however, is very different from how she does. He is very proud of having light skin and connects himself to ancestors in Spain and having money and haciendas and all that goes with that. He is also proud of being Mexican, but he associates himself with being like a "charro," a fancy Mexican cowboy. Interestingly, except for her and her mom and brother, everyone else in Mila's extended family in the United States is really tall, light skinned, and blond and have either green or blue eyes. Compared with them, her immediate family is much darker and shorter.

"My mom would get a lot of bad comments from her siblings saying, 'Hey, your kids are gonna be the uglier ones.'"

Mila connects with her indigenous roots in a number of ways. She considers herself a healing woman. When she was a little girl, her mother would tell her to not pick flowers or branches because it hurts the plants, that it was like tearing somebody's arm off. On reflection, she felt these perspectives linked to those of her ancestors so that she was starting to get involved with those connections without really knowing it. She sought out people and groups in her immediate area that taught her more about indigenous medicines and ways of living. "I've learned that it's the woman in the group that carries the smoke and the medicine for all the people," she said. "I've learned how to work with [the special kind of cup that holds] the incense. I've learned to work with different plants and [to make] medicine and burn them so that I can provide some harmony in, you know, our dances, in people's prayers, doing different cleansings for people. So, yeah, that's kind of how I've evolved over time and how I've kind of harnessed who I am a little bit more." She further described how she has learned about other cultures with different traditions in order to increase her understanding by going to various ceremonies. "I've been to teepee ceremonies, which is not what I'm used to. But I've been allowed to enter those spaces and be mindful and respectful and be able to pray with them." She also goes to Alcatraz Island every year for Indigenous People's Day to participate in that ceremony. Mila's mother is curious about Mila's attraction to Native cultural practices and perspectives and has attended a few ceremonies with her. However, her mother is Catholic and still would like for Mila to go to mass and ultimately adopt Catholic religious traditions, and that's an area of contention between them.

Another identity connection Mila makes to her ancestors is through dance. She started doing Aztec dancing when she was in middle school. She was invited by a friend who had been doing it for a while to join her in Aztec dance classes. She loved the classes and continued dancing throughout high school. These earlier dance classes did not make strong spirituality connections, but after high school she joined another dance group that had a teacher from Mexico who really emphasized the indigenous and spiritual aspects of the dance. She taught the philosophies behind the dance steps or why they were done to certain songs. Mila learned songs in an Aztec language and other sacred things that could be done and that were needed for a people to heal. She said, "We sing prayers and we give thanks, you know? We cry; we encourage one another. And so that's another thing that I've been really lucky to have and it's just kind of amazing for me to know that those practices can, you know, those things can still exist for us. Because a lot of people died in order for that to continue." Like Darien, Mila talked about the cultural exchange between different indigenous groups—the songs, the dances, the philosophies. She noted, for example, that there are a lot of Lakota philosophies embedded in those of her ancestors because there was a lot of knowledge exchanges between them and the indigenous people in Mexico.

In these Native cultural community settings, Mila learned many things that influenced her sense of herself. "It was kind of like college where individuals can come and learn the different sciences within our culture," she said. She learned about astronomy and about different energies intersecting the physical and social world. She participated in a ceremony in which she was given an indigenous name that reflects the time and space in which she was born and the nature of her personal energy that can be harnessed to direct her life. She said there are 20 energies, and in different people there are different energies. Everybody has all 20, but some of them are more prominent in each person. Water is one of these energies, and it's a big one for healing. But Mila noted that there is a whole science behind these concepts, and it takes a lot of study to really understand them. For example, rather than having a binary sense of gender, this orientation suggests that every person possesses male and female energies with aspects of each being dominant or subdued in different ways in different people. Since everyone already carries these energies, people would not be seen as fixed or needing to be fixed in any specific orientation, like a tightly defined sexual orientation, for example. From this perspective, she feels there is acceptance for the full range of orientations that people may have because it's understood that everyone already has all these energies within them. "It's been really important for me in having a more open view and just being mindful of other people. You know, maybe they're having a bad day or maybe there's something going on inside them that's not allowing them to heal. It's giving me a lifestyle and a mentality that I carry with me and express wherever I go."

RES-GIRL

Alexandra was born and lived until she was 5 on a Navajo reservation in Arizona close to states that come together as the Four Corners. Her mother and father worked outside the reservation, but Alexandra said her mother was definitely a "res-girl." During that time she was cared for by her grandmother, a sheep herder and master weaver. Then her family moved to a small city in Northern California. Her perception of this particular part of the state was, "It was all about how much money you could show that you had." There, also, it was automatically thought she was Mexican or Latina. Although people in society may sometimes see her as an American Indian, most often they think she is an immigrant from Mexico or Central America. She speaks a little Spanish, yet it was common growing up in California for other kids, or their parents, or sometimes teachers, or even strangers to start conversations with her in Spanish. She gave an example of being in a large grocery store and having a woman begin speaking to her in Spanish. She decided to tell her that she was Native American, but the way the woman looked at her, it was clear that she was thinking, "I can't believe you don't speak Spanish." These incidents have happened many times. At one point she asked a few Hispanic friends how she should respond when other Hispanics asked her where she was from, meaning what country. "Some of my friends didn't understand how to say you're Native American, you're indigenous to the Americas. You know, here, this is your home."

How Alexandra identifies and introduces herself is reminiscent of the point made in Chapter 2 of needing to go back at least seven generations. She begins by saying she is "Tótsohnii," born for the "Ke' tl' ah." These are from the Diné language, and Diné is the Native name for her Navajo tribe. "The way I was raised, you introduced yourself not only to people, but to the world, to the universe, to the elements, you know? I would identify my maternal mother's clan that is for me Tótsohnii, which translates into Big Water Clan. Then I would introduce my father's clan that is not Navajo. He's not Diné, but from another tribe in Southern Arizona. So Ke' tl' ah in Diné means 'one whose foot is sandal-ed.' Like, it's describing the type of sandal the desert people would wear. That's how my grandma named me because in my family that's what they called the Pima band of natives."

A tradition in Navajo culture is for the grandmother to give a name (or a nickname) to the child. She calls Alexandra "Miss Papago," which is another way of saying "Asdzaa Ke' tl' ah" where "Asdzaa" means "miss" or "woman." So a rough translation of her native name is the phrase "sandal-wearing Pima Indian person" or "the girl whose foot is sandal-ed." Therefore, her clan is Tótsohnii born for the Ke' tl' ah, while her mom's clan is Tótsohnii born for the Kinyaa'áanii—the "Big Water Clan" born for the "Towering House Clan." Consequently, in introducing herself, Alexandra would identify her clan and her mother's clan, and if her father was Diné, she would also introduce his mother's clan and his father's clan. "It's an introduction of where I'm from, who I am, who my ancestors are behind me, and the reason why I'm here," she said. "That's kind of the main introduction for me as a Diné woman. I identify as Diné because my mom is Diné, and my grandma's Diné, and so on. For everyone who is not part of my family, it's Navajo because it's the most known, but for me with my family, it's Diné, which basically means the ones, the people."

Introducing oneself in prayer and ceremony as well as in daily life is also done by acknowledging and calling on one's ancestors. As a Navajo woman, Alexandra was taught to be up early and greet each sunrise with prayer and offerings of corn pollen or white cornmeal in meditation and appreciation of the first beam of light giving birth to each new day. A Navajo woman blesses herself from the earth up. "Even your shoes represent that first dawn rising." A Navajo man, on the other hand, blesses himself from the sky down. Either way, the Navajo person shows connectedness to all the elements in the universe in prayers for herself or himself, for their families, for the human family, and for whatever may be in one's heart at the time. "Especially if you're in a Diné ceremony, you are constantly introducing your clan system, your mother's side, your father's side," she said. "And it's kind of like you have your maternal grandparents on your right and your paternal grandparents on your left. The paternal energies maybe are ready to discipline you and tell you what is good, what is right, and what is wrong. The maternal energies, they're more, you know, calm and nurturing. It's a balance." She talked about how her grandmother would tell her the characteristics of a Diné woman and how her goal was to be in harmonious balance." Alexandra called this "Diné being-ness. Being in balance in your surroundings, in your world, in your mind, in your body. That's also the reason Diné people stress praying in the morning is that balance in life. And ending your prayer, there's a word meaning everything is good, is beautiful, is harmonious. Everything is in balance."

Alexandra discussed the importance of traditional stories in shaping the identities of Navajo children. Some of these stories teach that there was a time when animals, birds, humans, fish, etcetera, all could speak to each other and understand each other. There are also stories of the trickster coyote that taught that things are not always as they appear. There are stories that go back to the beginning of time, to the beginning of the world and the coming together of sun spirits, earth spirits, wind spirits, and water spirits. "In the mornings we're praying to the spirits that come up, like the sun beings that come up as it's rising," she said. "And we're taught that these beings are, you know, very sacred, very holy. Our elders taught us that these beings are looking to see who's up and out there putting down offerings. Who's out there asking for blessings. And it goes into our whole lifestyle."

Alexandra made it clear, however, that prayers to these spirit beings are not just to ask for individual blessings. They also are moments of internal reflection on the individual's connectedness to everything else. "We grow up knowing that even putting down an offering of corn pollen, which is so delicate, and petite, and tiny, is expressing the idea that each cell is like that. They're in the forming of these tiny particles as well as the entire universe. The tiny particles are connected to everything else that's in the universe. Alexandra has a younger sister and brother who are 12 and 13 years younger, respectively, than she is. Born in California, they did not have experiences of living any significant part of their lives outside cities. Alexandra feels that some of the connectedness inherent in the cosmology of her people is lost when Native Americans move away from their lands into cities. Of course, additional dissipation of their cultures occurs through indoctrination into Christianity. She felt intense cultural dissonance herself coming to California as a child and having to try to adjust to very different people, a different language, different smells, just a completely different way of living. "I was completely culture shocked," she said, "trying to self-identify, trying to understand both worlds. When I meet with other Native people, they feel that same duality of how to act in a world that doesn't understand who or what Native American culture is." She feels she has learned how to act in this context because she embraces an identity not only as a Diné woman but also as a Native American indigenous woman. "In just regular-day society, I feel I have to represent such a large ancestral background that, you know, has almost been stained. So whether or not I'm teaching some person or just representing my people, it's like, 'I am here, you know; I'm very much like, I deserve to be here.'"

Like Mila, Alexandra talked about the acceptance of a range of energies or spirits in Native people. "In my culture," she said, "we have also been taught in our old creation stories that there are people with two spirits in one, male and female. You know, it wasn't totally looked down on to see a male do women's work. Basically, people with the two spirits were also part of, you know, our community. They held certain medicines, and maybe they were thought to be more spiritual or in tune to be able to be with both male and female spirits." Alexandra didn't feel that the term "bisexual" captured what she was trying to say about the sense of two spirits existing in one body. "I don't necessarily know that there were terms like that, similar to that," she said. "But it was more just thought of, you know, as people with two spirits, and I don't think it was so foreign to see a male maybe dress in a woman's skirt." Her grandfather told her that these considerations did not just occur all of a sudden in recent times. Instead, it was a part of the community, a part of life.

VIRTUAL PRESENCE

Lily was not an early adopter of digital media. She didn't start emailing until after college and didn't have a cellphone until she was in graduate school in 2004. She didn't get on Facebook until 2009, and even in 2016 she was not maintaining an active presence. "I'll share articles or post a picture of my dog," she said, "but I don't really do a lot of, like, selfies or anything like that." However, she does use Facebook to stay in touch and keep abreast of activities in the Native community as well as to sustain contact with people she has met professionally and activists who are Native or work on Native issues. "I read all of that stuff; I try to keep current on it, and, you know, sometimes I will bring it up if it's something that's related work, since I'm in education."

Like Lily, Darien was not an enthusiast of social media, even though his stepfather was on the front end of key technological innovations. Only after he was 30 did he join Facebook, and that was to stay in touch with Native student groups on campus. "They said you have to get Facebook, otherwise you won't know when we have events." At the time he was about a decade older than other undergrads and felt more like a big brother. He soon begin to see the utility of digital tools for research both for his personal focus on Native American issues and for his academic focus on science. This was particularly helpful for getting information on treaties and tribal council bylaws and other things not available in written texts. Yet he said his use of digital media was "less about culture and more about science."

Although she is 23, Mila doesn't use social media much. She doesn't have Facebook; she does have LinkedIn but does not use it. She will play games on her phone, however, such as the Pokémon Go game that was a craze around the time she was interviewed. Basically, she doesn't get very involved with social media "because sometimes it feels like a waste of time." Instead, she sees her time being better used in self-care, physically, emotionally, and mentally. "I don't have time and also it just seems like it consumes, it could consume so much of me when I could be focusing on myself." In this regard, it seemed like she would at least have followed her mentor's Facebook page because of all that she has learned from her mentor about Native cultures and energies, but Mila said, "I've decided not to. Yeah, I've decided not to."

Alexandra's feelings about digital culture are akin to Mila's. "I am not on social media that much because I can get like Facebook, for example, and then 2 hours of my life will be gone, and I don't even know what I got from all that scrolling up and down. So I kind of am not a big fan of Facebook." She thinks a lot of people use Facebook because they need personal validation through all their posts and pictures. Her mom is on Facebook, but they are not Facebook friends. Alexandra does text and go online when she has a specific purpose. "For the American Indian Film Institute, for example, I'm relearning how to put stuff out there—post, tweet, email, blast, you know." But she prefers to talk directly to people over the phone, or to actually meet and talk face to face. Prior to being interviewed, she had just returned from the Navajo lands in Arizona, and she described how despite continual rains, everything was so beautiful. Just being outside, breathing the air, and seeing the sheep, and thoroughly enjoying all these sights and sounds and smells—these are the experiences she cherishes.

PRESENCE OF HIP-HOP

Darien, Mila, and Alexandra talked about their engagement with hip-hop. I didn't explore this with Lily. Darien grew up in the 1980s and noted that it was called rap rather than hip-hop then. He gravitated toward those artists who were creating "conscious rap" rather than those rapping about money, guns, drugs, violence, and the denigration of women. He said that he always felt a part of hip-hop culture growing up, the breakdancing, the graffiti artists, the MCs, the DJs, but as he's gotten older, he feels he is not a part of it now. At her age, Mila definitely feels a part of what's happening now and said with a big smile, "I love hip-hop. I really like it. I like the music. I like the street culture that comes with it. Sometimes, even the clothing." She quickly qualified these statements by saying it was actually old-school hip-hop, listening to its story line, that she liked rather than what's out there now. "I think a lot of the hip-hop now is about the three same things, cars, money, and girls, and I get tired of hearing about these same three things." She listens to contemporary hip-hop music because "the beat is still cool" but prefers the older music. She sees no conflict between being into contemporary hip-hop and being into recovering and practicing indigenous Mexican Indian culture. "I have to be very flexible and versatile because I'm in a place where I just have to be like that. I can't be full-on indigenous. I can't be full-on American. I can't be full-on Mexican. I have to be very flexible."

Hip-hop was also big for Alexandra, particularly growing up in the Bay Area as a kid, a teen, and an adult. She would rock all the hip-hop radio stations, play her music loud, wear baggy jeans and tight shirts, use the brusque language, frequent the hip-hop clubs, and hang out with some of the up-and-coming artists. She also had older cousins who were DJs, so just visiting them was also immersion in hip-hop. She was attracted to the poetry in hip-hop. "Like, oh, what are they saying; what is he saying; what is she saying? Then like, oh wow, you get it. Mind blown!" Also, in looking back she said, "It was the beats, yeah, like in our culture. The drumbeat is like your mom's heartbeat, like the womb of the woman. It's the earth, right? And yeah, it's always been very much like how does this rhythm go? This rhythm sounds great!"

The earlier sections on Mila and Alexandra described their quests for Native culture recovery, learning about traditional medicines or spreading corn pollen to greet the sunrise, but their discussions here also show that there were significant intersections and interactions with hip-hop culture all along the way. This sometimes created odd cultural conflicts or novel cultural congruencies. Alexandra talked about spending summers with her uncle and his kids, going to different powwows, all the while with her headphones locked in place listening to rap music until she fell asleep. Or she would go to ceremonies with her mom but not follow the tradition of women wearing dresses. Navajo women also are never, ever supposed to cut their hair. "I definitely attribute hip-hop culture to being part of my rebellion during my teenage years," Alexandra said. "Yeah, baggy jeans, tight shirts, you know, this is also contradictory to my mom and how she raised me." Yet her mom also understood the hip-hop influences on almost all kids at the time. Beyond rebelling against family and tribal traditions, however, Alexandra, Mila, and Darien identified with the themes of rebellion against societal oppression in some of the rap music and other hip-hop practices. These three interviewees were from different Native tribes, but hip-hop was a culture and language they shared on the "urban res."

LISTENING TO SPIRITS

Alexandra talked about influences from the spirits of ancestors. Mila talked about drawing on energies of the sun, wind, water, and earth. Darien talked about the being-ness of animals like bears and how they can be our teachers. Lily talked about lost languages, lost cultures, and lost tribes and about hopes for her future kids. Each of these Native people is on a quest to reconnect and restore something essentially human that has been lost. It's a similar quest to those whose stories are told in previous chapters. Ultimately, it's a quest for all of us—to be connected, to be restored, to belong.

This quest is imperative, and perspectives of the interviewees in this book offer prospects for directions to take. Like those in previous chapters, the interviewees in this chapter delineate the hyperdiversity that's reflected and the stereotyping that's encountered as they construct their unique identities in relief to those ascribed by society. The hyperdiversity of Lily, Darien, Mila, and Alexandra is revealed through their complex positionalities in connection with different tribes, varying personal histories, and specific cultural and geographic contexts surrounding their development. They evidenced substantial "within-group distinctions" in their families and within and across tribes. Racial indeterminacy was prominently in play in each of their lives. Their work to construct their own identities challenged binaries and included specific identity rejections as well as self-selected practices and the creation of affinities with specific social, tribal, educational, and community groups. All this was enabled by varying uses of digital texts and tools, while hip-hop culture intersected with and influenced how they identified themselves. Through it all, each one suffered painful stereotyping and discrimination from being perceived in various relational identities or only in terms of homogenized groups, or not seen at all with respect to who they really are. The gross media images of Native people, the appropriation of their names for sports teams, mascots, and automobiles, the pollution of their lands and contamination of their water sources, these American inventions make us scream along with Lily, "Why is this still okay!" It's a question and also an accusation—of capitalism, colonialism, racism, and white supremacy toasting their feast on the earth's bounty and its people, with red rum.

One direction out of this morass is offered by Darien. In other parts of his interview, he pointed out that it was not just Lakota traditions that needed to be restored. "The way I was raised and the teachings I had are of how to be a good human being. Lakota just means a person," he said. "It doesn't mean a certain race of people. It's a person. The traders that came and lived with us and married in, we didn't say, 'Well, they're half.' . . . Instead of separating, we're talking about how to be good human beings." He further discussed how in addition to Native Americans and Africans being displaced from their lands and cultures, European American have also been disconnected from aspects of their identities and homogenized simply as Caucasians or whites. "In trying to understand who we are in terms of values and culture, we have to remember to be inclusive of these other people who have also lost their way. . . . We've all lost our culture in a lot of ways," he said. He also noted that it was not just his Native American ancestors that he was struggling to reconnect with. "I'd be very willing if my ancestors were closer to learn Hungarian. My mom grew up in the Alps, gathering in the woods. I'd love to learn about that as well. I'm also from other places, and I'd like to not only acknowledge that for myself, but also try to bring people into the conversation as well. It's human focused. It also embraces the diversity and differences of all beings."

The interconnectedness and interdependence of human beings and *all* things that Darien expressed are critical for our survival. He also talked about rediscovering old solutions to new problems, that hopeful directions for the future are rooted in the past. Scholars have convincingly argued that viable directions are not within the structure of the tree root and its image of vertical hierarchy, however. Rather, they are in the structure of the rhizome and limitless connectivity. For example, Deleuze and Guattari (1980) developed a theory that used the rhizome as a metaphor for modes of knowledge and models of society as an alternative to hierarchical and binary modes of organization and that allow for multiple, nonhierarchical connections and representations. A rhizome in the natural world is characterized by hyper-connectivity and novel, interdependent intersections, even across species. As a model for culture, a rhizomatic orientation resists hierarchies and simple binaries as productive structures for relationships among people. This way of understanding human potential for connectedness, balance, and virtue is clearly embedded in Native Indian cosmologies, though rarely attributed to them. It is as rarely seen as Alexandra laying out tiny corn pollen particles, and greeting the sunrise, and listening to spirits.

CHAPTER 9

Micro-Cultures

I doubt there's someone else out there who has the exact background that I do, my exact combinations. Those reference group definitions aren't helpful in defining my characteristics.

—Halle (March 30, 2016)

Findings from the interview data discussed in the previous five chapters as revealed through 13 coded themes indicated again and again that each person is utterly unique yet intricately connected to others in fluid relationships and dynamic cultural contexts. Their myriad constructions of identity cannot be productively accounted for within ascribed categories of race. Paraphrasing Halle's quote at the beginning of the chapter, there is no one out there with her exact combination of characteristics (identity components), and racial reference groups aren't helpful for defining her. Based on findings from the 20 interviews, I argue that the idea of micro-cultures, or any idea that similarly captures the significance of human variability in identity constructions, should replace the idea of race. I further suggest that deconstructing race starts with each person's rejecting ascribed racial identifications in their daily lives as well as in institutional frameworks. "Acceptance" of racial identifications is itself racist. It perpetuates the use of race as a classification for people and, therefore, contributes to racism's fundamental expression. I hasten to add that this view may not be held by the interviewees. My claim, however, is that this view is evidenced and justified by what I learned from their lives, collaterally with what I learned from scholarship and literature. A key piece of that scholarship is Banks's (2013) concepts of "microcultures" (without the hyphen) and "multiple group memberships," which I have built on and will address in the final section of this chapter.

At the end of Chapter 6, I offered a more viable way of identifying people in this country that borrowed from how Hispanics were identified as an ethnic group rather than a race in the U.S. census of 2010. This was consistent with what many interviewees were saying about needing to identify directly with their immediate families and ancestors. So I put forth the following consideration for identifying people in the census: *A person's identity can be viewed as the heritages, lineages, nationality groups, or country of birth of the person or the countries of birth of the person's parents or ancestors*. This definition allows people to identify themselves in connection with generations and geographies rather than in connection to race. This does not account for ways that activity-based identities also shape how individuals identify themselves, but it is specifically an attempt to redefine identity for purposes of the census and other societal institutions. Sexual orientation also is not addressed in this definition, and, of course, there are contexts in which it must be accounted for. Consequently, a more comprehensive sense of individual identity is the concept of micro-cultures.

As a framework for discussing the findings from the interviews, the concept of micro-cultures indicates the wide array of distinct components that make up the entire set of personal-cultural positioning, practices, choices, and perspectives engaged in and enacted by each individual in society. Micro-cultural identities are the mercurial combinations of "identity components" that merge at the intersection of individual, cultural, language, institutional, geographic, historical, and environmental experiences. It's critical to see that many micro-cultural components of identity are shaped or initiated through activity (Gee, 2013), through participatory practices that are consequences of specific choices made by individuals. In this chapter I relook at three considerations of how micro-cultural identities are manifested in the lives of the interviewees to make several concluding points from this research. One consideration is framed by Steele's (2010) concept of "identity contingencies." The other two considerations further address how the interviewees' participation in "digital culture" and "hip-hop culture" yielded additional components of their identities that problematize notions of race. I conclude this chapter with a discussion of how micro-cultural identities operate in "interstitial spaces" and use that to explore an idea of transitive belonging.

IDENTITY CONTINGENCIES

Steele (2010) and numerous other researchers building on his work have indicated how identity contingencies such as skin color, facial features, hair type, and body size are linked to how people are socially constructed and treated in society as well as how they interact with the world. Stereotypes associated with identity contingencies can forcefully and problematically shape people's identities and development. One problem is the stereotype response in which the stress of being seen stereotypically can actually increase the probability of responding consistent with the negative implications of the stereotype. It can also be argued that a person's stress can be increased by perceiving another person in line with a stereotype, with the implication of the stereotype generating discernible stress linked to this misperception. In introducing each interviewee, I indicated the complexion of their skin, the color of their hair and eyes, and their height because these are identity contingencies that can color what people see and result in inequitable penalties for some and unearned privileges for others. I will argue from the interview data, however, that things do not have to be this way.

It was important for Samantha, Sasha, James, and Ryan to acknowledge being perceived as white in order to visibilize and in some ways resist the unearned privilege that comes with that positionality. But their experiences within the veil of whiteness were strikingly different. As an immigrant, Sasha had been ambivalent about staking claim to that identity and there were times when she openly claimed that she was not white. James engaged whiteness from a different social class perspective and also learned what it was like to not be privileged by whiteness during his years in Taiwan. Ryan's identification as queer brought his being seen only as a white male into contention, and he actively rejected and challenged the construction of that stereotype.

Anton, Lily, and Darien were also generally perceived as white; however, they never saw a real need to make their access to privilege visible, perhaps because they had alternative experiences that made it clear how tenuous investments in the idea of whiteness can be in the United States. Either way, what might appear to be a defining contingency, like being a white person, is shown to not be definitional at all outside intentional forces within society to homogenize people in that category. As discussed in Chapter 2, Baldwin (1971) quoted Malcolm X to Margaret Mead to challenge her to see that "white is a state of mind. The great question, my dear, is how one begins to attack that state of mind?" (159). In this regard, I noted in Chapter 2 that more than making conferred privileges visible, Du Bois and Baldwin called on whites to disavow their loyalty to whiteness. This was seen in the identity rejections and challenges to binaries and stereotypes described for some of the interviewees. Identity rejections were ways that some interviewees consciously declined identification of themselves by race, gender, or sexual orientation, and intentional acts to disrupt reductive conceptions of themselves were seen as challenging binaries. Consequently, one way to attack whiteness as a state of mind is to become race traders—people who reject being identified within ascribed racial categories and actively clap back!

Although identity contingencies and the socio-cultural position one is born into contribute to how we are perceived, they do not have to be determinative of our identities. Identities are also shaped by the range of activities or practices that we participate in throughout our lives. These practices can stem from acculturation, but they can also reflect or extend from major and minor life choices we make as well as perspectives we develop about ourselves and others at the intersection of social and material worlds. This interaction of variable, fluid, and agentively formed components of identity is always in process despite the societal rhetoric of race.

For example, the interviewees have shown consciously motivated identity rejections throughout their stories. Interestingly, each of the interviewees who identified as queer actively resisted stereotypical and binary perceptions of their sexual orientations as demonstrations of agentive stances against being misperceived.

There were also examples of interviewees or people in their lives actively resisting and constructing alternatives to the racial identities ascribed to them. One thing that Ingrid, Joshua's wife, Samantha's daughter's blond, blue-eyed friend, and Rachel Dolezal demonstrated was that no physical contingency has to define one's identity. Importantly, trading race for personal-cultural identities that are more just actually benefits those defined as white as much as those defined into other racial categories. Darien noted, for example, how European Americans have also been disconnected from important aspects of their identities that need to be recovered and restored. In addition to rejecting whiteness as an identity, rejecting identification with the other color categories is equally needed. The identity contingencies of every interviewee revealed not only the inaccuracy but also the absurdity of using physical markers to mark identities of individuals in society.

DIGITAL CULTURE

Interviewees were selected who were born and became adults since the concurrent rise of the digital age and the birth of hip-hop in the early 1970s because these two cultural influences obviously contributed to shaping their identities, and I wanted to capture how they did. There are always tensions around the question of whether digital media can be used for authentic constructions and projections of identity or if its institutional influences continue to racialize and contrive how people are seen. Either way, digital media is pervasive in the lives of this group of interviewees in ways that were never imagined by their parents and others who came before. Their insights were reported for both these cultural forces in each of the five interviewee chapters. I bring these insights together in this section and the following one and discuss how they are additional illustrations of agentive, micro-cultural identity constructions that often work to circumvent static categories of race.

Gee's (2003) definition of the "Identity Principle," which is one of 36 Principles of Learning with New Media, provides one indication of how the use of digital tools increases micro-cultural components of identity. He noted that "learning involves taking on and playing with identities in such a way that the learner has real choices and ample opportunity to mediate on the relationship between new identities and old ones. There is a tripartite play of identities as learners relate, and reflect on, their multiple real-world identities, a virtual identity, and a projective identity" (p. 208). This ability to use digital media to reflect on real-world identities and exercise prerogatives in projecting virtual ones worked for most interviewees as extensions of their personal identities and cultural connections.

All the interviewees used digital media, but their levels and motives for participation indicated yet again how diverse the positioning, practices, choices, and perspectives of people are. If their participation in digital media were graphed, it would show striking differences in the duration of use, the variety and number of digital tools used, the purposes for use, and the personal stance each interviewee took regarding use. Chloe, Phil, and Felix were the most intensive users, while Relene, Ingrid, and Javier indicated the least amount of use. The others fanned out in between. Chloe said she used digital media 24/7. The youngest of all interviewees, she also noted that digital culture *is* the culture of her generation. Phil felt he was on the crest of the digital age and was an early adopter and avid user of just about all things digital. Felix said he was on social media "way too much." At the other end of the spectrum, Relene indicated that her use of digital media was moderate, while for different reasons, Ingrid rarely used social media and Javier never did. The oldest interviewee, Javier prefers to read on paper rather than on screen, and although he uses email for work, he said he has never gone on Facebook or used apps like Twitter or Snapchat. Despite the widely varying perspectives and levels of participation between Chloe on one pole and Javier on the other, distinctions in engagement with digital media cannot be simply mapped along generational lines. Mila, who doesn't use social media much and thinks it's basically a waste of her time, is just a year older than Chloe.

Excepting Javier, the interviewees' reflections on using digital tools and especially social media revealed how they understood their virtual identities as connecting to and extending their identities in the physical world. Or, as I suggest, they understood how virtual identities increased the components of their micro-cultural identities. Ryan noted, for example, "This definitely is a piece, a big piece, of how I approach digital media that connects to how I identify in the world. [It's] more around my own kind of personal ideologies of how I like to cultivate myself and my relationships." But Joshua, who is African American, noted his caution in "curating a persona because you don't have control over who is able to view it." He feels he has to continually be on guard about how he is socially constructed as an African American male in these spaces and feels restrictions that don't exist for others. However, he uses digital media to disrupt racialized stereotypes. Both Joshua and Ryan indicated that digital media enabled a political extension of their personal selves, and this is one of the key ways that many of the interviewees used these affordances. Others, like Ingrid and Mila, saw social media particularly as too egocentric. "I don't want to just focus on me," Ingrid said.

In the remainder of this section, I provide an example of each of the three main purposes for which the interviewees, with the exception of Javier, used digital media. This discussion also illustrates Gee's (2003) point that digital media enables choices regarding the mediation of newly constructed, projective identities in virtual space and an individual's multiple real-world identities. The three people are Sasha, Samantha, and Suzana and the three purposes are "personal production," "social connection," and "political action," respectively.

Sasha found digital media to be a powerful vehicle for her personal, creative productions. She had been an avid user of digital media starting when she was very young, and her desire to stay connected to her friends made the Internet a pervasive part of her life. She had learned on her own how to build websites, but then she went into the doldrums for a period until she decided to appropriate media platforms for her visual art and photography. As her digital activities evolved, she began creating online galleries to make her work publicly available. These activities in the virtual world also increased her self-confidence in the physical world. In other words, she was able to experiment, make choices, and play with various ways of representing herself in the virtual world through her artwork and photography, which also transformed how she identified and perceived herself in the physical world.

Samantha used various forms of digital media to effect and extend social relationships with her children, her athlete friends, her colleagues at work, and her relatives and friends in other countries. Of course, this is how most people use social media, but Samantha's example clearly reveals how mediating these relationships digitally had unusual and unanticipated impacts on these relationships as well as her projective identity as a parent, colleague, relative, and friend. The fact that her daughter's friend began to follow her, and that she was allowed to follow her daughter's friend on some media apps, gave her interpersonal insights that were not able to be reached in other ways. And the description of how her perceptions of herself in her role as a parent changed though ongoing dialogues with a friend in Argentina was a clear indication of how aspects of her digital identity were able to transform her identity as a parent in the real world. As she noted, "I've become more aware of how my Internet profile is really the main way that people get to know me. . . . I don't know if it's identity or relationships, but a lot of the primary contact, and sometimes the only contact, I have with others, is through the Internet."

Suzana talked about unique ways that digital media enabled her to represent and extend her identity as a social activist for work on Colombian human rights issues as well as for activist work on issues affecting queer women and women of color. She feels connected to these communities through the Internet and sees that a lot of digital spaces for women of color are driven by queer women. This impacts her own sense of herself as a queer woman, as a woman of color, and as a mother and wife. She is also impressed by how this medium allows her to reach out to communities she would not otherwise have access to, engage in difficult conversations on issues like race and sexual orientation, and get others who may not have access to certain perspectives to pay attention to them. Again, this ability to create virtual identities that open novel opportunities to reflect on possible positionalities and practices that are not readily available by any other means extends identity constructions into new realms.

Whether for personal production, social connection, or political action, digital media provided the interviewees with abundant opportunities to create or curate virtual identities that, like avatars, offered a range of projective identities. These representations, once created, were in dialogue with their real-world identities, even digitally dialogued with potentially numerous others in virtual worlds. As has been argued earlier regarding real-world identities, virtual identities and representations are crafted productions and performances that reflect people's personal-cultural perspectives and choices with respect to how they want to act and also be perceived in both virtual and physical social worlds. The interviewees were even more aware of how they defined and identified themselves as well as how they were externally identified and defined when options for both were significantly expanded digitally.

HIP-HOP CULTURE

Hip-hop culture is electrified, digitized, and spoken through rappers' mikes, DJ music mixes, dance styles, and graffiti. It's also controversial, particularly regarding one of its prevalent subgenres, gangsta rap. Gangsta rap lyrics are violent, confrontational, shocking, misogynistic, and profane. But the form is also much more. As one of the originators, DJ Kool Herc, noted, it is also "the way you walk, the way you talk, the way you look, the way you communicate" (quoted in Chang, 2005, xi). Essentially, DJ Kool Herc is invoking Gee's (1991) notion of discourse as "an 'identity kit.'" Yet identities and affinities with hip-hop culture can also be controversial. In digital culture, Gee (2003) noted that affinity groups are "bonded primarily through shared endeavors, goals, and practices and not shared race, gender, nation, ethnicity, or culture" (212). But since its inception, there have been heated debates regarding whether hip hop is mainly an African American cultural form, and elements of these debates still permeate hip-hop discourse. Kitwana (2005), for example, argued that hip-hop is a black thing, while others, like Chang (2005), contested exclusionary links to African Americans, noting that there are numerous people producing and transforming hip-hop who are neither black nor born in the United States. He suggested that hip-hop included "anyone who is down" (p. 2).

All the interviewees felt they were down with hip-hop, yet they were down in different ways. They fondly reflected on their affinities to hip-hop, and their participation in it revealed additional aspects of their microcultural positioning, choices, and perspectives, but its influences on them and their ways of participating were quite different, depending on things like age, ethnicity, gender, sexual orientation, and location. The one thing that was common across all these factors was that each person had to learn to perform key components of identity as a way to participate in hip-hop culture and have his or her affinity for it recognized and hopefully accepted. These performances were mostly revealed in ways of talking, dressing, and dancing and in the kind of music listened to. Interestingly, only James noted actually producing hip-hop music as opposed to mainly consuming it.

The first thing we generally see of others is the skin they're in, and one of the most prominent hip-hop influences on people's identity is the clothing that covers (or uncovers) that skin. Sasha dressed, talked, and acted like a B-girl and even identified with a B-girl name, "B-girl Trinity." James shoplifted Criss Cross clothes at the mall in order to dress in hip-hop style. Relene dressed and styled her hair in hip-hop fashions. Alexandra locked on headphones and wore baggy jeans and tight shirts even when attending powwows and other Native ceremonies. Joshua wore True Religion jeans and Air Jordans as a conversation starter with African American youth. Anton talked about how his daily attire was a cross between Cholo and hip-hop styles and how his first gang was a breakdancing crew, the Chain Breakers. Like Relene, Carmen looked to neighborhood and media projections of hip-hop for cues on how to wear her hair, how to dress, and how to talk. She said these performances of hip-hop culture helped "anchor" her in a black identity. Similarly, Ethan, enthralled with *To Pimp a Butterfly*, said that hip-hop gave him a better understanding of his racial identity. Felix felt that "hip-hop culture is almost like Filipino culture," and Suzana said hip-hop music was part of the soundtrack of her life. Anton also saw hip-hop as a bridge between Mexicano/Chicanos and African Americans. Phil, in connecting *Enter the Wu Tang (36 Chambers)* with the Bruce Lee classic *Enter the Dragon*, similarly saw hip-hop as a bridge for exploratory crossings of cultural divides because it resonated with the experiences of so many youth on the urban res.

Korean American Jonathan Park feels he is down with hip-hop as he raps to knock down racial walls. In stirring participants to go deep into cultural practices and also to bridge multiple cultural domains, hip-hop is something of a rhizome with myriad points of connectivity for identification, participation, and belonging.

INTERSTITIAL SPACE

How do we stir identification, participation, and belonging in our country more broadly? It can be argued that societal forces like digital culture and hip-hop culture increase the range of people's positions, practices, and choices such that it's more difficult to feel connectedness and belonging. This is the argument that Toffler (1970) made in his influential book, *Future Shock*. He addressed how the increase in diversity, novelty, and transience in society with regard to our relationships to things, experiences, and even people was creating psychological overload and inhibiting our sense of belonging.

Interestingly, this was before the digital age had really taken off. But there is a more identifiable "black snake" squeezing the life out of many people in this country—the institutional forces of white supremacy and its poisonous hierarchy of race. In the final chapter, I provide a number of considerations for multicultural education as a force that contributes to knocking down the racial walls. But here, I further address implications for identity, participation, and belonging in the context of micro-cultural positioning, practices, choices, and perspectives.

Banks (2013) described "microcultures" within the U.S. macroculture by showing how the overarching culture incorporates smaller cultural groupings within it that share most of the country's core values but may also have values and practices that are very different. At the same time, some of the core values of the dominant culture may be at odds with or may take different forms in certain microcultures. Banks (2013) continued this discussion at the level of the individual by describing how a person can have "multiple group memberships." He outlined considerations of individual membership in six major groups—nationality, race/ethnicity, religion, exceptionally/nonexceptionality, social class, and gender.

The concept of "micro-cultures" with the hyphen also operates at the level of the individual. However, *micro-cultures* sharpens the focus of identity to incorporate and be revealed through the myriad possible positionings, practices, choices, and perspectives exhibited and enacted by a person while also recognizing and accounting for fluid ways that each of these four aspects of a person's identity can change or be in a dynamic process of change, alone or in various combinations. The virtually limitless combinations of components reflect and define uniqueness of individuals that cannot be captured in static categories. In examining how various social, cultural, and biological categories of identity intersect, Crenshaw's (1989) concept of intersectionality also attempts to account for this uniqueness. Gee (2013) also attempts to focus attention on our uniqueness with his "Sub-Type Principle" that emphasized how the real diversity among people exists one or more levels down below any general label. The idea is to probe beneath the more static membership groupings that have been put forth (to slip between the notes, as Ellison's protagonist did) to apprehend the intricate levels of variability in identifications and experiences like those that have been evidenced in the stories of the 20 interviewees.

Felix (but every other interviewee as well) is an illustrative example of why this more sharply focused micro-cultural lens is needed. He looks almost exactly like his identical twin brother physically as well as when viewed through the lenses of the six major membership groupings that Banks noted. They have the same nationality, race/ethnicity, religion, social class, and gender, yet their individual identities are strikingly different, not only because of the identity component of Felix being gay while his brother is straight and married with a family, but also in terms of the fluid practices, choices, and perspectives that each brother individually enacts. The hyphen is a space where all the components of identity that distinguish Felix from his twin brother reside. It's a dynamic space that changes in shape and specific components of personal-cultural identity as Felix himself changes. The nature and speed of these changes can be influenced by choices and practices he initiates with respect to things like digital media, hip-hop culture, learning another language, travel to other countries, enrolling in graduate school—the list is nearly infinite. Yet one way to understand his identity at any moment in time is to see the specific combination of all his identity contingencies intersecting with all his identity affinities. This intersection is the space of the hyphen, the space of in-between-ness, the interstitial space of "being" that each person uniquely resides in while simultaneously being connected to or attempting to connect through every aspect of the positionality, practices, choices, and perspectives that makes that person who he or she is. The hyphen is in between things, but it's also its own thing. It's the space where bridges originate—to family, other individuals, societal institutions, affinity groups, selected and required communities, ancestors, the universe—on which cultural content and meaning move in both directions in vehicles like digital media and hip-hop, and numerous others.

Identifying himself as "a Chinese American, transnational, ethnically cosmopolitan mix," Phil said. "I live in a Hyphen." Based on each interviewee's negotiation of identity and search for belongingness through participation in dynamic contexts of families, interpersonal relationships, different languages, diverse communities, multiple affinity groups, and various societal institutions, I saw that each one lives in a hyphen, as we all do. From the interviews, I came to see their identities beginning and over time being affirmed in the space of the hyphen and extending through participation in all the different things that all the interviewees connect to as they actively worked from the inside out to define themselves and find their sense of belonging.

CHAPTER 10

Challenges of Multicultural Education

Let America be the dream the dreamers dreamed—
Let it be that great strong land of love
Where never kings connive nor tyrants scheme
That any man be crushed by one above.

—Langston Hughes, "Let America Be America Again" (1935)

Every fall semester in my urban education course, we have sustained focus on the work of scholars who shaped multicultural education. We explore and design implementations for the progressive principles and viable approaches for increasing equity and inclusion, for prejudice reduction, and for creating greater congruence between students' cultural backgrounds and schooling experiences in order to increase academic achievement and personal-social development. The two sections of this course have a total of 50 students each year composed of preservice teachers working on their master's degrees in education and teaching credentials in English language arts, science, math, and multiple subjects (for elementary school) with a few doctoral students sprinkled in. My co-instructors and I work to ground these students in core principles of multicultural education and also provide them with opportunities for application of some of the approaches within the class context as preparation for their integration into teaching practices soon to come.

As I discussed in Chapter 2, however, the core principles and approaches of multicultural education often accept operating within ascribed racial categories and thus contribute to these categories being sustained in schooling as markers of difference. This acceptance implies (and is actually claimed in critical race theory) that race is permanent. The argument of this book is that because race is socially constructed, it *can* be deconstructed. Schooling has a crucial role to play in this process along with other entities and institutions in society, and multicultural education plays a crucial role in schools. But it can be a more potent force in challenging and transforming this country's racial paradigm to bring America closer to honoring and practicing democratic values and principles.

I've experienced and thought about race my entire life, but things crystallized a decade ago when I went to the Science Museum of Minnesota in

St. Paul to see the exhibit titled *Race: Are We So Different?* which ran from January to May in 2007. This exhibit has since been featured at many museums around the country, including the Oakland Museum, which is close to the university where I teach. Developed by the American Anthropological Association in collaboration with the Science Museum, the exhibit was organized into interrelated, interactive exhibits that explored the idea of race from the perspectives of history, science, and lived experiences. We learn from science that we all share a common ancestry and that differences we see are not as significant as they may seem. Instead, they are natural variations, results of migration, marriage, and adaptation to different environments. Racism is a consequence of how we assign meaning to the differences we see and, importantly, how we assign meaning to difference is learned. To conclude the syllogism, racism is learned.

The exhibit had displays that explained how genetic analysis (e.g., DNA testing) is able to indicate that approximately 94% of physical variations among people lies within ascribed racial groups. However, these groups differ from each other in only about 6% of their genes. So there is significantly greater variation *within* than *between* groups. Since different groups have always interbred and shared genetic materials whenever they came into contact, humankind has continued as a single species. Yet as a one-off combination of parents', grandparents', and family ancestry, every person is unique. As Halle noted, no one out there has her exact combinations. Every person also has differing life experiences. Their positioning, practices, and choices situates them in unique interstitial spaces even though each may bridge overlapping entities in society.

Although there is no scientific justification for race, it continues to be socially constructed to serve specific political and profit interests. As a reminder of what was discussed in Chapter 2, the idea of race in the United States was invented during the 18th century. European Americans, who were leaders in the early stages of colonialism in this country, propagated numerous fictitious and exaggerated beliefs about the European settlers, the people brought from Africa to provide slave labor, and the Native peoples encountered here. One claim was that these groups constituted different species. These fictions, these formulations of the ideology of white supremacy, have no relationship to the reality of human capabilities or behavior; they became institutionalized and ingrained in society and were used to justify the retention of slavery as well as the conquering, displacement, and killing of Native peoples. Tragically, this ideology of fictive human differences spread to other areas of the world and has been used to justify subsequent genocides.

This is why the "black snake" of white supremacy must be defanged—to rid the world of its poisonous venom of race. Multicultural education is essential in this process because myths and fictions about human diversity and abilities are learned before behaviors stemming from them are operationalized. Rather than using and, thereby, perpetuating racial categories, multicultural education must prioritize principles and approaches to teaching and learning that target deconstructing the idea of race. The SciEd extension of the *Race: Are We So Different?* exhibition provided an educator guide for middle and high school teachers that has curricular and other learning resources for linking classrooms to the information in the museum exhibit. This guide is very useful for educators who want to design rigorous learning experiences across disciplines that teach truths about the lies of race.

Multicultural educators can seamlessly incorporate the exhibit's three primary themes into a wide range of content areas and learning experiences. These themes are "the science of human variation," "the history of the idea of race," and "the contemporary experience of race and racism." Understanding the facts of human variation and the inhuman impacts of the idea of race across time are fundamental literacies that must take their place beside and through the literacies of reading, writing, speaking, listening, and digital communication. The guide suggests a particular focus in the third theme on how race and racism have become virtually invisible in the laws, customs, and institutions of the United States. Making these processes visible is perhaps more important than making privilege visible. The latter will not provide the substance of things hoped for because it is mostly confessional without challenging the racial categories on which unearned privilege is based. But the former will provide evidence of things unseen by lifting the veil of white supremacy.

In the coming sections, I suggest how things I've learned from others as well as things that have been explored in my urban education classes can contribute to principles and practices that shift the paradigm of multicultural education. Science has clarified how, regardless of genetic propensities, human personalities and dispositions are learned and developed within the context of culture. A key point of this book is that it is also important to have educational experiences that facilitate learners' seeing and understanding the nearly limitless range of micro-cultural positionalities, practices, choices, and perspectives of individuals below the surface of broad notions of culture. This is akin to Gee's (2013) "Sub-Type Principle" noted in the previous chapter, that the real diversity among people exists one or more levels below more general and static labels or groupings. It's akin to Ethan in Chapter 6 going "in deep." Consequently, in addition to students learning about cultures broadly defined, they also explore their own uniqueness as personal-cultural beings in conjunction with more complex and nuanced understandings of others.

To address how this can look in classrooms, I discuss two of the projects that were handed in for one of the assignments in my 2015 and 2016 urban education classes. The prompt was for students to design a culturally responsive learning experience for implementation in an urban classroom that effectively used one or more digital tools, connected to one or more of the Common Core State Standards or other relevant learning standards, and reflected five principles of learning with new media (based on the 36 Principles of Learning with New Media at the end of Gee, 2003). Shivani Savdharia in my 2015 class and Yael Friedman in my 2016 class agreed that I discuss the learning designs they handed in for this assignment and also include their write-ups of the projects in the appendixes of this book. Ms. Savdharia returned to the 2016 classes to give a presentation on design thinking and to talk a bit about her own learning design for the previous year's class. She noted how she used her learning design as a key part of her materials submitted for teaching positions and as a primary document for discussions in her job interviews. "Personal Perspectives Projects" was designed to facilitate students' understanding their individual positionalities in relationship to others through research and presentation on their families and ancestors. Ms. Friedman's project, "From Beirut to Oakland," was designed to facilitate students' deep learning about themselves and about distant others through heightened understanding of historical and contemporary immigration issues. Additionally, I discuss the work of Eva Marie Oliver in "Integrating Restorative Discipline Principles" in her Oakland public school over several years. As Lily noted in Chapter 8, people who have been oppressed over centuries may experience historical trauma and long for healing, but have been taught to see the source of their stress and frustration in others who are more proximal and may be experiencing similar consequences from trauma. Ms. Oliver was a student in my urban education class 5 years earlier, and we have continued to collaborate on teaching and educational research projects. It is interesting to compare the level of her current work to her master's thesis, which was revised for publication in *The First Year of Teaching* (Mahiri & Freedman, 2014). Her chapter reflected the beginning of her work on the use of restorative discipline principles at her Oakland public school. She presented the current stage of her work to my urban education classes in 2015 and 2016. I provide a closing discussion on meeting the challenges of multicultural education in a section titled "Multicultural Education 2.0" and conclude this final chapter with a section titled "A-mericans."

PERSONAL PERSPECTIVES PROJECT

Before she decided to be a teacher, Shivani Savdharia worked for a number of years with IDEO, a company in Palo Alto, California, that combines the capabilities of designers, engineers, and researchers to tackle complex problems and rapidly bring product solutions into existence. I talked in the class about the perspective of designing learning experiences, and we also had work in class with design thinking. It became clear that the class could learn a lot about design from Ms. Savdharia. As I reviewed and responded to her Personal Perspectives Project (Appendix A), I could see how skillfully she had incorporated all four of the kinds of knowledge we had addressed in the class—content knowledge, pedagogical knowledge, technological knowledge, and cultural knowledge—as did Ms. Friedman and Ms. Oliver.

Ms. Savdharia's learning experience (Appendix A) was designed to engage students in identity explorations using a multimedia app called Tellagami, with the first goal being to allow students to take safe risks while developing a sense of personal-cultural understanding and self-efficacy. The project facilitated students' going deep into their own positionality, but the share-out portion also allowed all class members to learn more about others as they learned more about themselves, their families, and their ancestors. Her second goal of connecting media literacy to identity and multicultural education is one aspect of what multicultural education 2.0 looks like. At the same time, the rigor of the learning experience reflected in its connection to external standards and internal assessment is key and nicely revealed in Ms. Savdharia's design. Additionally, the component of research is central to how students must learn for themselves and become producers of knowledge rather than merely consumers.

To summarize the stages of the project, the design began with the metaphor of the "cultural iceberg" in order for students to visualize how their identities constitute much more than is seen on the surface. Next, students brainstormed about eight different aspects of diversity (age, gender, sexual orientation, ability, race, ethnicity, religion, and socioeconomic status). After this, the students were to answer a series of questions from Christine Sleeter's Critical Family History, such as: What is the structure of your family? Who are members of your family and what roles do they play? Next, students reflected on which aspects of their identities others can and cannot perceive. Students were then given the opportunity to create an online avatar, or animated character, using a free Tellagami app. The program gives students the freedom to design physical attributes, mood, background environment, and music as well as record a voiceover explaining who they are. The project culminated in classwide presentations of students' avatars.

In addition to stimulating reflection and awareness and creating community, Ms. Savdharia's learning design embraced digital media as a creative, shareable, exciting space for remixing representations of one's own identity. This is what is meant by reframing multicultural education to more directly illuminate and build on students' unique micro-cultural identities. Although race is one of the categories that Sleeter's Critical Family History offered, it is only one of eight categories, and importantly the category of sexual orientation is also one. Ultimately, the educator would want to eliminate the racial category, or if left in, to use it as a window into discussion of what we know about the science and history of the idea of race. Recognizing the potential to activate a component of a student's identity in a safe and exciting way in conjunction with gaining significant insights into the identities of others while developing rigorous academic skills inherently contributes to positive personal-cultural and intellectual development.

FROM BEIRUT TO OAKLAND

Since Yael Friedman and her colleagues in the 2016 urban education classes heard Ms. Savdharia's presentation on her learning design, some requested to see it as they considered their own work on the assignment. I decided not to share the write-up of her project because I didn't want students in the subsequent classes to map onto it a template for the design of a project. I wanted them to use their own creativity to design original learning experiences that addressed the assignment prompts. Ms. Friedman's is an example of an original design (Appendix B), yet conceptually it bears similarities to Ms. Savdharia's in that they both facilitate students' going deep into understandings of their personal positionality and yet wide to understandings of others. In Ms. Friedman's design, the others were collaborating students in Beirut. Given the divisive rhetoric on immigration in the United States, Ms. Friedman's students had much to gain from hearing the personal perspectives of peers who live in a deeply divided country experiencing a refugee crisis. With goals of exploring immigration and nativism in California and in their own families prior to engaging in sustained conversations with student in Beirut, a key objective of the learning was for students to be able to make connections between the refugee crises in the Middle East and the sociopolitical reality of the United States with respect to similar issues.

As in Ms. Savdharia's design, Ms. Friedman's mediated the learning with appropriate digital tools, creating, in effect, a digital, multimodal classroom that allowed conversations between the two groups of students, who were physically thousands of miles apart. The project actually would not have been possible without the use of digital tools. Similar also was the centrality of research in the project for students on both continents that included interviews of parents or caretakers, but also investigations for the U.S. students to find out who their earliest known ancestor in this country was. Key considerations for the larger conversation of multicultural education revealed in this learning design was the focus on customizing the learning experience for each learner and how the design allowed for low-stakes risks while discussing controversial issues. Yet the customized focus was able to widen to larger political and societal considerations through synthesis and reflection such that the national and global understandings were able to be grounded in local and personal experiences and insights, all while gaining affinities with distant others.

Technology was also critical for doing the research and accessing the prompted sites as a starting point to link to wider and wider connections to the central focus. Finally, one thing that came up in the interviews of the people whose stories were heard in earlier chapters was the importance of travel in enlarging their perspectives of themselves and others. Ms. Friedman's learning design allowed for some of the kinds of learning that can result from travel, but the trips of these urban students in Oakland and Beirut were made virtually.

INTEGRATING RESTORATIVE DISCIPLINE PRINCIPLES

Eva Marie Oliver's curricular project (Appendix C) on integrating restorative discipline principles throughout every aspect of teaching and learning with her students provides an additional set of perspectives that can inform the ongoing evolution of multicultural teaching perspectives and approaches. It was interesting to see how her approach evolved from her teacher research that she documented in her master's thesis. It became more systematic, comprehensive, and conceptually rich as she iterated it year after year.

Some educators are using terms like "trauma-informed schools" to indicate school and classroom contexts in which some members participate in unexpected ways. Their actions can disrupt the desired flow of learning, and when extreme, they can actually cause serious emotional or physical harm. Ms. Oliver observed a series of extreme incidents of cyberbullying between two of her 12th-grade female students early in her teaching career that propelled her on the path to integrating restorative discipline principles and practices in her classes in every aspect of teaching and learning.

A central principle of restorative discipline is that instead of applying punitive responses to harmful acts, have students take responsibility for their actions as the first step in a process of restoring the community as a safe and supportive place for learning. One goal is to have students learn the importance of healthy human relationships. When her school expanded to a 6–12 program, she was asked to develop the language arts curriculum for the middle school. She realized that middle school–aged youth are in a fragile space as they struggle to figure out how they want to identify and to what they want to belong. And they make mistakes. She decided to infuse the entire content of her curriculum with the key restorative discipline principles of agency, ownership, and accountability, thereby putting the humanity of students at the core of every instructional act. These three principles were used as lenses for looking at the characters her classes encountered in fiction and in life. By critically evaluating choices of the protagonists, their allies, and their adversaries, students began to think about their own choices and the agency, ownership, and accountability they needed to exercise in their own lives. They learned that their progress toward liberatory personal spaces was marked by healthy human development and empathy with others.

In Ms. Oliver's approach, we see the significance of healthy human development as the central goal and focus of all curricular activities. Multicultural education can shift a greater, more explicit focus on healthy human development beyond its focus on specific racial-cultural groups. Students certainly go deep in understandings of their unique personal cultural positioning and perspectives. But the purpose of these deep dives is to explore and appreciate the pearls and perils in the sea of humanity and to make deliberate choices to embrace one and avoid the other. Other principles might be used, but in Ms. Oliver's classes, students are guided in their quests by a trifocal lens—agency, ownership, and accountability—grounded in close analysis of the motives and consequences of choices and practices of characters encountered in literature and life.

MULTICULTURAL EDUCATION 2.0

One of the challenges of multicultural education *is* moving beyond the color-bind. I visited Ms. Oliver's middle school classes in East Oakland on several occasions and her diverse students would be identified in each ascribed racial category. It was interesting that when she talked, wrote, and presented about her work with them, she never referred to them in terms of color. Ms. Savdharia and Ms. Friedman also did not make characterizations of students by color. Contingencies like skin color should not define and distort people's identities. The three learning designs indicated how rich identity work could take place in schools that required reflection, research, meaningful collaborations, and emphatic consideration of others. This is clearly seen, for example, in Ms. Oliver's students' "Growth Essay," in which they explained how they had grown as readers, writers, thinkers, and humans through middle school. Many students described how their growth was driven by learning to hold themselves and others accountable for their choices, how they had developed more empathy, how they believed they were capable of being activists, how they didn't want to oppress anyone, and how they wanted to liberate their communities. All three learning designs revealed intensive identity work on the part of students, not only for themselves, but also to understand the identities and circumstances surrounding the lives of others. As Halle noted in Chapter 6, people should be able to define themselves because it's problematic being defined by other people or feeling a need to counter the definitions they have imposed.

Ways of focusing deeply on students' understanding and development of their identities and the identities of others beyond the color-bind is one of the components of multicultural education 2.0. Another is the effective use of digital media to extend learning in new ways that cannot be achieved without it. A challenge for multicultural educators is to be leaders in designing learning that increases students' abilities and understanding of the production and consumption of information and images in new media. As Ms. Savdharia stated in her learning design, "Media literacy is critical to multicultural education because our conceptions of multicultural identities have been influenced by surrounding media. Our relationship and perceptions of race, ethnicity, gender, sex, socioeconomic status, religion, age and ability impact the way we see ourselves as well as others, and these opinions and experiences are often created through our interpretations of media. Therefore, it's important we teach young learners how to read images critically, interpret sounds and build an awareness of how media can be interpreted in a multiplicity of ways."

During the final months of writing this book, I was also curating articles for two special issues of *Multicultural Education Review* as a guest editor on a theme that gave the issues their title "Cyber-Lives: Digital Media and Multicultural Education." Considerations I put forth in the proposal for the issues' focus were that multicultural educators and researchers needed to increase understanding of how new media texts and tools affect identity construction as well as interactions with and perceptions of others in both local and global contexts. The other side of that consideration was that multicultural educators needed to effectively incorporate more of the appropriate digital technologies into pedagogical approaches and perspectives in order to truly build on identities and extend learning experiences for contemporary youth. The articles for these two issues, set for publication in the summer and fall of 2017, explore how digital media practices reveal important ways that people's actual lives and learning are much more complex, nuanced, and multifaceted than essentialized racial/ethnic categories admit. These articles explicate how individual and social identity construction, interpersonal and work relationships, and ways of learning and constructing new knowledge are dramatically transformed through the pervasive use of digital texts and tools. They variously show how digital media has expanded, virtually connected, and complicated people's personal-cultural identities, group affinities, and ways of knowing as well as the sense of place and space.

The learning designs of Ms. Savdharia and Ms. Friedman exemplified seamless integration of digital tools into learning and identity development. Ms. Oliver's did also, although this aspect of her teaching was not made explicit in her write-up. Ms. Savdharia's students used Tellagami to learn through multiple sign systems, including written text, animated video, and digital symbols and attributes in representing their identities and presenting them to others in this multimedia project. Ms. Friedman's students researched the history of immigration in their own families and in California, making connections between these histories and presenting their learning using Prezi. The second phase of their learning revolved around a collaborative, digital classroom partnership with a collaborating teacher and class in Beirut, Lebanon, via the online forum ePals. They also used online, interactive curricula, including the Angel Island Immigration Station's curriculum on the Chinese Exclusion Act, and other digital resources like the Chinese Exclusion Act, the Bracero Program, Jewish Holocaust refugees, and the Vietnamese boat people sites to work in small groups to find primary sources to contextualize the history of restrictive immigration policies in California.

A third consideration for multicultural education 2.0 that is intricately connected to digital mediation of learning is the role of student research. Student research should be seen as a primary principle and practice of multicultural education. To really become independent learners, students have to develop the ability and agency to find information, sort and evaluate it, and then integrate and synthesize findings that can be clearly communicated to others. Using appropriate technology is becoming more and more critical to intellectual inquiry. All three learning designs provided innovative examples of students conducting various inquiries: Ms. Savdharia's students being apprenticed in ethnography to get the information needed to complete their Critical Family Histories, Ms. Friedman's students researching immigration and nativism in California and in their own families, Ms. Oliver's students spending an entire year exploring the language of oppression and how it masks or normalizes societal problems like sexism, heterosexism, racism, classism, religious intolerance, ableism, and ageism.

Controversial issues like those addressed in Ms. Oliver's and Ms. Friedman's projects are a fourth consideration for multicultural education 2.0. They are controversial because they index how white supremacy sustains its oppression and control. They have to be brought into classrooms in safe ways for students to learn about how these issues come into play in their immediate lives as well as in local, national, and global contexts. Multicultural education should help students go beyond empathy to seeing their own capabilities and opportunities to disrupt these modes of denigration and oppression. Interestingly, in the three learning designs as well as in the stories of the interviewees, things like travel and speaking and appreciating different languages beyond English were also important aspects of identity development

In conjunction with research and the use of digital tools, a fifth consideration for multicultural education 2.0 is to more definitely forefront the roles of collaboration in learning. We saw extensive collaborative activities designed into the three examples, and the point that each implied, but needs to be made explicit, is that classrooms must be places where opportunities for relationships to form are intentionally incorporated into the learning experiences. When collaborative work is well designed it extends beyond the classroom and is a crucial part of learning about others through working with others. Again, the use of technology can be instrumental in facilitating meaningful collaborations as well as the actual production of the work in both physical and virtual space.

A sixth consideration is for multicultural education to focus more attention on exploring and understanding significant examples of global youth culture. The importance of this was shown with respect to hip-hop culture, specifically in terms of its influences on every one of the interviewees. It was a kind of common place of cultural participation and production that suggests that other common places can exist or be made to exist in which people are motivated to participate across differences. I use a video clip of a 16-year-old student named Geoff Murihia, also known as Masai, that beautifully captures how a person his age experiences and understands hip-hop as a common culture for youth. He said, "As a person who is very much into hip-hop I realize that culture is beyond African American. It is more of what the world should be. It's a worldly culture. I have Latino brothers and sisters; I have Asian brothers and sisters; I have, you know, Samoan partners and all kinds of nationalities that I can look at as brothers and sisters regardless of anything just because they are a part of that culture."

The seventh consideration of making the science of human variation and the history and experiences of race central to the formulation and foci of multicultural education 2.0 was addressed at the beginning of this chapter. Obviously, education alone is not a panacea for the consequences of a society in which lies dominate truth, in which fictions define reality, and where profit is taken over people. But it is one of the vital forces through which people can contribute to creating a reality that profits from the truth.

A-MERICANS

I have argued that the idea of race was invented and socially constructed to serve the political and economic interests of white supremacy and its black snake of capitalism that squeezes the life out of humans. Some see no alternative to this way of constructing society and even suggest that race is permanent. However, race can be deconstructed, and we can heal from the poison it spreads. We can actively work to counter its devastating consequences in favor of more human alternatives. On the other hand, continuing to perpetuate the idea of race by identifying ourselves within the colorized categories of white, or black, or brown, or red, or yellow is itself a racist act. Instead, like Phil in Chapter 6 who talked about living in a hyphen, we can acknowledge that we all are hyphenated "A-mericans" living in a "hyphen-nation."

I ask students in my urban education classes to write and share "Personal Profiles" to give everyone an initial sense of who we actually are below the waterlines of our cultural icebergs. With her permission, I included Kylie Garcia's profile (Appendix D) as one final example of why we cannot assume anything about a person until we develop relationships, share experiences, engage in conversations, and open ourselves to surprises. I use pictures of my students to learn their names, but Ms. Garcia's picture was not available. When I finally matched her to her name, I found out that she was Japanese American, Filipino, and Pacific Islander, and not Hispanic. Her Personal Profile, like the stories of all 20 interviews, exemplifies microcultural positioning. She begins by saying, "Each person has a story to tell. Understanding each other's stories and making empathetic connections provides us the opportunity to learn with and from each other. It is an important aspect of helping diverse students thrive as learners." She talks about how she and her sister look like opposites, and how differently they are perceived as a result. She concludes with the reflection, "These experiences influenced my perspective on diversity, and prompted me at an early age to embrace my multicultural identity. I have gained a deeper understanding of seeing others beyond what is merely presented at a first glance, and being interested and intrigued with the stories each person holds within."

The heart of this book is the intriguing stories gleaned from ethnographic interviews of Samantha, Sasha, James, Ryan, Relene, Ingrid, Joshua, Ethan, Chloe, Halle, Phil, Felix, Carmen, Suzana, Anton, Javier, Lily, Darien, Mila, and Alexandra. You know who you are. Thank you for sharing! It was Spradley (1979) who taught me that rather than studying people, ethnography means learning from them. I didn't know I would also be learning from spirits.

This book began with the stories of Hélio and Santi, who along with their siblings, Nina and Amado respectively, are my grandchildren. What will the world be like in seven generations for them and for all children? Will it be a shareable, sustainable world? Will it be a place where no person is crushed by someone above, as Langston Hughes dreamed? What we do now will determine the world generations will inherit and inhabit.

Personal Perspectives Project

Shivani Savdharia

**DESIGN OF LEARNING PROJECT FOR URBAN EDUCATION
(DECEMBER 2015)**

This lesson, or learning experience, is designed for upper elementary school students, 4th grade and up. I refer to it as the "Personal Perspectives Project," created to help students examine and represent their individual identities through the use of multimedia app Tellagami (tellagami.com/app/). The Personal Perspectives Project supports the following Learning Principles as outlined by James Gee: Semiotic Principle, "Psychosocial Moratorium" Principle, Identity Principle, Cultural Models About Learning Principle, and Insider Principle.

Learning Goals

I. Engaging students in a meaningful, authentic, and deeply personal learning experience by giving them the opportunity to take safe risks and feel a sense of personal agency.

Through students being allowed to feel control over what they're doing and creating, they develop a sense of agency and ownership, thereby feeling an intrinsic motivation to put forward their best efforts. This lesson is scaffolded to help students take personal inventory, synthesize their findings, and share out what they've learned in a supported environment as a means to connect with others.

II. Connecting media literacy to identity and multicultural education.

Media literacy is critical to multicultural education because our conceptions of multicultural identities have been influenced by surrounding media. Our relationship and perceptions of race, ethnicity, gender, sex, socioeconomic status, religion, age, and ability affect the way we see ourselves as well as others, and these opinions and experiences are often created through our interpretations of media. Therefore, it's important we teach young learners how to read images critically, interpret sounds, and build an awareness of how media can be interpreted in a multiplicity of ways.

III. Building ISTE (International Society for Technology in Education) standards competencies by developing multimedia technology skills.

This lesson connects with ISTE standards, created to help students learn effectively and live productively in an increasingly global and digital society. Through the Tellagami app, students will learn to express themselves using text, images, and sounds. They will use critical thinking, decision-making, communication skills, research and information fluency, technology operations/concepts/systems, and creativity to develop both hardware and software skills needed to stay connected and current in the digital age.

Project Phases

// RESEARCH //

The initial phase of this Personal Perspectives Project is designed for students to deep dive into personal research. Before jumping to creation, it's important that students take time to inquire. Since this project is designed for students to get to know themselves better, I have provided various frameworks below for learners to use as a way to take personal inventory. In this phase, students will be encouraged to journal or sketch out their reflections to the following three categories aimed to get individuals thinking more deeply about who they are and where they come from. Students will need to be assured that they won't be forced to share their findings.

1. Eight Dimensions of Diversity

Students will take a look at the eight dimensions of diversity below and think about how each one applies to them. Teachers will need to clarify terms for common understanding.

Ability	Age	Ethnicity	Race
Gender	Sexual Orientation	Religion	Socioeconomic Status

2. Critical Family History

Learners will answer the following questions inspired by Christine Sleeter (http://christinesleeter.org/critical-family-history/):

- What is the structure of your family? Who are members of your family and what roles do they play?
- How is leisure time spent in your family?

- What role does religion play in your family?
- What do you and others in your family read, listen to as music, enjoy as art?
- Who works at what? Are there occupations common in generations of your family?
- Where did your family originate, and how did you come to live in CA? Are there any common experiences that tie you, your family, and others in a larger group together?
- What languages are spoken?
- What does your diet consist of? What are the times and routines of your meals?
- Are there any visual symbols of your family or larger culture (clothing, jewelry, etc.)?
- Are there any organizations or rituals that are important in your family life?

3. The Cultural Iceberg

Students will use the template below to create their own cultural iceberg. Above the water they will draw/write what others see and below they will share the nonobservable.

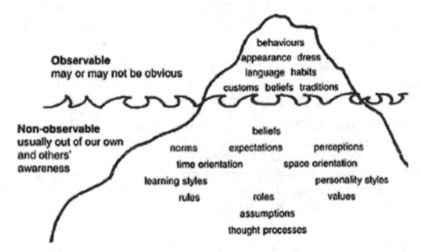

// CREATE //

After investing time researching and reflecting, students will proceed to create an animated character (or avatar) using the Tellagami app (available for free download on all mobile and desktop devices). This app allows students to embody their synthesized findings by using what they've learned about themselves and directly translating it to a virtual avatar. The Tellagami avatar allows students to design the character's physical attributes, moods, background environment, and music and record a voiceover dialogue explaining who this character is. The idea is that students feel comfortable putting themselves and their personal identities out there by having the option to "hide" behind their embodied creations.

// CONNECT //

Finally, students will come together to share their Tellagamis with the classroom community. Before beginning, the teacher will lay out and explain the following three agreements: Don't criticize others, use empathetic listening, and maintain confidentiality. As the facilitator, the teacher will highlight points of connection as well as emphasize that students who "look the same" may actually have very different individual identities, since culture is granular and highly personal.

Gee's Learning Principles

The following five principles were held in mind while creating the Personal Perspectives Project.

Semiotic Principle. Students learn through multiple sign systems in this multimedia project. Through the Tellagami creation process, students use written text, animated video, and digital symbols and attributes to represent their identities.

"Psychosocial Moratorium" Principle. Since there are no real-world consequences in the creation of avatars, students can safely explore and take risks around how they want to represent their personal identities.

Identity Principle. This project allows students to make real choices, negotiating real-world identities they have discovered about themselves, the virtual identity they would like to depict, and a projective identity that allows the individual to trade parts of his or her own psyche with those desired attributes depicted through their virtual identities, thereby giving the students an "opportunity to meditate on the relationship between new identities and old ones."

Cultural Models About Learning Principle. Reflection and introspection are at the crux of this project, thereby allowing learners ample space to think consciously and critically "without denigration of their identities, abilities, or social affiliations, and juxtapose them to new models of learning and themselves as learners."

Insider Principle. This project makes the learner the creator or producer rather than the media consumer. Each student creates his or her own avatar and embarks on individual research, thereby making him or her the expert and leader of the learning experience.

From Beirut to Oakland

Long-Distance Shared Inquiry on Immigrants and Refugees

Yael Friedman

DESIGN OF LEARNING PROJECT FOR URBAN EDUCATION (DECEMBER 2016)

Purpose

This unit implements project-based, multimodal learning to counter the current climate of baseless anti-immigrant/-refugee and Islamophobic rhetoric. Over the course of this unit, students will:

- Explore histories of immigration and nativism in California and in their own families
- Identify and investigate definitions of immigrant and refugee
- Engage in sustained and meaningful cross-cultural contact with peers in Beirut, Lebanon
- Make connections between the refugee crises in the Middle East and the sociopolitical reality in the United States

Overview

During this course of expeditionary learning, 4th-grade students will perform a comprehensive study on past and present conceptions of immigrants and refugees. First, students will research the history of immigration in their own families and in California, making connections between these histories and presenting their learning using Prezi.

The second phase of the project revolves around a collaborative, digital classroom partnership with a teacher in Beirut, Lebanon, via the online forum ePals. Located a stone's throw from the greatest humanitarian crisis in the world, Beirut is a developed, diverse, and cosmopolitan city. British and French colonization in Lebanon has yielded a trilingual system of education, in which English and French are the mandated languages for math and science instruction. Accordingly, educated Lebanese children are bilingual, allowing cross-cultural connections to be made with minimal language barriers. According to the UNHCR, over one million Syrian refugees are seeking asylum in Lebanon. Given the divisive rhetoric surrounding immigration in the United States, specifically related to Syrian refugees, students in the United States have much to gain from hearing the personal perspectives of peers who live in a deeply divided country experiencing a refugee crisis. The students in Lebanon will separate fact from fiction and reflect on the state of affairs in their country by preparing presentations on the Syrian refugee crisis. Students in both classrooms will engage in direct, online dialogue regarding their experiences with and opinions on immigration within the context of their background knowledge and their concurrent learning, posting discussions and presentations on a shared blog maintained by the two classes.

Part I: Immigration in the United States

Students will research migration in the United States from two perspectives: with regard to their own family, and with regard to California's history. Our study of California will focus on 4th-grade California Department of Education content standards 4.4.3 and 4.4.4, examining historical immigration to California and the wider United States. Using simplified, age-appropriate versions of curricula such as the Angel Island Immigration Station's curriculum on the Chinese Exclusion Act, students will use primary sources to contextualize the history of restrictive immigration policies in California. In small groups, students will create a Prezi delineating the responses to and causes and consequences of the Chinese Exclusion Act, the Bracero Program, Jewish Holocaust refugees, and the Vietnamese boat people. Making conclusions using primary sources optimizes Gee's **Discovery Principle**, in that rather than being told overtly, students actively seek and record information to construct their own knowledge. These presentations will be shared on the blog to be viewed by the students in Lebanon as an introduction to immigration issues in the United States. Both American and Lebanese students will complete the Universe of Obligation handout (available at facinghistory. org/sites/default/files/Universe_of_Obligation_0.pdf) to analyze national responses to these migrants and refugees.

Concurrently, through interviews with their parents or caretakers, students will obtain information on their first *known* ancestor(s) in the United States, including:

- Who they were
- Where they came from, where they arrived, or both
- Why they left their country of origin
- How they made the journey
- What they did, where they worked, or where they attended school on arrival

While it is unreasonable to expect that every student will have access to this information, the objective would be for students to learn as much as possible. Students will then conduct Internet research to collaboratively construct definitions of *immigrant* and *refugee* and determine how their relatives might have been classified. Students will be encouraged to think about American Indians and African Americans, whose narratives may include people who might not have been labeled "immigrants" or "refugees" at all. Using Prezi, students will visually represent their data and post it to the blog. By situating their own family histories within the wider context of migration in the United States, students demonstrate Gee's **Self-Knowledge Principle**, coming to know more about themselves while and through learning about content.

Part II: A Window into Lebanon

Students in Lebanon will create Prezis introducing aspects of the Syrian conflict and refugee crisis as they experience them. American and Lebanese students will be matched with one another, as close to 1:1 as possible, and students will have the opportunity to send informal, more personal messages in the style of pen pals, via email. Students will be introduced to the issues surrounding the Syrian refugee crisis through online, interactive curricula and given the opportunity to ask their peers in Lebanon for opinions and perspectives on this issue. By drawing on one another's knowledge and opinions, students embody the **Insider Principle**, teaching, producing, and customizing the learning experience for each other. Questions they might ask their counterparts include:

- (How) Are you affected by the huge number of Syrian refugees in Lebanon?
- Where is your family from?
- What is the difference between a refugee and an immigrant?

Strict norms will be established regarding acceptable language and conduct online. Students' making themselves vulnerable by asking and answering difficult questions in an online conversation with their peers on a controversial topic demonstrates Gee's **"Psychosocial Moratorium" Principle**. This format allows students to take low-stakes risks discussing a controversial and possibly emotional or inflammatory topic in a safe space, as they develop the language and social skills to make sensitive, reasoned arguments for their ideas.

Part III: Synthesis and Reflection

Students will complete a second Universe of Obligation graphic organizer, this time outlining the U.S. stance with regard to Syrian refugees, as

Lebanese students do the same for their government. We will compare student responses and discuss the analyses, writing personal reflections about what we have learned during this course of study. Our goal at this stage is to have demonstrated the **Affinity Group Principle,** by uniting these students who have never interacted in person through the shared experience of this project. Responses will be posted on the blog and students will be assigned to comment on at least three other reflections.

Integrating Restorative Discipline Principles into Classroom Content

Eva Marie Oliver

(DECEMBER 2016)

Restorative discipline is effective because instead of punitively punishing students, it creates space for them to own their choices, recognize the harm they caused to others, and work to right that harm for all those affected in the community. Additionally, it provides the opportunity for all those affected by a harmful event to learn and grow from the experience—all the while retaining their humanity.

During the 2011–2012 school year, I witnessed the restorative discipline process take the toxicity out of a very painful situation between two 12th-grade students and create an opportunity for humanization, accountability, growth, and the reification of school culture. Inspired and transformed, I wrote my master's thesis for the University of California–Berkeley's Multicultural Urban Secondary English program on restorative discipline. I came to deeply appreciate the values and principles of restorative discipline, and, as a result, I began to work to integrate them into my teaching practice and curriculum.

Soon after completing my master's degree, I was given the opportunity to build a middle school English language arts curriculum as my school expanded from a high school to a 6th–12th school. Quickly, I realized that middle school students—who are in the crux of developing their identities and figuring out who they want to be in their own bodies and in the world—make a lot of mistakes, some of which create tremendous harm for those around them. While our administrators were mostly committed to addressing this harm in a restorative way, it was still reactive, in that the process only begins once harm has been done rather than being proactive and ultimately preventing future harm.

Thus, I decided that this restorative work couldn't just happen outside the classroom. Students in 6th–8th grade needed continual opportunities to encounter and collaboratively think through ideas about harm, restoration, accountability, dehumanization, and empathy in safe, intellectual, nonpunitive spaces. Consequently, I infused the actual content of my classes with restorative discipline principles—namely the concepts of *agency, ownership*, and *accountability*. I was determined to make the humanity of my students the center of our class such that they *learned* to negotiate and navigate the humanity of themselves, each other, their supporters, and the characters (both fictional and real) whom we read about together.

Agency—6th-Grade English Language Arts

THEMATIC SCOPE AND SEQUENCE FOR MS ENGLISH-6TH GRADE

Tracing the Hero's Journey and Empathy-Building with:
1. *The Lightning Thief*
2. *Hatchet*
3. *Charlie and the Chocolate Factory*
4. *Seedfolks*

When developed in 2012, the first iteration of the year's essential questions were: *What does a hero's journey look like? How can I participate in my own hero's journey?* These questions were explored through four books and five major projects. As we traced the hero's journey in each of these books, we looked closely at the choices the heroes made—how these heroes shaped their own destiny and, often, the destiny of others through their agency. With the protagonist of *The Lightning Thief*, Percy, we examined the difference between prophecies and choices. By observing the protagonist of *Hatchet*, Brian, we talked about how and why he changed and made deliberate decisions in order to survive. While waiting to find out who Willy Wonka would give the chocolate factory to in *Charlie and the Chocolate Factory*, we learned about the qualities of a leader and thought about which character had most of these and whether or not we had them too. Finally, in *Seedfolks*, while reading about how one girl changed her community by starting a community garden, we wrote about the power young people hold within their communities.

Each book and each project empowered students to think about choices and the impact/consequences of those choices. By doing this work, my hope was that students would realize and embrace their own agency. We all make choices that affect our lives and, more often than not, the lives of others.

And by critically evaluating the choices of our protagonists, their allies, and their adversaries, I believe that my students began to think about their own choices with the same kind of weight. Thus, by the end of the year, students understood they had agency in their own lives (and in the world) and began to take more ownership of their own choices.

Ownership—7th-Grade English Language Arts

THEMATIC SCOPE AND SEQUENCE FOR MS ENGLISH-7TH GRADE

Levels of Oppression	Types of Oppression
Institutional	Sexism
Interpersonal	Heterosexism
Internalized	Racism
	Classism
	Religious Intolerance
	Ableism
	Ageism

Evaluating Oppression in:

1. *The Giver*
2. *Monster*
3. *Persepolis*
4. Lit Circle **Choice** Book (all protagonists suffer from a Mental Illness)

For my 7th-grade curriculum, I wanted to build on this idea of ownership and to complicate the idea of agency, specifically how some people choose to use their agency to take away the power of others. Part of understanding the world around us, recognizing harm, and owning our own choices is having the language to talk about what we are doing, seeing, and experiencing. So my students and I spent an entire year exploring the language of oppression and building our ability to empathize with people whose lives may be very different from ours. Through *The Giver*, we discussed institutional oppression and whether or not it's acceptable to take people's power away for the "greater good." With *Monster*, we talked about the racism and ageism present within the American justice system, and students ultimately were tasked with developing a policy proposal for how serious youth offenders should be treated by the justice system. *Persepolis* gave us the opportunity to discuss sexism, classism, and religious intolerance. And our literature circle unit enabled students to better understand ableism and the stigmatization of people with psychiatric illnesses. This final unit ended with students making their empathy public by organizing a Mental Health Awareness Night, where each of my 64 students went up to the microphone in the hopes of raising money for the National Alliance on Mental Illness (NAMI). Over the past 3 years, my 7th-graders have raised over $1,000 for NAMI!

Through each unit, I watched my students' understanding of power and privilege deepen and strengthen. They were recognizing the impact of others' choices, which led to them owning their own choices more consistently. By the end of the year, I heard my students say things like "We need to talk about mental illnesses more because people keep judging them and they face enough internalized oppression without all that," and "Don't say faggot; that's heterosexist," and "Is it religious intolerance that we don't celebrate any Muslim holidays at school?" These statements and questions revealed to me that my students understood the concepts of agency, ownership, oppression, and harm. Now they needed the tools to do something about the "bad" that they saw and experienced; they needed the tools and language of liberation.

Accountability—8th-Grade Humanities

Thematic Scope and Sequence for MS English–8th Grade

Tactics of Liberation
Emotional Manipulation
Information Sharing
Civil Disobedience
Violence
Self-Sacrifice
Public Protest
Escape

Evaluating the Use of the Tactics of Liberation in:
1. Film Study of *Catching Fire* and *12 Years a Slave*
2. *Absolutely True Diary of a Part-Time Indian*
3. *Narrative of the Life of Frederick Douglass*
4. Book Circle **Choice** Book (Activist Biography)
5. Lit Circle **Choice** Book (all protagonists identify as Trans)

To achieve the goal of providing students with the tools and language of liberation, we evaluated the tactics of activists/heroes as they worked to liberate themselves and others. We examined how they held themselves and others accountable for harm, and we ruminated on the strategies they used to right those wrongs and return power/dignity/humanity back to the people who had been harmed and oppressed. Through critical conversations about Solomon Northup (*12 Years a Slave*), Katniss Everdeen (*Catching Fire*), Arnold "Junior" Spirit (*Absolutely True Diary of a Part-Time Indian*), Frederick Douglass, Che Guevara, Cesar Chavez, Ida B. Wells, and Malala Yousafzai, students decided for themselves which tactics of liberation were the most effective and successful and why. Therefore, by the end of the year, students were prepared to become activists themselves—to hold oppressors accountable for their harm. After reading one of four novels featuring a transgender protagonist, students were asked to create a policy that would lead to equity for transgender teens. To defend their policy, they had to show that harm had been done to their protagonist, explain the types and levels of oppression their protagonist faced, inspire others to empathize with their protagonist, choose a policy that would benefit their protagonist, and use the tactics of liberation (and anything else they had learned) to prove that the policy would bring about the most equity.

At the end of 8th-grade humanities, students were asked to compose a "Growth Essay," where they had to explain how they had growth as readers, writers, thinkers, and humans through middle school. In the final paragraph, many students explained how they had grown because they held themselves and others accountable for their choices, how they had more empathy, how they believed they were capable of being activists, how they didn't want to oppress anyone, and how they wanted to liberate their community. I believe that many of my students walked into 9th grade understanding that their voices mattered, that their choices carried weight, and that there is harm in the world but we have power to recognize it and—in many cases—make it right.

On the Path of Empathy

Through nearly 5 years as a middle school teacher, I have found that, when students recognize their own agency, are capable of evaluating the weight/consequence of their choices, own their decisions, and choose to hold themselves and others accountable to creating and maintaining liberatory spaces, students make fewer harmful mistakes. My hope is that my students hold on to these ideas (and ideals) in high school and beyond and that, as they gain more power and privilege with age and education, they remember our study of heroes and activists and choose to stay on the path of empathy.

Personal Profile

Kylie Garcia

URBAN EDUCATION (DECEMBER 2016)

Each person has a story to tell. Understanding each other's stories and making empathetic connections provide us the opportunity to learn with and from each other. It is an important aspect of helping diverse students thrive as learners. Stories from my multicultural upbringing lend to my understanding of diverse perspectives. I identify myself culturally as "Hapa," meaning, my ethnic background is Japanese American, Filipino, and Pacific Islander. One would never guess that my grandparents' families lost their homes and were relocated to Manzanar and Utah during the Japanese internment, or that my father was born in Hawaii before it was granted statehood. From the strong Hawaiian influence of my father's family, I easily fell into the comfort of speaking "pidgin" English before I started elementary school. Although my parents constantly corrected my language, I was thankfully scooped into speech therapy in 1st grade to modify my language skills.

The families in the community where I grew up were predominantly Chinese and Hispanic. There were times where this caused confusion for me in early elementary school as students of Hispanic background would ask, "If your last name is Garcia, why do you look Asian?" I also recall asking my mother if I was Chinese, and when she responded that we were not, I replied, "Why not?" Like every child, I just wanted to be like everyone else. I remember when two kids in 3rd grade found out I was Japanese, they called me a "dirty Jap," only to be reprimanded by the teacher after I reported what they had said. I think I was viewed as a "cultural misfit" by the kids growing up in my hometown. As I've gotten older, the response I often receive from strangers is that I look "exotic." Interestingly, my sister and I look like opposites. She has fair skin, light-brown hair, and green, round-shaped eyes in contrast to my tan skin tone, black hair, and hazel-brown, almond-shaped eyes. While she is often asked if she is half white, I am asked if I am Hispanic or Filipino. I have learned that society has a need to categorize people into a specific singular race.

These experiences influenced my perspective on diversity, and prompted me at an early age to embrace my multicultural identity. I have gained a deeper understanding of seeing others beyond what is merely presented at a first glance, and being interested in and intrigued by the stories each person holds within. Being ethnically unique or "different" and experiencing challenges because of this has given me a sense of confidence in myself and in my ability to relate to others who struggle to "fit in."

References

Ajrouch, K. J., & Jamal, A. (2007). Assimilating to a white identity: The case of Arab Americans. *The International Migration Review, 41*(4), 860–879.

Alexander, M. (2012). *The new Jim Crow: Mass incarceration in the age of color-blindness* (2nd ed.). New York, NY: The New Press.

Allen, T. W. (2012). *The invention of the white race, volume 2: The origin of racial oppression in Anglo-America.* London, UK: Verso Books.

Areskoug, L., & Asklund, H. (Eds.). (2014). *Berättelsens möjligheter. Lärares reflektioner över fiktion [The possibilities of storytelling: Teachers' thoughts on fiction].* Stockholm, Sweden: Studentlitteratur.

Asher, N. (2007). Made in the (multicultural) U.S.A.: Unpacking tensions of race, culture, gender and sexuality in education. *Educational Researcher, 36*(2), 65–73.

Banks, J. A. (2004). Multicultural education: Historical development, dimensions and practice. In J. A. Banks & C. A. McGee Banks (Eds.), *Handbook of research on multicultural education* (2nd ed., pp. 3–29). San Francisco, CA: Jossey-Bass.

Banks, J. A. (2013). Multicultural education: Characteristics and goals. In J. A. Banks & C. A. M. Banks (Eds.), *Multicultural education: Issues and perspectives* (pp. 3–32). Hoboken, NJ: Wiley.

Banks, J. A., & McGee Banks, C. A. (Eds.). (1995). *Handbook of research on multicultural education.* San Francisco, CA: Jossey-Bass.

Banks, J. A., & McGee Banks, C. A. (Eds.). (2004). *Handbook of research on multicultural education* (2nd ed.). San Francisco, CA: Jossey-Bass.

Bell, D. A. (1992). *Faces at the bottom of the well: The permanence of racism.* New York, NY: Basic Books.

Bever, L. (2017, January 27). Muslim employee attacked at airport. *San Francisco Chronicle,* p. A6.

Bonnell, V. E., & Hunt, L. (Eds.). (1999). *Beyond the cultural turn: New directions in the study of society and culture.* Berkeley, CA: University of California Press.

Brodkin, K. (1998). *How Jews became white folks and what that says about race in America.* New Brunswick, NJ: Rutgers University Press.

Cardinal, M. (1983). *The words to say it.* Cambridge, MA: VanVactor & Goodheart.

Carter, P. (2012). *Stubborn roots: Race, culture, and inequality in U.S. and South African schools.* New York, NY: Oxford University Press.

Castagno, A., & Brayboy, B. (2008). Culturally responsive schooling for indigenous youth: A review of the literature. *Review of Educational Research, 78,* 941–993.

Chang, J. (2005). *Can't stop won't stop: A history of the hip-hop generation.* New York, NY: St. Martin's Press.

Cleary, L. M. (2008). The imperative of literacy motivation when native children are being left behind. *Journal of American Indian Education, 47*(1), 96–97.

Coates, T. (2015). *Between the world and me.* New York, NY: Spiegel & Grau.

Cobb, J. (2015, June 15). Black like her: Rachel Dolezal. *The New Yorker.* Retrieved from newyorker.com/news/daily-comment/rachel-dolezal-black-like-her

Confessore, N., & Yourish, K. (2016, March 15). $2 billion worth of free media for Donald Trump. *The New York Times.* Retrieved from nytimes.com/2016/03/16/upshot/measuring-donald-trumps-mammoth-advantage-in-free-media.html?_r=0

Conrad, J. (1910). The secret sharer: An episode from the sea (part I). *Harper's Magazine.* Retrieved from harpers.org/archive/1910/08/the-secret-sharer/

Crenshaw, K. (1989). Demarginalizing the intersection of race and sex: A black feminist critique of antidiscrimination doctrine, feminist theory, and antiracist politics. *The University of Chicago Legal Forum, 140,* 139–167.

Cross, W. E. (1991). *Shades of black: Diversity in African-American identity.* Philadelphia, PA: Temple University Press.

Deleuze, G., & Guattari, F. (1980). *A thousand plateaus* (B. Massumi, Trans.). London, UK, and New York, NY: Continuum.

Denzin, N. K., & Lincoln, Y. S. (Eds.). (2003). *Collecting and interpreting qualitative materials* (2nd ed.). Thousand Oaks, CA: Sage.

Derrida, J. (1981). *Positions* (A. Bass, Trans.). Chicago, IL: The University of Chicago Press. (Original work published 1972)

Derrida, J. (2005). *Writing and difference* (A. Bass, Trans.). London, UK: Routledge. (Original work published 1967)

Diversity of Native American Groups. (2014). Independence Hall Association in Pennsylvania. Retrieved from ushistory.org/us/1a.asp

Du Bois, W. E. B. (1968). The song of smoke. In A. Chapman (Ed.), *Black voices: An anthology of Afro-American literature* (p. 348). New York, NY: New American Library.

Du Bois, W. E .B. (1994). *The souls of black folk.* New York, NY: Dover. (Original work published 1903)

Ellison, R. (1947). *Invisible man.* New York, NY: Vintage Books.

Ennis, S. E., Rios-Vargas, M., & Albert, N. G. (2011). The Hispanic population: 2010. United States Census Bureau. C2010BR-04.

Feagin, J. R. (2010). *The white racial frame: Centuries of racial framing and counter-framing.* New York, NY: Routledge.

Fields, K. E., & Fields, B. J. (2012). *Racecraft: The soul of inequality in American life.* London, UK: Verso.

Fleming, W. C., & Juneau, C. (2006). Myths and stereotypes about Native Americans. *Phi Delta Kappan, 88*(3), 213.

Fordham, S. (2010). Passin' for black: Race, identity, and bone memory in postracial America. *Harvard Educational Review, 80*(1), 4–30.

Fraga, L., & Garcia, J. A. (2010). *Latino lives in America: Making it home.* Philadelphia, PA: Temple University Press.

Frank, C. (2009). *Ethnographic interviewing for teacher preparation and staff development.* New York, NY: Teachers College Press.

Freire, P. (1970). *Pedagogy of the oppressed.* New York: Continuum.

Fryberg, S. A., Markus, H. R., Oyserman, D., & Stone, J. M. (2008). Of warrior chiefs and Indian princesses: The psychological consequences of American Indian mascots. *Basic and Applied Social Psychology, 30*(3), 208–218.

García, O., & Kleifgen, J. (2010). *Educating emergent bilinguals: Policies, programs, and practices for English language learners.* New York, NY: Teachers College Press.

Gates, H. L. (1988). *The signifying monkey: A theory of Afro-American literary criticism.* New York, NY: Oxford University Press.

Gay, G. (2010). *Culturally responsive teaching: Theory, research, and practice* (2nd ed.). New York, NY: Teachers College Press.

Gay, G., & Howard, T. C. (2000). Multicultural teacher education for the 21st century. *The Teacher Educator, 36*(1), 1–16.

Gee, J. P. (1991). What is literacy? In C. Mitchell & K. Weiler (Eds.), *Rewriting literacy: Culture and the discourse of the other* (pp. 3–12). New York, NY: Bergin & Garvey.

Gee, J. P. (2003). *What video games have to teach us about learning and literacy.* New York, NY: Palgrave Macmillan.

Gee, J. P. (2013). *The anti-education era: Creating smarter students through digital media.* New York, NY: Palgrave/Macmillan.

Gee, J. P. (2015). *Literacy and education.* New York, NY: Routledge

Gilroy, P. (2000) *Against race.* Cambridge, MA: Belknap Press of Harvard University Press.

Gomez, M. A. (1998). *Exchanging our country marks: The transformation of African identities in the Colonial and Antebellum South.* Chapel Hill, NC: The University of North Carolina Press.

Gregory, A., & Weinstein, P.S. (2008). The discipline gap and African Americans: Defiance or cooperation in the high school classroom. *Journal of School Psychology, 46*(2), 455–475.

Gross, M. P. (1979). Indian self-determination and tribal sovereignty: An analysis of recent federal Indian policy. *Immigration and Nationality Law Review, 3,* 295–344.

Guevarra, R. (2012). *Becoming Mexipino: Multiethnic identities and communities in San Diego.* Rutgers, NJ: Rutgers University Press.

Gutierrez, K. D., & Rogoff, B. (2003). Cultural ways of learning: Individual traits or repertoires of practice. *Educational Researcher, 32*(5), 19–25.

Hanley, M., & Noblit, G. (2009). Cultural responsiveness, racial identity and academic success: A review of the literature. *The Heinz Endowments.* Retrieved from heinz.org/userfiles/library/culture-report_final.pdf

Hayden, R. (1966). *Selected poems by Robert Hayden.* New York, NY: October House.

Hernández Sheets, R. H., Howard, G., Dilg, M. A., & McIntyre, A. (2000). Advancing the field or taking center stage: The white movement in multicultural education. *American Educational Research Association, 29,* 15–20.

Hoeffel, E. M., Rastogi, S., Kim, M. O., & Shahid, H. (2012, March). The Asian population: 2010. United States Census Bureau. C2010BR-11.

Hoffman, M. A., II. (1991). *They were white and they were slaves: The untold history of the enslavement of whites in early America* (4th ed.). Coeur d'Alene, ID: Independent History and Research.

Ignatiev, N., & Garvey, J. (Eds.). (1996). *Race traitor.* New York: NY: Routledge.

Inskeep, S. (Host). (2016, August 5). Former Klan leader David Duke on his Senate run and Donald Trump [Radio broadcast]. In *Morning Edition.* NPR.

Jackson, L. (2014). *Muslims and Islam in U.S. Education: Reconsidering multiculturalism.* New York, NY: Routledge.

Johnson, K. C., & Eck, J. T. (1995). Eliminating Indian stereotypes from American Society: Causes and legal and societal solutions. *American Indian Law Review, 20*, 65–109.

Keyes, R. (2004). *The post-truth era: Dishonesty and deception in contemporary life.* New York, NY: St. Martin's Press.

Kim, G. M. (2016). Practicing multilingual identities: Online interactions in a Korean dramas forum. *International Multilingual Research Journal, 10*(4), 254–272. doi:10.1080/19313152.2016.1192849

Kina, L., & Dariotis, W. M. (2013). *War baby/love child: Mixed race Asian American art.* Seattle, WA: University of Washington Press.

Kitwana, B. (2005). *Why white kids love hip hop: Wanksters, wiggers, wannabes, and the new reality of race in America.* New York, NY: Basic Civitas Books.

Knight, M., Bangura, R., Chen, C., Desai, K., Jean-Baptíste, N., & Diabate, W. (2014). Cultural grounded inquiry: Examining literacy practices with/for African immigrant girls 2013–2014. Report.

Ladson-Billings, G. (2006). From the achievement gap to the education debt: Understanding achievement in U.S. schools. *Educational Researcher, 35*, 3–12.

Ladson-Billings, G. (2009). *The dreamkeepers: Successful teachers of African American children.* San Francisco, CA: Jossey-Bass.

Ladson-Billings, G., & Tate, B. (1995). Toward a critical race theory of education. *Teachers College Record, 97*(1), 47–68.

Lee, C. D. (2003). Why we need to re-think race and ethnicity in educational research. *Educational Researcher, 32*(5), 3–5.

Lee, C. D., Spencer, M. B., & Harpalani, V. (2003). "Every shut eye ain't sleep": Studying how people live culturally. *Educational Researcher, 32*(5), 6–13.

Lee, S. J. (2015). *Unraveling the "model minority" stereotype: Listening to Asian American youth.* New York, NY: Teachers College Press.

Lensmire, T. J. (2017). *White folks: Race and identity in rural America.* New York, NY: Routledge.

Leonardo, Z. (2009). *Race, whiteness, and education.* New York, NY: Routledge.

Leonardo, Z. (2010). After the glow: Race ambivalence and other educational prognoses. *Educational Philosophy and Theory, 43*, 675–698.

Leonardo, Z. (2013). *Race frameworks: A multidimensional theory of racism and education.* New York, NY: Teachers College Press.

Lew, J. (2006). Burden of acting neither white nor black: Asian American identities and achievement in urban schools. *Urban Review, 38*, 335–352.

Lewis, A. E. (2004). What group? Studying whites and whiteness in the era of "color-blindness." *Sociological Theory, 22*(4), 623–646.

Lewis, D. L., & Willis, D. (2005). *A small nation of people: W. E. B. Du Bois and African American portraits of progress.* Washington, DC: The Library of Congress.

Lieberson, S., & Waters, M. C. (1986). Ethnic groups in flux: The changing ethnic responses of American whites. *Annals of the American Academy of Political and Social Science, 487*(79), 82–86.

Lipsitz, G. (2006). *The possessive investment in whiteness: How white people profit from identity politics.* Philadelphia, PA: Temple University Press.

Locke, A. (Ed.). (1925). *The new Negro: Voices of the Harlem Renaissance.* New York, NYL Simon & Schuster.

Mahiri, J. (2011). *Digital tools in urban schools: Mediating a remix of learning.* Ann Arbor, MI: University of Michigan Press.

Mahiri, J. (2015). Micro-cultures: Deconstructing race/expanding multiculturalism. *Multicultural Education Review, 7*(4), 1–11.

Mahiri, J., & Freedman, S. (Eds.). (2014). *The first year of teaching: Classroom research to improve student learning.* New York, NY: Teachers College Press.

Mahiri, J., & Ilten-Gee, R. (2017, April). In-human development: A micro-cultures alternative. *Journal of Human Development, 59*(6), i–iv.

Mahiri, J., & Kim, G. (2016). *Micro-cultures and the limits of multicultural education.* Revista de Ciencies de l'Educacio. Universitas Tarragonenis, Tarragona, Spain.

Marable, M. (1995). *Beyond black and white: Transforming African-American politics.* London, UK: Verso.

McCamon, S. (Host). (2016, August 29). For some Trump loyalists, it's personality over policy [Radio broadcast]. In *Morning Edition.* NPR.

McCarty, T. L., Romero, M. E., & Zepeda, O. (2006). Reclaiming the gift: Indigenous youth counter-narratives on native language loss and revitalization. *The American Indian Quarterly, 30*(1&2), 28–48.

McPherson, J. A. (1986). *Elbow room.* New York, NY: Fawcett.

Mead, M., & Baldwin, J. (1971). *A rap on race.* New York, NY: Dell Publishing.

Mendoza, M. (2017, February 16). Korean American rapper knocks down racial walls. *San Francisco Chronicle*, p. E1. Retrieved from sfchronicle.com/music/article/Dumbfoundead-knocks-down-the-racial-walls-10935086.php

Mills, C. (1997). *The racial contract.* Ithaca, NY: Cornell University Press.

Morín, J. L. (2008). Latinas/os and U.S. prisons: Trends and challenges. *Latino Studies, 6*(1), 11–34.

Morrison, T. (1992). *Playing in the dark: Whiteness and the literary imagination.* Cambridge, MA: Harvard University Press.

Mwakikagile, G. (2007). *Relations between Africans and African Americans: Misconceptions, myths, and realities.* Johannesburg, South Africa: New Africa Press.

Nakayama, T. K., & Krizek, R. (2010). Whiteness: A strategic rhetoric. In C. Burgchardt (Ed.), *Readings in rhetorical criticism* (4th ed.). State College, PA: Strata Publishing.

Nasir, N. S., & Saxe, G. B. (2003). Ethnic and academic identities: A cultural practice perspective on emerging tensions and their management in the lives of minority students. *Educational Researcher, 32*(5), 14–18.

Nieto, S. (1992). *Affirming diversity: The sociopolitical context of multicultural education.* New York: Longman.

Nieto, S. (2013). *Finding joy in teaching students of diverse backgrounds: Culturally responsive and socially just practices in U.S. classrooms.* Portsmouth, NH: Heinemann.

Nieto, S., & Bode, P. (1992). *Affirming diversity: The socio-political context of multicultural education.* Boston, MA: Pearson.

Noguera, P. (2008). *The trouble with black boys and other reflections on race, equity, and the future of public education.* San Francisco, CA: Jossey-Bass.

NoiseCat, J. B. (2015, July 30). 13 issues facing Native people beyond mascots and casinos. Retrieved from huffingtonpost.com/entry/13-native-american-issues_us_55b7d801e4b0074ba5a6869c

Norris, T., Vines, P. L., & Hoeffel, P. L. (2012). The American Indian and Alaskan Native population: 2010. United States Census Bureau. C2010BR-10.

Nucci, L. (2016). Recovery: The role or reasoning in moral education to address inequity and social justice. *Journal of Moral Education, 45*(3), 291–307.

Obama, B. (Special Ed.). (2016, November). *Wired, 24*(11), 72–74.

Ocampo, A. C. (2016). *The Latinos of Asia: How Filipino Americans break the rules of race.* Stanford, CA: Stanford University Press.

Olsen, L. (2008). *Made in America: Immigrant students in our public schools.* New York, NY: The New Press.

Orellana, M. F., & Bowman, P. (2003). Cultural diversity research on learning and development: Conceptual, methodological, and strategic considerations. *Educational Researcher, 32*(5), 26–32.

Painter, N. I. (2010). *The history of white people.* New York, NY: W. W. Norton.

Palmié, S. (2007, May). Genomics, dinination, "racecraft." *American Ethnologist, 34*(2), 206.

Pang, V. O., Han, P. P., & Pang, J. M. (2011). Asian American and Pacific Islander students equity and the achievement gap. *Educational Researcher, 40*(8), 378–389.

Pantoja, A. (2013). Reframing the school-to-prison pipeline: The experiences of Latino youth and families. *Association of Mexican American Educators Journal, 7*(3), 17–31.

Paris, D. (2012). Culturally sustaining pedagogy: A needed change in stance, terminology, and practice. *Educational Researcher, 41*(3), 93–97.

Purkayastha, B. (2005). *Negotiating ethnicity: Second-generation South Asian Americans traverse a transnational world.* New Brunswick, NJ: Rutgers University Press.

Rastogi, S., Johnson, T. D., Hoeffel, E. M., & Drewery, M. P., Jr. (2011). The black population: 2010. United States Census Bureau. C2010BR-06.

Reason, R. D., & Evans, N. J. (2007). The complicated realities of whiteness: From color blind to racially cognizant. *New Directions for Student Services, 120*, 67–75.

Rios, V. M., & Galicia, M. G. (2013). Smoking guns or smoke and mirrors? Schools and the policing of Latino boys. *Association of Mexican American Educators Journal, 7*(3), 54–66.

Rushdie, S. (2016, December). *Professional Traveller,* 109–115.

Saldaña, J. (2009). *The coding manual for qualitative researchers.* Los Angeles, CA: Sage.

Samuels, A. (2015, July 19). Rachel Dolezal's true lies. *Vanity Fair.* Retrieved from vanityfair.com/news/2015/07/rachel-dolezal-new-interview-pictures-exclusive

Santa, A. O. (2002). *Brown tide rising: Metaphors of Latinos in contemporary American public discourse.* Austin, TX: University of Texas Press.

The Santa Cruz Feminist of Color Collective. (2014). Building on "the edge of each other's battles": A feminist of color multidemensional lens. *Hypatia, 29*(1), 29–40.

Shriver, M. D., Parra, E. J., Dios, S., Bonilla, C., Norton, H., Jovel, C., Pfaff, C., Jones, C., Massac, A., Cameron, J. N., Baron, R., Jackson, T., Argyropoulos, G., Jin, L., Hoggart, C. J., McKeigue, P. M., & Kittles, R. A. (2003). Skin pigmentation, biogeographical ancestry, and admixture mapping. *Human Genetics, 112*, 387–399.

Sleeter, C. (2013). Confronting the marginalization of culturally responsive pedagogy. *Urban Education, 47*(3), 562–584.

Sleeter, C., & Grant, C. (1987). An analysis of multicultural education in the United States. *Harvard Educational Review, 57*(4), 421–445.

Southern Poverty Law Center. (2016). Update: Incidents of hateful harassment since Election Day now number 701. Retrieved from splcenter.org/hatewatch/2016/11/18/update-incidents-hateful-harassment-election-day-now-number-701

Spradley, J. P. (1979). *The ethnographic interview.* Belmont, CA: Wadsworth.

Steele, C. (2010). *Whistling Vivaldi: And other clues to how stereotypes affect us.* New York NY: W. W. Norton.

Stevenson, B. (2015). *Just mercy: A story of justice and redemption.* New York, NY: Spiegel & Grau.

Taylor, P., Lopez, M. H., Martínez, J., & Velasco, G. (2012). When labels don't fit: Hispanics and their views of identity. *Pew Research Center, Hispanic Trends.* Retrieved from pewhispanic.org/2012/04/04/when-labels-dont-fit-hispanics-and-their-views-of-identity/

Toffler, A. (1970). *Future shock.* New York, NY: Bantam Books/Random House.

Trainor, J. S. (2008). *Rethinking racism: Emotion, persuasion, and literacy education in an all-white high school.* Carbondale, IL: Southern Illinois University Press.

Trump, D., & Schwartz, T. (1987). *Trump: The art of the deal.* New York, NY: Random House.

U.S. Census Bureau. (2000). American fact finder: Profile of general demographic characteristics: 2000. Retrieved from factfinder.census.gov/faces/tableservices/jsf/pages/productview.xhtml?pid=DEC_00_SF1_DP1&prodType=table

U.S. Census Bureau. (2010). American fact finder: Profile of general population and housing characteristics: 2010. Retrieved from factfinder.census.gov/faces/table-services/jsf/pages/productview.xhtml?pid=DEC_10_DP_DPDP1&src=pt

Valenzuela, G. (1999). *Subtractive schooling: U.S.-Mexican youth and the politics of caring.* Albany, NY: State University of New York Press.

Wacquant, L. (2008). *Urban outcasts: A comparative sociology of advanced marginality.* Cambridge, MA: Polity Press.

Walbert, K. (2009). American Indian vs. Native American: A note on terminology. Retrieved from learnnc.org/lp/editions/nc-american-indians/5526

Waters, M. C. (1990). *Ethnic options: Choosing identities in America.* Berkeley, CA: University of California Press.

Wiedermann, M., & Berg, Q. (Producers), & von Donnersmarck, F. H. (Director). (2006). *The lives of others* [Motion picture]. Germany: Buena Vista International.

Wilson, J. (1980). *The declining significance of race: Blacks and changing American institutions* (3rd ed.). Chicago, IL: University of Chicago Press.

Wood, M. C. (1994). Indian land and the promise of native sovereignty: The trust doctrine revisited. *Utah Law Review, 4,* 1471–1569.

Wu, F. H. (2002). The model minority: Asian American "success" as a race relations failure. In *Yellow: Race in America beyond black and white* (pp. 39–77). New York, NY: Basic Books. Retrieved from faculty.umb.edu/lawrence_blum/courses/CCT627_10/readings/wu_model_minority.pdf

Wyszecki, G., & Stiles, W. S. (2006). *Color science: Concepts and methods, quantitative data and formulas.* New York, NY: Wiley.

Yosso, T. J. (2005). Whose culture has capital? A critical race theory discussion of community cultural wealth. *Race, Ethnicity and Education, 8*(1), 69–91.

Zack, N. (1993). *Race and mixed race.* Philadelphia, PA: Temple University Press.

Index

About the Author

Jabari Mahiri is a professor of education and the William and Mary Jane Brinton Family Chair in Urban Teaching at the University of California, Berkeley. He is faculty director of the Multicultural Urban Secondary English Program, Faculty P.I. for the Bay Area Writing Project, and a board member of the National Writing Project. He also is a board member of the American Educational Research Association, 2014 through 2017.